THE CATHOLIC UNIVERSITY OF AMERICA
CANON LAW STUDIES
NUMBER 48

The Canonical Status of the Orientals in the United States

A DISSERTATION

Submitted to the Faculty of Canon Law of the Catholic University of America in partial fulfillment of the requirements for the Degree of

DOCTOR OF CANON LAW

by the

REVEREND JOHN ALOYSIUS DUSKIE, A.B., J.C.L.
of the Diocese of Concordia

THE CATHOLIC UNIVERSITY OF AMERICA
WASHINGTON, D. C.
MCMXXVIII

Nihil Obstat:

✠THOMAS J. SHAHAN, S. T. D., J. U. L.,

Washingtonii, D. C., die VI Junii, 1928.

Imprimatur:

✠MICHAEL J. CURLEY, D. D.,

Archiepiscopus Baltimorensis.

Baltimorae, die VI Junii, 1928.

To the

Right Reverend Francis J. Tief, D.D.
Bishop of Concordia

this work is dedicated
with esteem and gratitude

TABLE OF CONTENTS

PAGE

Foreword vii

CHAPTER

I. Historical Review of the Church in the Orient........ 1

II. The Oriental Uniate Rites........ 9
- § 1. Liturgy 9
- § 2. Rite 13
- § 3. A Catholic Rite........ 17
  - 1. Schema of the Uniate Oriental Rites and their Liturgical Languages 19

III. The Attitude of the Church Towards Oriental Discipline...... 20

IV. Legislation for the Orientals in the United States........ 30
- § 1. Legislation for the Greek-Ruthenian Clergy........ 31
- § 2. Past and Present Status of the Other Oriental Priests 35
- § 3. Oriental Alms Collectors and the Instruction of 1894.. 36
- § 4. The Oriental Laity........ 38
- § 5. The Status of the Greek-Ruthenian Catholics in the United States 40
  - 1. The Bishop of the Greek-Ruthenian rite........ 44
  - 2. The Greek-Ruthenian Clergy........ 46
  - 3. The Greek-Ruthenian Laity........ 50
  - 4. Marriages between the Faithful of Different rites 52

V. The Oriental Churches and the Discipline of the Latin Church 54
- § 1. The Code in Relation to Orientals........ 57
- § 2. Instances of Latin Legislation Which May Affect Orientals 64
- § 3. Latin Legislation as a Source of Oriental Discipline 64
- § 4. The Orientals in the United States........ 65
- § 5. The Orientals Under the Jurisdiction of Latin Ordinaries 67
- § 6. A Vicar General for the Oriental Rites........ 70

VI. The Determination of Persons According to Rite........ 72
- Canon 98, § 1 72
- Canon 98, § 2 76
- Canon 98, § 3 77
- Canon 98, § 4 80
- Canon 98, § 5 83

VII. The Rite of Baptism........ 85
- Canon 756, § 1 85
- Canon 756, § 2 87
- Canon 756, § 3 89

VIII. The Sacrament of Confirmation........ 91
- § 1. The Minister of Confirmation Among the Orientals.. 91
- § 2. The Subject of Confirmation Among the Orientals.. 98
- § 3. The Reception of Holy Communion by Infants after Confirmation Among the Orientals........ 99

TABLE OF CONTENTS

PAGE

IX. The Celebration of Mass and the Holy Eucharist............ 101

§ 1. The Credentials of a Strange Priest Wishing to Celebrate Mass 101

1. Greek-Ruthenian Priests 104

2. The Other Oriental Priests.................... 105

§ 2. The Credentials of Alms' Collectors and the Celebration of Holy Mass................................ 106

§ 3. The Matter of the Holy Eucharist: Unleavened and Leavened Bread 110

§ 4. The Place for the Celebration of Holy Mass.......... 112

§ 5. The Minister of Holy Communion................. 117

§ 6. The Reception of Holy Communion in the Different Rites 120

1. Devotional Communion 120

2. The Paschal Precept.......................... 122

3. The Holy Viaticum 123

X. The Sacrament of Penance................................ 125

§ 1. The Reception of the Sacrament in Different Rites.. 125

1. The Jurisdiction of the Confessor............. 125

2. Freedom of the Penitent...................... 127

§ 2. The Orientals and the Reservations of the Code...... 129

§ 3. Episcopal Reservations and the Orientals in the United States 138

§ 4. Faculties to Absolve from Reservations............. 139

1. Oriental Confessors subject to Latin Ordinaries 139

2. The Greek-Ruthenian Confessors................ 140

§ 5. Indulgences 143

XI. The Sacrament of Extreme Unction........................ 145

XII. The Form of Marriage.................................... 149

§ 1. Orientals not bound to observe a juridical form...... 152

§ 2. The Orientals bound by the decree Tametsi.......... 158

1. The Maronites 158

2. Italo-Greeks 162

§ 3. The Decree Ne Temere, the form of Marriage for the Greek-Ruthenians in the United States............... 164

§ 4. Certain Principles with Reference to the Marriage of Orientals 167

1. Marriage Form when Orientals contract among themselves 167

2. The Form of Marriage when Orientals contract with Latins 169

3. Requisites for the Licit Celebration of Marriages for Catholics of Different Rites................ 169

4. Mixed Marriages 171

5. The Assistance of a Schismatic Minister........ 174

§ 5. Faculties to Dispense Orientals from Matrimonial Impediments 175

Bibliography 181

Theses 193

FOREWORD

A considerable number of the Oriental Catholics have settled in this country within the past fifty years, and at the present time some of the Oriental Churches are well represented in membership in the United States. Each of the various Oriental Churches, as it is known, observe their proper liturgy and are also governed by a distinct ecclesiastical discipline.

Although the author of this monograph proposes to discuss certain canonical aspects of the status of the Orientals in this country, a suitable orientation demands, it seems, that the preliminary chapters be devoted to other introductory matter not entirely connected with the canonical discipline of the Eastern Churches. The initial chapter presents a few historical facts pertinent to the foundation and the struggle of Catholicism in the Orient. Another follows with a brief explanation of two important terms: "liturgy" and "rite." A third and final introductory chapter recalls the constant solicitude of the Holy See to protect and to promote the liturgy and discipline of the Uniate Eastern Churches.

When considering the ecclesiastical legislation proper to the different Oriental Churches, a paramount principle must not be overlooked. An Oriental, as long as he remains a member of his Rite, is subject to its respective canonical discipline. The observance of the canon law of any particular Oriental Church does not entail unusual difficulty in the Orient where they have their own Ordinaries, priests and churches. In the United States the ecclesiastical organization of most Orientals is not so complete, consequently their canonical status naturally offers some complications. In this country the Orientals who have no Ordinary of their Rite are subject to the jurisdiction of the local Latin Ordinaries, and their status is regulated by certain norms provided by the Holy See.

The Greek-Ruthenians, the most numerous of the Oriental Catholics in this country, are now under the jurisdiction of Ordinaries of their Rite, and, moreover, they are fairly well supplied with their own priests and churches. Hence, the observance of the ecclesiastical discipline proper to their Church is greatly facilitated by such organization. The Holy See, too, has established certain rules to promote the status of the Greek Ruthenians in harmony with local conditions, and especially to regulate the inter-communication between them and the Latin Catholics.

Finally, the relation of the Code to the Orientals must also be considered. Ordinarily the discipline of the Latin Church does not affect the Oriental Church, however, the first canon enunciates certain principles which determine the extent of the Code to the Orientals. These must also enter into this study.

It is quite impossible within the domain of this treatise to discuss even all the more practical cases relative to this particular field of canonical jurisprudence. Likewise, a definite solution cannot be expected of all questions proposed, since authentic norms applicable to this country are not available in every case. No doubt, further study and interest relative to the Oriental Churches and their discipline would bring to light many useful principles of the Holy See in dealing with the Oriental Catholics; when such knowledge is gained possibly many of the local canonical difficulties will be solved.

The author welcomes this opportunity to express his gratitude to the faculty of Canon Law of the Catholic University for their kind assistance during his course at the University, and more especially for their direction in the preparation of this monograph. The writer is also indebted to the Right Reverend Constantine Bohachevsky, D. D., Philadelphia, Penna., Ordinary of the Greek-Ruthenians from Galicia in the United States, Monsignor Henrico Benedetti, of the Vatican Library, Rome, and the Reverend Paul Sandalgi, Baltimore, Md., for their generous cooperation and interest.

CHAPTER I

HISTORICAL REVIEW OF THE CHURCH IN THE ORIENT

A thorough knowledge of Church history makes the study of ecclesiastical laws and customs more agreeable, gives the student living pictures of the past, and furnishes him with a more accurate interpretation of ecclesiastical legislation.[1] This is especially true with reference to Oriental laws and customs. There is much which the ordinary Catholic of the Latin rite does not understand about his Eastern brethren, who are members of the same universal Church. He may regard them with a certain suspicion, doubting whether they are really Catholics.[2] A few facts, however, marshalled from the past should dispel this unhappy attitude. The Eastern Catholic Churches have a small membership in comparison with the Western Church, but the former still retain the divine deposit of doctrine and tradition which links them with the true fold whose vitality issues from the same perennial stem.[3]

A brief survey of the spread of Christianity, especially in the East, and its more important centers, must convince the impartial student that the Oriental Catholics of the present day command respect and admiration, since they can point to a distinguished Christian ancestry. Recall their martyrs, their scholars, their saints; but even a mere mention of them and of their deeds

1 Augustine, *A Commentary on Canon Law*, I, 7.

2 Fortescue, *The Eastern Uniate Churches*, p. 22.

3 Fortescue estimates the membership of the Eastern Catholic Churches to be over six and one-half millions (*op. cit.*, p. 21). Estimates, however, show considerable variation. The Western Church numbers approximately three hundred million. Streit (*Atlas Hierarchicus*, p. 123) gives detailed statistics of the various Oriental Churches. *The American Ecclesiastical Review* (73 [1925], 570), and the *Revista Illustrata Della Exposizione Missionaria Vaticana* (Rome, 1927, p. 373), may be consulted for more recent surveys.

would be an unwarranted digression from the subject. However, certain historical facts of the Church in the Orient are inseparably connected with the proposed field and must be considered.

When the leaders of the Jewish synogogue at Jerusalem by their persecutions forced the dispersion of the Apostles, the antagonists of truth only accelerated the spread of Christianity. Then, two by two, symbolizing the bond of fraternal charity, the Apostles departed for fields afar, and preached charity supreme, Jesus Christ and Him Crucified. Quite naturally, the Apostles and their co-laborers hastened to bring the Gospel news to the chief cities of the vast Roman Empire. By the end of the first century well established Christian communities were to be found. In these cities the local bishop presided in the place of God, and the entire hierarchy of divine origin was represented.[4] The exhortation of the martyr-bishop St. Ignatius (c. 107) gives confirming evidence: "Let everyone reverence the deacons, as Jesus Christ, so also the Bishop, who is the type of the Father, and the priests, as the senate of God, and the council of the Apostles."[5] There is also noticeable a superior rank and precedence of certain bishops, exercising a limited jurisdiction over other ordinaries. But the paramount fact to bear in mind is that the Bishop of Rome possessed and exercised universal authority.[6]

When the Council of Nice assembled in 325, the Fathers recognized three great ecclesiastical provinces or patriarchates: Rome, Alexandria and Antioch.[7] Rome represented the Western or Latin Church, and the other two the Eastern Churches.[8] Later the province of Antioch was divided when Jerusalem was recognized as a

---

4 Fortescue, *The Orthodox Eastern Church*, p. 5.

5 Ignatius, ad Trall., cap. III, Migne, P. G., V, 678; Conc. Trident., *sess.* XXIII, *de sacramento ordinis*, c. 6.

6 Cf. Denzinger-Bannwart, *Enchiridion Symbolorum*, nn. 163, 1824, 1825; Funk, *Manual of Church History*, I, 59 seq.; Fortescue, *The Early Papacy*, cap. IV, V, VI.

7 I Conc. Nicea, can. 6, Mansi, II, 670; Hefele, *Conciliengeschichte*, I, 378-88.

8 "Eastern Churches," *The History of Religions*, IV, p. 1 seq.

patriarchate at the Council of Chalcedon, 451.[9] It was only after Constantinople became the capital of the new Empire that she gradually assumed and obtained recognition as the second ranking patriarchal see of Christendom.[10] The precedence of the Roman See both of honor and of jurisdiction for the universal Church may be taken for granted; however, the careers of the others have a very vital bearing upon the rise and fall of Christianity in the Orient.

The important Eastern metropolis, Alexandria, which enjoyed precedence as the second see of Christendom until the rise of Constantinople, was even more famous than Antioch or Rome in its heyday. It was the superlative city of the Orient, and among the foremost in riches, splendor, civilization and scholarship. Christianity made its admission with St. Mark, who, according to local tradition was ordained by St. Peter and delegated for this special mission.[11] Here, too, was found the first Christian school of philosophy and catechetics. Unfortunately, its renown was short-lived, as Monophysitism wrought havoc and swept away Catholic influences in Egypt. Dioscur, successor of St. Cyril of Alexandria, espoused this heresy and soon Catholicism was repudiated.[12] He was condemned in 451 at the Council of Chalcedon.[13]

The Church of Antioch is considered the first of all Christian foundations in Syria, and her traditions are most venerable.[14] This city was also known as a center of ecclesiastical learning, and the study of Sacred Scripture

---

9 Mansi, VII, 178; D. XXII, c. 6, 7; Funk, *op. cit.*, I, 182; Fortescue, *The Orthodox Eastern Church,* p. 25 seq.

10 Funk, *op. cit.*, I, 181; Fortescue, *op. cit.*, p. 28 seq.

11 Funk, *op. cit.*, I, 32; Fortescue, *The Orthodox Eastern Church,* p. 11.

12 Fortescue, *op. cit.*, p. 13; Duchesne, *The Churches Separated from Rome,* p. 21 seq.

13 Conc. Chalcedon (451), *sess.* III, Mansi, VI, 1098.

14 Fortescue, *The Orthodox Eastern Church,* p. 15. The esteemed title "Christian" seems first to have been given to the followers of Christ in this city. (Acts XI, 25; Funk, *op. cit.*, I, 23). Tradition has it that St. Peter reigned there some years prior to his going to Rome. (Funk, *op. cit.*, I, 27; Fortescue, *op. cit.*, *loc. cit.*).

flourished there, especially in the early centuries.[15] Eusebius of Nicomedia, Eustathius, defender of the faith at Nice, and St. John Chrysostom were all leaders of the Antiochene School. Despite its fame, there were men who brought the school into disrepute, and who were eventually responsible for Nestorianism in Syria. Theodore of Mopsuestia, the father of Nestorius (d. 429) and Theodoret of Cyrus, must share most of this ill fame. Their influence was practically the death knell of the true faith in Syria. Then came Monophysitism under Sergius, who had been unlawfully consecrated by James Zanzalos (d. 543), a Monophysite bishop.[16] The Syrian Monophysites honored the latter by calling their sect "Jacobites." The ravages of these heresies almost left the true shepherd of Antioch without a flock. Monophysitism also dismembered the Catholic fold of Jerusalem, the smallest of the patriarchates. The subsequent invasions of the Mohammedans in the seventh century practically swept away the Church in Syria and Palestine.[17]

The foundation of Constantinople and its position as the capital city of the empire forced a change in the ranking of the patriarchal sees. The Byzantine city and its rulers would not be ignored. They were now first in importance. The emperors, anxious for even more prestige, finally prevailed upon its bishop to maintain a similar status ecclesiastically.[18] This plan became somewhat an assumed reality in the first Council of Constantinople (381) when its bishop was given a rank inferior only to the bishop of Rome,[19] despite the protests of the Roman Pontiff, who did not accept the declaration of this canon.[20] When the fourth general council assem-

---

15 Fortescue, *The Orthodox Eastern Church*, p. 18.

16 Fortescue, *op. cit.*, p. 20; Funk, *op. cit.*, I, 160.

17 Fortescue, *The Orthodox Eastern Church*, pp. 26, 27.

18 *Codex Just.*, 1, 2, 24. In this passage, the church of Constantinople is referred to as the mother of all the churches. This indicates the ambitious attitude of the emperor. Funk, *Manual of Church History*, I, 181.

19 I Conc. Constantinop., can. 3, Mansi, III, 559; Duchesne, *op. cit.*, p. 126 seq.

20 Hefele, *op. cit.*, II, 17 seq; D. XXII, c. 3.

bled at Chalcedon (451), the position of Constantinople was quite definite; its bishop is mentioned immediately after the Bishop of Rome. In Canon 28, the Council defines the extent of his jurisdiction, as Patriarch of Constantinople, over other dioceses and provinces.[21] After these events the friction between East and West became more acute. In 853, Ignatius, the lawful patriarch, was deposed, and under Photius, the usurper, there is an open conflict with Rome.[22] Subsequently the historic "Filioque" clause furnished the occasion for all other differences which were mostly concerned with matters of ecclesiastical discipline.[23] Historians contend quite correctly that not only disagreements of doctrine but also political motives were very real factors behind the schism.[24] The Eastern church, controlled by such influences, was for several centuries previous to its rupture with Rome a threatening menace to the unity of the Church.[25] This was indeed a sad event in the history of the Church; since the schism, the largest portion of the Orientals adhere to their schismatical and heretical Churches.

With fairness to all, it might be mentioned that the failure of the East and West to come to mutual terms may be founded also on the fact that they did not understand each other; language was a difficulty: one spoke Greek, the other Latin.[26] After the death of Photius (891) peace was again restored to the Church. Although the great mass of Christians were united with Rome at this time, still there remained a strong anti-Western sentiment. Apparent union existed between the East and West for a century and a half, but Michael

---

21 Conc. Chalcedon, canon 28, D. XII, c. 6; Mansi, VII, 370; Hefele, *op. cit.*, II, 527.

22 Duchesne, *op. cit.*, 147.

23 "Eastern Churches," *The History of Religions*, IV, p. 19; Funk, *op. cit.*, I, 275 seq.; Fortescue, *The Orthodox Eastern Church*, p. 95; Duchesne, *The Churches Separated from Rome*, p. 139 seq.; infra chap. III.

24 Fortescue, *The Orthodox Eastern Church*, p. 89; Shahan, *Outline of Church History*, p. 34.

25 Duchesne, *op. cit.*, p. 109 seq.

26 Fortescue, *The Orthodox Eastern Church*, p. 88; Duchesne, *op. cit.*, p. 151 seq.

Cerularius reopened the wounds of friction in 1053.[27] Old animosities and almost forgotten difficulties renewed the rivalries of the past, which at that time festered into a fatal intensity. Whatever his motives, the objective evidence of his deeds and dealings with Rome revealed a very intolerant attitude; so much so, that the East and the West since that unhappy rupture have not known complete ecclesiastical unity.

It is manifest from this resumé of Christianity in the Orient that schism and heresy proved fatal to Catholic unity. Monophysitism and Nestorianism in Syria, Palestine and Egypt, and the Eastern Schism in the Byzantine Empire, made terrible inroads into the true fold.[28] But one must not be too hasty in his conclusions and forget entirely the noble past of his Christian ancestry in the East. There were men during all these times who have stood firmly and devotedly for loyalty to Rome and for all that the primacy implied.[29] The Eastern Catholics of today belong to that class. They defend and confess the primacy of the Roman See, established by St. Peter, vicar of Christ, whose successor enjoys the plenitude of jurisdiction over the universal Church.[30]

What is to be said about the Catholics in those parts which the heresies and schisms have so dismembered? There are still members of the true fold to be found in the once famous patriarchial divisions. Many of the Eastern Churches wholly or in part returned to the true fold at the Council of Florence. The Uniate Churches may be said to date from that time,[31] moreover, others have since reunited with the Holy See.[32] The vast numbers of Christians in the Orient, however, belong to var-

---

27 Fortescue, *op. cit.*, p. 172; Shahan, *op. cit.*, p. 35; Funk, *op. cit.*, I, 279 seq.

28 "Eastern Churches," *The History of Religions*, IV, p. 3 seq; Duchesne, *op. cit.*, pp. 13-40; 109 seq.

29 Allies, *See of Peter*, p. 78 seq.

30 Denzinger-Bannwart, *loc. cit.;* Fortescue, *The Uniate Eastern Churches*, p. 6 seq.

31 Eugene IV, Const. *Laetentur Coeli*, 6 Julii 1449, *Fontes*, n. 51; Eugene IV, Const. *Exultate Deo*, 22 Nov. 1439, *Fontes*, n. 52; Fortescue, *The Orthodox Eastern Church*, p. 205 seq.

32 "Eastern Churches," *The History of Religions*, IV, p. 25 seq.

ious branches of heretical or schismatical churches. Hence the distinction must always be kept in mind between the Oriental Catholics and the so-called Orthodox (really schismatical),[33] and the Nestorian and the Monophysite Christians. The Catholics in those regions and the converts from any of the separated groups are known as Oriental Catholics. Sometimes the word "Uniate" is used to designate such Catholics; the term is quite expressive, and as is intended, stresses the fact that the Uniates are in communion with the Apostolic See.

Notice must be taken of the fact that the separated Churches are not in communion with one another; there is no mutual recognition amongst them. The distinction made between the Uniate Catholic and the Latin Churches is quite different. They are really *one;* they profess the same faith, recognize the same Supreme Pontiff, the Vicar of Christ, and are in complete and perfect communion with one another. The various uniate groups, however, have their particular canonical law, customs, and liturgical rites, which gives a basis of

---

33 "The Orthodox Church is the technical name for the body of Christians who use the Byzantine Rite in various liturgical languages and are in union with the Patriarch of Constantinople, but in schism with the Pope of Rome." Cf. Fortescue, "Orthodox Church," *Catholic Encyclopedia,* XI, 329; Fortescue, *The Orthodox Eastern Church,* pp. 365-372. The term "orthodox" which signifies "right believer" was in use long before the Eastern schism. It was used to distinguish the Orthodox (Catholic) Christians from the Nestorian and Monophysite heretics. When the Church of Constantinople fell into schism, both names were claimed by the East and West. Gradually "Catholic" became the common name for the Western Church, and "Orthodox" designated the schismatical Church of Constantinople. This is rather an unhappy use of the word "orthodox" since it does violence to its radical significance. The terminology of the Holy See is clearer and more accurate. In the official documents the members of the separated Oriental Churches are called "*Orientales schismatici*" or "*heretici.*" Cf. e. g., S. Cong. Officii, 10 Maii 1753, *Coll. Lac.,* II, 532; S. Cong. de Prop. Fide, a. 1729, *Coll.,* n. 311; S. Cong. de Prop. Fide, 15 Julii 1876, *Coll.,* n. 1458; Leo XIII, Const. *Orientalium,* 30 Nov. 1894, footnotes 1, 2, *Coll.,* n. 1883; The Orientals united to the Holy See are called "*Orientales Catholici,*" sometimes "*Orientales uniti.*" Cf. Pius IX, allocutio, *Probe noscitis,* 3 Julii 1848, *Coll. Lac.,* II, 557; S. Cong. de Prop. Fide, 7 Feb. 1624; 7 Julii 1624, Heiner, *Benedicti XIV Papae Opera Inedita,* pp. 4-5; Leo XIII, Const. *Orientalium, loc. cit.* From the Latin term "unitus" the form "uniate" developed; apparently it was first used in the Slav languages for the Ruthenians; later it was introduced in other modern languages. Cf. Fortescue, *The Uniate Eastern Churches,* p. 1.

distinction, and improperly each may be called a Church, but in reality they are each a part of one and the same true Church.[34]

The term "Uniate," although a very good one, is somewhat inaccurate. Since it is used to designate the Oriental Catholic groups united with the Holy See, it is reasonable and logical to infer that there are non-Catholic Eastern Christian groups. Generally speaking, for every Catholic Oriental body, there is a schismatical counterpart using the same rite, probably the same liturgical language, but with the vital differences in matters of faith.[35] There is an exception, however; the Syro-Maronites, as a group, are entirely Catholic; they are all united with the Supreme Head of the Church. Here the term, "Uniate," might lead to some confusion. The same might be said of the Italo-Greeks. Again one might object: Why apply the term "Uniate" merely to the Oriental Catholics? Are not the Catholics of the whole world united with the Vicar of Christ? The question of terminology offers its difficulties; certainly a correct and uniform classification is to be desired. This would at least create a favorable impression and give the proper perspective of Oriental Church history and tradition.[36]

---

34 Fortescue, *The Uniate Eastern Churches*, p. 1 seq.

35 "Eastern Churches," *The History of Religions*, IV, p. 23 seq.

36 Cf. Asman, "Variety of Rites in Unity of the Universal Church," *A. E. R.*, 73 (1925), 561 seq.; Fortescue, *The Uniate Eastern Churches*, p. 7 seq.; Scott, *The Reunion of the East*, chap. I, II, III.

CHAPTER II

THE ORIENTAL UNIATE RITES

The very concept of a divinely founded Church which has the assurance of infallible guidance postulates unity in matters which pertain to the constitution of that society. In other words, whatever touches faith or morals belongs by its very nature to the essence of Catholic unity; in this there must be agreement, for the Church is "the pillar and ground of truth." Nevertheless, the outward liturgical expression of this oneness of faith need not be and is not uniform for all Catholics. The approved variations of the public liturgy used by the different Catholic rites manifest clearly that this diversity is no menace to the unity of belief which characterizes and distinguishes the Catholic Church. A few elementary notions of "liturgy" and "rite" may be helpful to avoid confusion. The terms are often used more or less synonomously; however, an analysis reveals different significations and applications.

§ 1. Liturgy

The word liturgy is of Greek derivation; its elements are λεῖτος meaning public, and ἔργω, to do; hence, the composite λειτουργός, designates one who performs a public duty, and the service rendered is called λειτουργία.[1] Among the Greeks, liturgy in its broad connotation embraced all services to the state of a public character.[2] In the sacred text of the Old Testament, liturgy signified the public functions of the priests, or the temple service proper.[3] In the New Testament times,

1 *Th. Code,* 11, 24, 6.
2 "Liturgia," *Dict. of Greek and Roman Antiquities,* I.
3 Numb. XVI, 9; XVIII, 4; VIII, 22, 26.

liturgy has a religious usage, which was definitely established.[4]

It it only natural that in early Christian times liturgy referred to the official service of the Church. But does the term "liturgy" include all the religious services of the Church? It is necessary to distinguish a two-fold application: a) "Liturgy" may embrace all sacred functions, with their respective ceremonies, which are used by the ministers of the Church while they offer to God a divine and public service which is due to Him.[5] This general definition embraces the whole complex of official services: Holy Mass, administration of the Sacraments, blessings, etc., as opposed to merely private devotions. This would include the complete array of ecclesiastical functions according to the approved prescriptions and rubrics which are used officially by a certain Church as its proper liturgy. In this general connotation one may speak of the "liturgy" proper to the Roman Church in contradistinction to the "liturgy" used by the Uniate Byzantine Church at Constantinople. It is in this sense that liturgy also means rite, and hence one may speak of the Byzantine liturgy or Byzantine rite, and have in mind the identical definition and its application as noted above. This free and interchangeable usage sometimes engenders confusion. b) There is a more restricted signification of the word "liturgy," which is the common acceptance in the Eastern churches even at the present time. Among the Oriental Catholics the term "liturgy" is limited to the chief official and public service of the Church, the Holy Sacrifice of the Eucharist, or the Mass, as it is known in the Western Church. Hence, when an Eastern Catholic speaks of the "Holy Liturgy," he re-

---

4 Luke I, 23; Heb. IX, 21; VIII, 6; Rom. XV, 16; Phil. II, 17; "Liturgies," *Catholic Dictionary;* Fortescue, "Liturgy," *Cath. Encycl.,* IX, 306-313.

5 Wernz-Vidal, *Jus Canonicum,* II, n. 21; Wapelhorst, *Compendium Sacrae Liturgiae, Introductio,* art. I.

fers to the Eucharistic Sacrifice only.[6] It is important to note that Eastern Catholics never employ the word "Mass" for the Holy Sacrifice, as it is used among the Latin Catholics. It is quite clear from this usage that "Liturgy" in the Orient is the corresponding term for "Mass" in the West. Among the Latins, "liturgy" has a more extensive application; it may refer to the various functions or only to specific ones of a public and sacred character.

The history of the infant Church verifies the restricted application of the term "liturgy." The Apostles continued the injunction of the Master to break the Bread of Life; hence, the New Testament narratives furnish the obvious sources of the essential elements of the Holy Liturgy or the Mass.[7] The Holy Sacrifice is perennial in the Church. The Scriptural accounts of the Last Supper ever remain the nucleus of the liturgy connected with the Mass despite growth and elaboration of its ceremonial in different parts of Christendom. Today each Oriental group in the Catholic fold has a prescribed and approved liturgy. This formal and detailed arrangement of prayers, ceremonies, and rubrics which had to do with the celebration of the Sacred Mysteries is not evident in Apostolic Liturgies; still to repeat the Banquet of the Lord, certain actions and words were indispensable. At first these were performed by the officiating minister without advertence to a gradually developing ritual. Preparatory prayers, bread and wine, the matter of the Sacrifice, were brought to the altar when needed; the ablutions of the hands were necessary because they were soiled, etc. From these indispensable actions a ceremonial developed.[8]

---

[6] Hedley, *The Holy Eucharist*, p. 174 seq.; Bona, *Rerum Liturgicarum*, lib. I, cap. III; Van der Stappen, *Sacra Liturgia*, I, 1; "Liturgies," *Catholic Dictionary*; Fortescue, "Liturgy," *Cath. Encycl., IX*, 306-313; Braun, "Liturgie," *Liturgisches Handlexicon*.

[7] Matt. XXVI, 26-28; Mark XIV, 22-24; Luke XXII. 19-20; I Cor. XI 23-25; Fortescue, *The Mass*, p. 1 seq.; Hedley, *op. cit.*, cap. I; Wapelhorst, *op. cit.*, cap. XIII, art. II.

[8] Fortescue, "Liturgy," *Cath. Encycl., IX*, 306-313; Hedley, *op. cit.*, p. 173 seq.; Bona, *op. cit.*, lib. I, cap. VI.

During the period of the Apostolic Fathers, the liturgy became clearer; yet there was no fixed formulary for the celebration of the Holy Sacrifice as in the missals of subsequent times, or as in present liturgical books of the Eastern Churches. Even before a prescribed ritual was used for the celebration of the Sacred Mysteries, it is well to note that the essential action was always the same, and hence, the prayers, petitions and ceremonies must have been very similar time after time. A speaker who expounds the same subject repeatedly, will unconsciously present his topic with almost identical words, phrases and emphasis. This analogy is applicable with reference to the liturgy of the Mass. Through constant repetition the ceremonies became more or less fixed.[9] There was a noticeable uniformity in principal Churches such as at Rome, Alexandria, Antioch, each forming their proper liturgy for the Sacrifice. The essentials were uniform, but in details the different centers reflected variations. Gradually these minor points became defined and a matter of tradition in their respective localities. It was quite logical that missionaries sent out from the central cities should copy and conform to the liturgy and practices of the mother Churches.

The Christian liturgies, undefined and vague in the first three centuries, are finally crystallized during the fourth century into the four parent liturgies, namely: those of Antioch, Alexandria, Rome and Gaul.[10] All present modifications of the sacred liturgy both in the East and the West had their origin in these.[11] Even the much used Byzantine liturgy of today traces its origin to Antioch.[12]

---

9 Fortescue, *loc. cit.; ''Liturgies,'' Catholic Dictionary.*

10 Fortescue, *The Mass*, p. 76 seq.; Duchesne-McClure, *Christian Worship*, p. 46 seq.; 86 seq.; Cheetham, ''Liturgy,'' *Dictionary of Christian Antiquities*, II; Wapelhorst, *Compendium Sacrae Liturgiae*, cap. XIII, art. I.

11 Fortescue, *The Mass*, p. 108.

12 Fortescue, *op. cit.*, p. 84 seq., 108.

§ 2. Rite

The Latin word "ritus" signifies primarily the form and manner of any religious observance. It may indicate various religious customs, usages or ceremonies. Such connotations were common with reference to the public services of the pagan temples and altars.[13] The English word "rite" conveys the same idea, and is defined as a solemn religious ceremony performed according to established prescriptions. It may denote the words or actions which constitute or accompany the ceremony, or it may apply to any formal practice or custom of a sacred character. The term is used to designate the ceremonies, prayers and functions of any religious body, pagan, Jewish, Moslem or Christian.[14]

It will be sufficient for the present to consider the term *ritus* as applied in Catholic liturgy. "*Ritus stricte significat modum rite actus liturgicos peragendi, seu debitum ordinem externum liturgiae.*"[15] This application has reference to the proper manner of performing the liturgical functions.[16] Accordingly "rite" may denote the entire complex of sacred functions or form of liturgy proper to some Church. Thus one may distinguish the Roman rite, the Byzantine rite, the Alexandrian rite, etc. In this sense the term "rite" is equivalent to "liturgy" in its broad connotation.[17] Hence, any approved Catholic rite represents the proper manner of performing all public liturgical functions for the glory of God and the sanctification of mankind. This definition embraces the following: a) The Holy Sacrifice of the Mass; b) The Divine Office or Canonical Hours; c) The administration of the Sacraments; and d) Functions which require the ministry of the Church such as Sacramentals, blessings, etc.

---

13 Facciolati-Torcellini, "Ritualis," *Lexicon Totius Latinitatis.*

14 Pouget, *Institutiones Catholicae*, tom. 12, appendix, p. 130; Antoine, *Theologia Moralis*, IV, 353 seq.; Fortescue, "Rites," *Cath. Encycl.*, *XIII*, 64-78.

15 Wernz-Vidal, *op. cit.*, II, n. 21.

16 Wapelhorst, *Compendium Sacrae Liturgiae, Introductio*, art. I.

17 Wernz-Vidal, *op. cit.*, II, n. 21; Wapelhorst, *loc. cit.*

It is evident that the term "rite" is preferable when the entire series or complex of liturgical functions proper to any Church is to be considered. In the subsequent discussion of the parent rites, this signification as just described is to be understood.

In the West there was a stronger tendency towards uniformity of rite. This was due not so much to the pressure or direct influence of Rome but rather to the desire of the Western bishops themselves.[18] How explain, then, the disappearance of the Gallican rite prevalent in Gaul during the fifth, sixth and seventh centuries?[19] Its passing was not the result of direct pressure or influence of Rome. The gradual tendency to uniformity was rather the work of local bishops and even of the kings of the eighth and ninth centuries, who were the active agents. In the frequent visits of the bishops to the Eternal City, they saw the Roman ritual observed and naturally there was the desire to imitate. Hence, on their return to their proper dioceses and in subsequent synodal legislation they effected uniformity with Rome.[20] Generally speaking the old principle that rite follows patriarchate finds its fulfillment in the West. There are, however, local exceptions in the Western Church; the Mozarabic rite at Toledo in Spain, the Lyonese rite (Gallican) in France,[21] and the Ambrosian rite used in Milan, are examples.[22] There are also minor differences found in the rites practiced by certain religious orders in the celebration of Holy Mass, and in the recitation of the canonical hours.[23] Wherever

---

18 Augustine, ep. XI, 64, Migne, P. L., LXXVII, 1186-1187; Hedley, *The Holy Eucharist*, p. 194; Fortescue, "Rites," *Cath. Encycl.*, XIII, 64-78.

19 Fortescue, "Rites," *Cath. Encycl.*, XIII, 64-78.

20 Duchesne-McClure, *Christian Worship*, p. 55; Fortescue, *The Mass*, p. 177 seq.

21 Funk, *Manual of Church History*, II, 252; Fortescue, *The Mass*, p. 97 seq.

22 Benedict XIV, Const. *Allatae Sunt*, 26 Julii 1755, n. 3, *Coll.*, n. 395; Wernz-Vidal, *op. cit.*, II, n. 21; Duchesne-McClure, *Christian Worship*, p. 86; Hedley, *op. cit.*, 191 seq.; Zitelli-Solieri, *Apparatus Juris Eccl.*, nn. 1161-1164.

23 Fortescue, "Rites," *Cath. Encycl.*, XIII, 64-78.

the Roman Rite is used, there is the desire of the Holy See that it should be maintained in its pure form. The Council of Trent made such provisions with all due respect to the ancient traditions of the West. Pius V, in 1570, brought about the results of the Council very prudently. He permitted all rites that could prove an existence of two centuries to remain intact. This safeguarded any local use and provided for the above exceptions found in the Western Church.[24]

Public worship in the Eastern Churches was never marked by that uniformity which gradually obtained in the West. On account of their individuality and their distance from Rome there was not that unifying influence. Moreover, the ancient rites which developed and were used at Alexandria, Antioch, and Jerusalem, traced their origin to the Apostles.[25] Even the later Byzantine rite came from Antioch and hence its antiquity demands the same respect.[26] In the course of time, when these important sees were recognized as patriarchates, there was the obvious tendency of all the churches to conform to the rites of their respective patriarchal see.[27] In Egypt there is the prevalent Alexandrian rite; in Syria, the Antiochene; in Asia Minor, Greece, Russia the Balkan States, the Byzantine rite of Constantinople, etc.[28] This in general represents the patriarchal or geographical divisions of Christianity in the East before the schism, together with their respective rites. The Church never demanded a uniformity of rites so long as these liturgical expressions had as a basis the unity of faith.[29]

After all, these differences found in the Eastern Catholic Churches are supported by reason and have the ap-

---

24 Pius V, Const. *Quem Primum*, 19 Julii 1570, *Fontes*, n. 135; Fortescue, *The Mass*, p. 205 seq.

25 Fortescue, *The Mass*, p. 76 seq.

26 Duchesne-McClure, *Christian Worship*, p. 65 seq.; Fortescue, *The Mass*, p. 108.

27 Wernz-Vidal, *op. cit.*, II, n. 22

28 Fortescue, *Eastern Orthodox Churches*, p. 111 seq.; *The Mass*, p. 76 seq.

29 Benedict XIV, Const. *Allatae Sunt*, 26 Julii 1755, n. 6 seq. *Coll.*, n. 395.

proval of the Holy See. Their prayers and their ceremonies are the result of the local conditions suited to the people in question, and in the last analysis are expressions of the same fundamental truths. Hence when any Eastern group which had fallen from the unity of the Church through schism or heresy again sought admission to the true fold, Rome did not demand a substantial change of rites. The only requisite was a profession of faith in the Catholic Creed and the abjuration of any heretical doctrines. When the expression of their liturgy conformed to orthodoxy, Rome was satisfied.[30]

Beyond the necessary changes, the Holy See has always been anxious for the preservation and continuance of the Eastern rites.[31] It is interesting to note what the Council of Trent says in regard to the growth and possibilities of liturgy. It distinguishes what is divine, substantial, and unchangeable, because ordained by Christ Himself, from that which is left to the Church to determine in her prudent judgment as necessary for the faithful, considering the circumstances of time and place.[32]

The schism of Photius (853) and of Cerularius (1154) and then finally, the conquest of this vast empire by the Turks, left Christianity very much disorganized throughout the Orient. Today the ancient patriarchal divisions exist only in name.[33] No longer can it be said that there is a uniform rite observed in these once thriving Christion provinces. Now many Eastern Catholics of different rites may be found in the same city or locality [34] and they continue the glorious liturgies of the past, although some have introduced certain modifications.

---

30 Benedict XIV, Const. *Allatae Sunt*, n. 18.

31 Benedict XIV, Const. *Allatae Sunt*, 26 Julii 1755, n. 6, *Coll.*, 395; Maximilianus, *Praelectiones De Liturgiis Orientalibus*, p. 4 seq.; Pouget, *Institutiones Catholicae*, tom. 12, appendix, cap. VII; Fortescue, "Rites," *Cath. Encycl.*, XIII, 64-78.

32 Conc. Trident., *sess.* XXI, *de communione*, c. 2; Denzinger-Bannwart, *op. cit.*, n. 309; Wernz-Vidal, *Jus Canonicum*, II, n. 22.

33 Fortescue, *The Uniate Eastern Churches*, p. 14.

34 Fortescue, *op. cit.*, p. 20. In Beyrut there are a Catholic Maronite Archbishop, a Catholic Syrian Bishop, and a Catholic Melkite Bishop, each ruling his own flock; while the Latins are subject to their own ordinary.

§ 3. A Catholic Rite

There is another connotation of this term which it is important to observe. In a secondary or derivative sense, a "Catholic rite" may designate a group of Catholics who have a proper liturgy for all sacred functions, a proper liturgical language, and are governed by a particular ecclesiastical discipline; e. g., Catholics of the Byzantine rite of Constantinople.[35]

The acceptance of the same faith, and the recognition of the supreme jurisdiction of the Vicar of Christ, are vital and fundamental; hence theologically, all Catholic rites or groups must be in agreement.[36] The liturgical expression of the one universal faith, however, may vary according to the approved liturgies of the different Catholic rites. But even in their various liturgies, the essential elements must be the same. The Holy Sacrifice must be celebrated according to the mind of Christ, who instituted the august Mystery; the proper matter, bread and wine, must be used; an ordained priest must pronounce the words of Consecration. The Sacrament of Baptism must be conferred with water and the simultaneous invocation of the Trinitarian form, etc. It is the variation of the essential elements by more or fewer prayers, by simpler or more solemn ceremonies, which have produced the variations found in the traditional and approved rites.[37]

The Oriental rites may be distinguished thus: the Byzantine, Alexandrian, Antiochene, Chaldean and Armenian; all except the last named are again subdivided, which results in a so-called modified rite of the original. The Chaldean rite is ordinarily classed as a modification

35 The term rite used in this restricted sense, which refers only to a Catholic group, must not be confused with the broader and more technical application; e. g., the Greek Catholic and Greek Orthodox (schismatic) are of the same rite, use the same liturgical language, and have many similar church laws. But the Greek Orthodox is not a Catholic rite, since there is no union with the Apostolic See. Cf. Scott, *Reunion of the East,* p. 8 seq.

36 Fortescue, *The Uniate Eastern Churches,* pp. 2, 11.

37 Fortescue, "Rites," *Cath. Encycl.,* XIII, 64-78.

of the Antiochene; although it came directly from the Church of Antioch, new surroundings and conditions in Persia and Mesopotamia, effected different liturgical uses.[38]

The several liturgical languages used by the Oriental Churches seem to offer a difficulty. The approved liturgical tongue of any particular rite, however, is not a basis of distinction.[39] The Byzantine rite, as a general rule, is celebrated in the Greek language; but there are exceptions. The Melkites of Syria and Egpyt conform to the Byzantine rite; together with Greek, Arabic is also used as a liturgical tongue. The Russians, Slavs, Ruthenians, Serbians, Bulgarians are members of the same rite, but Old Slavonic is the church language.[40] The Oriental Churches are also governed by a particular ecclesiastical discipline, approved by the Holy See.[41] But the acceptance of the natural law and its principles, the divine positive law, and legislation which of its very nature pertains to all Catholics, is necessarily the foundation of any ecclesiastical Code.[42]

Hence, the term "Catholic rite" with reference to the Orientals, designates a group of Oriental Catholics or a local Church within the unity of the Catholic fold. This "rite" or group is distinguished by certain characteristics of a proper liturgy, liturgical language, and ecclesiastical discipline.[43]

---

38 Duchesne-McClure, *Christian Worship*, p. 59.

39 Fortescue, *The Uniate Eastern Churches*, p. 19 seq.

40 Brightman, *Eastern and Western Liturgies*, I, 590; Fortescue, "Rites," *Cath. Encycl.*, XIII, 64-78. The distinction above is made clearer, if one recalls that even the Roman rite is celebrated in Old Slavonic in Dalmatia, and in Greek in a few places in Italy. Cf. Fortescue, *Eastern Uniate Churches*, p. 19.

41 Cf. infra chap. III.

42 Cicognani, *Commentarium ad Lib. Ium Cod.*, 9 seq.; Maroto, *Institutiones Juris Can.*, nn. 173, 198.

43 Scott, *Reunion of the East*, p. 8 seq.; Fortescue, "Rites," *Cath. Encycl.*, XIII, 64-78.

1. *Schema of the Uniate Oriental Rites and their Liturgical Languages*[44]

Rite		Language
I. Armenian		Armenian (Classic)
II. Antiochene	Syrian (pure)	Syrian with little Arabic
	Maronite	Syrian with much Arabic
III. Alexandrian	Alexandro-Egyptian (Coptic)	Coptic, Greek, Arabic
	Alexandro-Ethiopian	Geez (Ethiopian)
IV. Chaldean	Chaldean (pure)	Syro-Chaldean
	Chaldeans of Malabar	Syro-Chaldean
V. Byzantine	Greeks (pure)	Greek
	Italo-Greeks	Greek
	Georgians	Georgian
	Melkites	Greek, Arabic
	Rumanians	Rumanian
	Hungarians	Hungarian (Magyar)
	Ruthenians	Old Slavonic
	Bulgarians	Old Slavonic
	etc.	

---

44 The Byzantine is the most extensively used of the Oriental rites; it is found among various peoples, and in several liturgical languages. The writer is indebted to the Reverend Cirillo Korolevskij (Editor of the *Stoudion*, Rome) for valuable information which furnished the basis of the above schema. Other sources which may be consulted with profit are: Streit, *Atlas Hierarchicus*, p. 68 seq., map, p. 34; Cappello, *De Curia Romana*, I, 236 seq.; Zitelli-Solieri, *Apparatus Juris Eccl.*, nn. 1160-1168; Braun, "Ritus," *Liturgisches Handlexikon*; Fortescue, "Rites," *Cath. Encycl.*, XIII, 64-78; Maximilianus, *Praelectiones de Liturgiis Orient.*, I, p. 13 seq.; 31 seq.; *AkKR*, LXXI (1894), 193 seq.; Silbernagl, *Verfassung und gegenwärtiger Bestand sämtlicher Kirchen des Orients*, p. 325 seq.

CHAPTER III

THE ATTITUDE OF THE CHURCH TOWARDS ORIENTAL DISCIPLINE

The diversity of liturgical rites evident among the Oriental groups does not constitute the only difference between the Western and the Uniate Eastern Churches. There are also variations in their respective disciplinary codes. The present purpose does not demand a specific enumeration or comparative examination of these legal differences, but it will suffice to indicate the traditional attitude of the Apostolic See towards the discipline of the Uniate Oriental Churches. The latter, generally speaking, date from the Council of Florence, 1439;[1] hence, it will suffice to consider the mind of the Holy See towards Oriental legislation since the reunion Council. By way of introduction, a few factors with reference to the origin of the diverse discipline may be noted.

The ecclesiastical legislation of the early centuries which obtained in the East and in the West was necessarily much the same, since it was based upon divine positive and Apostolic laws. Also many of the disciplinary canons of the first eight general Councils provided for the universal Church.[2]

There are indications, however, that even before the Eastern schism, ecclesiastical discipline was not uniform throughout Christendom. The attempted program of the Church of Constantinople at the Council of Trullo (692) gives conclusive evidence. The Eastern Church presumed at this time to dictate to Rome and elsewhere in matters disciplinary, and tried to bring about a uniformity of diverse ecclesiastical customs. The Armenians, for example, did not refrain from the use of eggs

---

1 Fortescue, *The Orthodox Eastern Church*, p. 219 seq.

2 Maroto, *Institutiones Juris Can.*, I, n. 198; Cicognani, *Commentarium ad Lib. Ium Cod.*, p. 9.

and cheese during the Lenten Sundays. In Rome, Mass was celebrated every day of Lent; at Constantinople, only on Sundays and Saturdays. The Latins fasted on Saturdays of Lent; not so the Greeks. The Byzantine law permitted priests and deacons to live in conjugal state, provided they had married before ordination; this was not lawful for the clergy of the Western Church.[3] Such were variations, which were purely a matter of ecclesiastical discipline which Constantinople did not approve, and considered as abuses or local peculiarities.

It appears that a marked tendency of a dual discipline is quite well defined at the advent of the schism, which made harmonious intercommunication beyond question. Then, the schismatic patriarchs of the East, as circumstances required, gradually introduced new laws or modified the ancient discipline. During the prolonged schism, the East was naturally adverse to anything of Latin origin; hence, prevalent church legislation of the West was not adopted in the East. It must be noticed also, that after the schism of Cerularius, there began in the Western Church a scientific legal epoch, which promoted immeasurably the advancement of ecclesiastical discipline. The East unfortunately did not share this wholesome legal development. The schism at least furnished an opportune occasion for the inauguration of a dual discipline.[4]

Differences of discipline which existed between the East and the West at the time of the Photian schism are revealed in certain accusations which the schismatics made against the Western church. Photius charged that: 1. The Latins fast on Saturdays. (This was a general custom in the Roman Patriarchate). 2. They use butter, cheese, milk the first week of Lent. (Note that the

---

3 Duchesne, *The Separated Churches*, p. 140 seq.

4 Petit-Martin, *Acta Conc. Vatic. I Acta praesynodalia, XIII*, 1087-1091 (aliter Mansi, XLIX, 1087-1091); Azor, *Institutiones Morales*, part I, lib. V, c. 11; Maroto, *op. cit.*, I, n. 198. For sources of Oriental Legislation and Collections cf. Milasch, *Kirchenrecht der abendländischen Kirche*, p. 79 seq.; Bardenhewer-Shahan, *Patrology*, p. 349 seq.; Augustine, *A Commentary on Canon Law*, I, 20; Vering, *Theologische Bibliothek*, p. 32 seq.; Wernz, *Jus Decretalium*, I, n. 204 seq.

Byzantine Church began Lent Quinquagesima Monday, and the Roman Church not until Ash Wednesday; in other words Latins did not conform to Eastern discipline). 3. They despised a married clergy. (Latin discipline demanded a celibate clergy, but they did not condemn the Oriental legislation). 4. Latins did not recognize Confirmation administered by Greek priests. (It is true Latin priests were forbidden to confirm, but Rome did not object to the Easern custom). 5. Latins have changed and corrupted the Creed by adding to it the *Filioque.*[5] It must be noted that the points mentioned were mostly concerned with local Latin legislation, and the Holy See in no way whatsoever asked or forced the Eastern Catholics to conform to the Latin discipline.[6] When Michael Cerularius reopened the Eastern schism he objected to the use of unleavened bread for the Holy Eucharist by the Latins, and maintained that only the Byzantine practice, which required leavened bread, was licit and valid.[7]

The examples enumerated indicate a difference of ecclesiastical discipline. The Byzantine Church constantly manifested a bitter attitude towards diverse Latin customs. On the other hand, however, Rome has always recognized that ecclesiastical customs are not the essential elements, so long as there is unity in Catholic doctrine and teaching. The fact that the Eastern Churches have different customs and ecclesiastical laws vindicates the general principle of the Church, that she does not arbitrarily impose uniformity in these matters. A law, properly speaking, is an ordinance of reason, and as such it must consider the circumstances of person, time and place. Legislation enacted with such consideration should result in prudent provisions. A few statements taken from the pronouncements of the Holy See and the Roman Pontiffs, plainly manifest that the Uniate Oriental rites

5 Fortescue, *The Orthodox Eastern Church,* pp. 153, 421.

6 Fortescue, *op. cit.,* p. 153; Funk, *Manual of Church History,* I, 275 seq.

7 Fortescue, *The Uniate Eastern Churches,* p. 30; Will, *Acta et Scripta,* p. 105; Fortescue, *The Orthodox Eastern Church,* p. 179 seq.

and customs have not only been tolerated, but approved, protected and preserved.[8]

When Photius started his quarrel with the Latins by attacking Western customs,[9] Pope Nicholas I (858-867), reminded the schismatics that there is no objection to the fact that people have different rites, if they contain nothing opposed to the sacred canons.[10] Leo X wrote to Cerularius in 1053, that in and outside of Rome, many monasteries and churches of the Greeks are found, but none of them have been disturbed or hindered in the traditions or customs of their ancestors, but rather they are advised and encouraged to preserve these.[11] Pope Innocent III, assured the Greeks who had returned to the Catholic fold, that the Holy See intended to cherish and honor them, and to maintain their rites and customs as far as possible with the help of the Lord.[12]

In the Council of Florence provisions are made for distinct disciplinary regulations. Rome does not force the Catholics of the East to change their ancient rites and laws so long as they are in no wise opposed to Catholic doctrine or practice. Eugene IV admits their venerable liturgies and particular discipline, and renews all rights and privileges of the recognized patriarchal sees of the East: "*Renovantes insuper ordinem traditum in Canonibus caeterorum venerabilium Patriarcharum, ut Patriarcha Constantinopolitanus secundus sit post sanctissimum Romanum Pontificem, tertius vero Alexandrinus, quartus autem Antiochenus, et quintus Hierosolymitanus, salvis*

---

8 Fortescue, *The Eastern Uniate Churches*, p. 31 seq.

9 Fortescue, *The Orthodox Eastern Church*, p. 152 seq.; Funk, *Manual of Church History*, I, 275 seq.

10 Nicholas I, ep. XII *ad Photium*, Migne P. L., CXIX, 789; Fortescue, *The Eastern Uniate Churches*, p. 30.

11 Will, *Acta et Scripta*, p. 81.

12 "Licet Graecos, in diebus nostris ad oboedientiam Sedis Apostolicae revertentes, fovere ac honorâre velimus, mores ac ritus eorum, in quantum cum Domino possumus, sustinendo, in his tamen illis deferre nec volumus nec debemus, quae periculum generant animarum et ecclesiasticae derogant honestati * * *"—IV Lateran Council (1215), c. 4, Mansi, XXII, 990; Denzinger-Bannwart, *Enchiridion Symb.*, n. 435.

videlicet omnibus privilegiis et juribus eorum.''[13] This pronouncement of the Church reflects the constant attitude of the Holy See towards the Oriental Catholics. There is firmness in regard to points of faith and morals. In matters of rite and discipline, justice and wisdom are manifested in continual protective legislation.[14]

There is abundant confirmation in the numerous documents of many Popes, which enunciate distinct legislation for the Oriental Catholics. A casual review of the Constitution of Benedict XIV, *Allatae Sunt,* will readily impress the reader that the Orientals are not, generally speaking, held to the ecclesiastical laws of the Western Church.[15]

Already in the early part of the seventeenth century, canonists held that Orientals were not embraced by pontifical constitutions save in matters which of their nature pertained to them; hence, it may be inferred that the Orientals are governed by a particular canonical discipline. Benedict XIV refers to an important commission of canonists and theologians headed by Cardinal Pamphili, July 4, 1631, which considered the question whether Orientals were bound by pontifical constitutions. Their decision was in the negative, with the following exceptions: *''Primo, in materia dogmatum fidei; secundo, si Papa explicite in suis Constitutionibus faciat mentionem et disponat de praedictis; tertio, si implicite in iisdem Constitutionibus de eis disponat, ut in casibus appellationum ad futurum Concilium.''*[16] The pre-Code legislation showed no tendency to subject the Uniate Eastern Churches to merely disciplinary laws of the

---

13 Eugene IV, Const. *Laetentur Coeli,* 6 Julii 1439, § 9, *Fontes,* n. 51; Eugene IV, Const. *Exultate Deo,* 22 Nov. 1439, pro Armenis, *Fontes,* n. 52; Papp-Szilagyi, *Enchiridion Juris Eccl. Orient.,* § 23.

14 Fortescue, *The Uniate Eastern Churches,* p. 29 seq.

15 26 Julii 1755, nn. 5-17, *Coll.,* n. 395.

16 Const. *Allatae Sunt,* 26 Julii 1755, n. 44, *Coll.,* n. 395. S. Cong. de Prop. Fide, 8 Nov. 1882, *Coll.,* n. 1578; S. Cong. de Prop. Fide, 6 Aug. 1885, *Coll.,* n. 1640. Cappello, *De Curia Romana,* I, 242; Ayrinhac, *The Constitution of the Church in the Code of Canon Law,* n. 55.

Latin Church, save in the above restrictions. The Code evidently reiterates the same principle.[17]

The fact remains that the Oriental Catholics are governed by a distinct ecclesiastical discipline. But it must also be noted that the Holy See has always insisted that the Uniate Eastern Churches must maintain their rites and customs and strictly adhere to whatsoever has the sanction and approval of the Church. Benedict XIV in his Constitution *Allatae Sunt* refers to certain questions proposed to the Congregation of the Propaganda by missionaries among the Syrians and Armenians. It seems that certain laws of abstinence of the above mentioned rites were disregarded, partly through weakness of human nature, and partly on account of their acquaintance with the milder discipline of the Latins in their regions. The missionaries at this time applied for faculties to dispense in particular cases, and to substitute other works of piety. The matter was proposed to the Congregation of the Propaganda and to the Congregation of the Inquisition. Benedict XIV gave the result of their deliberation, which insisted upon this general principle in regard to Oriental laws and customs: "*Nihil esse innovandum.*" The requested faculties in this case, however, were granted, but to be used with certain precautions.[18]

This principle which the Pontiff declared and developed was of great practical importance; it became a legal axiom with reference to the Oriental laws and customs. The pope insisted upon their integrity and preservation. Benedict XIV based his decision on a previous response of the Congregation of the Propaganda. Similar difficulties had been submitted by missionaries in the Orient. Application for dispensations were requested from fasts, prayers, change of ceremonies and the like, which were prescribed for the Oriental Churches. All doubts were dispelled by an exact and definite de-

---

17 Canon 1; Cicognani, *Commentarium ad Lib. Ium, Cod.*, p. 5 seq.; Blat, *Commentarium*, liber I, n. 50; Maroto, *Institutiones Juris Canonicis*, I, nn. 173, 198.

18 26 Julii 1755, nn. 2, 3, 47, *Coll.*, n. 395.

cree of the Sacred Congregation, January 31, 1702, which forbade any departure, whatsoever the pretext. "*Praetera eadem Sacra Congregatio censuit, non licuisse, nec licere praefatis Catholicis* (*Orientalibus*) *ullatenus a proprii ritus, a Sancta Romana Ecclesia ut supra appobati, consuetudine et observantia recedere.*"[19]

This decision of the Sacred Congregation is the reason of the response of Benedict XIV, "*Nihil innovandum esse,*" with reference to the rules and customs of the Oriental Catholic groups. The Pontiff in the same Constitution has given the historical basis of the above decision. This he did by repeating the decrees of a long list of his illustrious predecessors in the pontificate since the separation between the East and West. It may clearly be seen from their positive pronouncements, quoted by Benedict XIV, that they were all in favor of the preservation of Oriental Catholic rites.[20]

The Eastern Catholics in the Orient have always been strictly enjoined to observe and maintain their proper rites and customs according to the ruling of the Church.[21] But it must also be noticed that the same obligation binds the Oriental Catholics in localities where the Latin rite is predominant. This is evident from the various documents issued by the Holy See for that express purpose. Already Innocent IV (1254) provided for Greek Catholics subject to Latin bishops.[22] In the course of time, when every effort was bent towards reunion, many decrees were issued to protect and promote the Oriental Catholic rites and customs outside of their native lands. The Constitution of Benedict XIV is a typical example of such legislation;[23] it determined the status of the Italo-Greeks in Lower Italy and adjacent islands where the Latin rite was the rule. It established especially

19 *Ibidem*, n. 3.

20 Benedict XIV, Const. *Allatae Sunt*, 26 Julii 1755, nn. 3-17, *Coll.*, n. 395; Fortescue, *The Uniate Eastern Churches*, p. 35 seq.

21 Benedict XIV, *loc. cit.;* Benedict XIV, ep. encycl. *Demandatum*, 24 Dec. 1743, *Fontes*, n. 338; Fortescue, *op. cit.*, p. 34.

22 Ep. *Sub Catholicae*, 6 Martii 1254, *Fontes*, n. 34.

23 Const. *Etsi Pastoralis*, 26 Maii 1742, *Coll.*, n. 338; Fortescue, *Uniate Eastern Churches*, p. 33; *AkKR*, 71 (1894), 222.

certain norms which enabled the Latin bishops to govern their Oriental subjects without injury to their rite. The Pontiff recalled the legislation of his predecessors for the Italo-Greeks and embodied the same in the Constitution *Etsi Pastoralis.* Thus he confirmed, explained, and supplemented previous legislation for the peculiar circumstances of the Greek Catholics of Lower Italy.[24]

The Apostolic letter *Ea Semper,*[25] which provided a separate status for the Greek Ruthenians in the United States, contained many similar points of legislation. This arrangement, since it was not entirely satisfactory, was of short duration.[26] The Decree *Cum Episcopo,*[27] which followed and still continues in force, has given the Greek Ruthenians in the United States a status more in harmony with that of their native land.[28] The Holy See has taken into consideration the traditions of the Orientals even beyond the confines of their respective countries or patriarchates.[29]

The same attitude is manifested towards the Greek-Ruthenians in the dioceses of Poland and Austria-Hungary. When they sought for a reunion with the Holy See at the close of the sixteenth century, their traditions were given every possible consideration. They requested that their Greek rites and customs be retained, and Clement VIII gladly accepted their condition, save the necessary changes which would prove a hindrance to Catholic unity. The Bull *Magnus Dominus*[30] of the Pontiff commemorated the happy event.[31] Shortly afterwards, dur-

---

24 Zitelli-Solieri, *Apparatus Juris Eccl.*, n. 1182.

25 14 Junii 1907, *A. S. S.*, XLI (1908), 3 seq.; *A. E. R.*, 37 (1907), 459 seq.

26 *Stoudion*, IV (1927), 15; cf. infra chap. IV.

27 S. Cong. de Prop. Fide pro Negotiis R. O., 17 Aug. 1914, *A. A. S.*, VI (1914), 458 seq.

28 S. Cong. de Prop. Fide, 6 Oct. 1863, *Coll.*, n. 1243.

29 The Holy See in recent years has provided a special status for the Greek-Ruthenians in Canada. Cf. S. Cong. de Prop. Fide pro Negotiis R. O., 18 Aug. 1913, *A. A. S.*, V (1913), 393-398. The legislation for the Greek-Ruthenians in South America is similar; however, they are under the jurisdiction of the local Latin Ordinaries. Cf. S. Cong. de Prop. Fide pro Negotiis R. O., 27 Mar. 1916, *A. A. S.*, VIII (1916), 105-107. Cf. also *AkKR*, 71 (1894), 231 for other examples.

30 23 Dec. 1595, *Bullarium Romanum*, X, 239.

31 *Dublin Review*, 161 (1917), 215-243; *AkKR*, 71 (1894), 194.

ing the reign of Paul V, rumor had it that through the union with Rome, the Greek-Ruthenians would gradually have their ancient rites and customs suppressed. Again the Holy See in the person of Paul V championed the cause of the Oriental Catholics. This is evident from a very explicit declaration which leaves no doubt in the matter that their rites are to be maintained.[32] Over a century later Benedict XIII approved the decrees of the Provincial Synod of the Greek-Ruthenians.[33]

The Constitution *Orientalium Dignitas* of Leo XIII is another memorable document for the Eastern Catholics. The Pontiff approved and sanctioned the protection given to the Orientals by his predecessors. This Constitution was prompted to conteract the imprudent zeal of certain Latin missionaries who were severely censured and threatened with certain penalties,[34] because they endeavored to latinize their Eastern converts. The mind of the Holy See towards Oriental customs is well expressed in this Constitution; the Church has never condemned them, but rather has frequently commanded their observance.[35]

---

32 "Dummodo veritati et doctrinae fidei catholicae non adversentur et communionem cum Romana Ecclesia non excludant, per unionem praemissam tollere aut extinguere Ecclesiae Romanae intentionem, mentem, et voluntatem non fuisse nec esse, neque id dici vel conseri potuisse nec posse; quinimmo dictos ritus eisdem Ruthenis episcopis et clero ex apostolica benignitate permissos, concessos et indultos esse, sicut ex litteris praedictis et Concilio Florentino apparet, et ex instituto collegii Graecorum Urbis nostrae, necnon aliorum qui de ritu huiusmodi servando, sicut accepimus, iuramentum praestant, apostolica auctoritate, tenore praesentium, decernimus et declaramus."—Breve Paul V, 10 Dec. 1615, *Bullarium Romanum*, XIII, 341; Benedict XIV, Const. *Allatae Sunt*, 26 Julii 1755, n. 14; *Coll.*, n. 395; Dublin Review, 161 (1917), 215-243.

33 Breve Benedict XIII, 19 Julii 1724, *Coll. Lac.*, II, 2, 3.

34 Leo XIII, Const. *Orientalium*, 30 Nov. 1894, *Coll.*, n. 1883; Benedict XIV, ep. encycl. *Demandatum*, 24 Dec. 1743, § 13, *Fontes*, n. 338. The New Code does not mention this penalty, but the spirit of the law remains the same. Cf. Canon 98, § 3; infra chap. VI.

35 "At-inquit Leo XIII (*loc. cit.*)—Ecclesiis Orientalibus Romana potissimum, ecclesiarum omnium caput, sane quantum honoris et caritatis inde a memoria apostolica tribuere consuevit et quam fideli obsequio vicissim laetari * * * Neque ultimum illud fuit vigilantiae officium, ut proprias cuiusque Orientalis gentis consuetudines sacrorumque rationes, quas pro potestate et sapientia sua legitimas edixisset, integras in eis perpetuo custodiret ac tueretur: cuius rei documenta multa sunt quae Decessores Pontifices, cum primis Pius IX fel. rec. vel suis ipsis actis, vel per sacrum Consilium christiano nomini propagando prudentissime censuerunt."

In the light of history, the conclusion is warranted that the Oriental Catholics are exempted from the discipline of the Latin church, save in the matters which of their nature must include them. On the other hand, the Orientals must follow their proper rite and discipline approved by the Holy See. In countries where Latins and Orientals intermingle, this also applies. In such cases the Holy See has provided norms to safeguard the rite and discipline of each group. The legislation approved for the Italo-Greeks and the Greek-Ruthenians furnishes historical evidence in this regard.[36]

36 The Holy See has made persistent efforts to give adequate attention to the problems of the Oriental churches. When Gergory XV established the Congregation of the Propaganda (Const. *Inscrutabili,* 22 Junii 1622, *Coll.,* n. 3), one of its two sections was devoted to the affairs of the Oriental rites. Pius IX (Const. *Romani Pontifices,* 6 Jan. 1862, *Coll.,* n. 1223), provided a complete organization; practically speaking, it was in itself a congrêgation but it had no proper prefect and remained affiliated with the Propaganda. This condition was not changed by Pius X. (Const. *Sapienti Consilii,* 29 Junii 1908, *A. A. S.,* I [1908], 7 seq.). Benedict XV, however, recognized the importance and particular character of Oriental affairs, and as a consequence created the Congregation for the Oriental Church, which is presided over by the Roman Pontiff as prefect. (Const. *Dei Providentis,* 1 Maii 1917, *A. A. S.,* IX [1917], 529). The new Code declares that this Congregation is competent to deal with all matters which pertain to the rites, discipline or persons of the Oriental Church, even of a mixed character. The only exception is made in favor of the Holy Office whose jurisdiction remains intact. Cf. Canons 257, 247; Ayrinhac, *Constitution of the Church in the Code of Canon Law,* n. 55; Fortescue, *The Uniate Eastern Churches,* p. 38; Vermeersch-Creusen, *Epitome,* I, n. 333.

CHAPTER IV

LEGISLATION FOR THE ORIENTALS IN THE UNITED STATES

The Oriental Catholics, representing several rites and especially the Greek Ruthenians, began to reside in the United States in considerable numbers after 1880.[1] Some years elapsed, however, before the Sacred Congregation of the Propaganda for the Affairs of the Oriental Church provided canonical legislation either for the Oriental laity, or for the clergy in this country. Prior to the action of the Holy See, which definitely placed the Oriental Catholics under the jurisdiction of the local Latin Ordinaries, many questions arose of a very practical import to bishops and priests with reference to their Oriental subjects.[2] A few historical facts which are merely mentioned in the early decrees record that the canonical status of the Oriental Catholics was rather a perplexing problem to the Latin Ordinaries in this country. The Holy See in 1890 and subsequent years by means of several decrees established certain provisions for the Oriental Uniate clergy[3] and laity[4] in the United States. Although they were subject to the jurisdiction of the local Latin Ordinaries, the Orientals were free to observe their rites and customs in so far as circumstances permitted. This was not always possible since the Oriental clergy were not adequate; in such cases the faithful were privileged to conform to the Latin rite.

---

[1] Hitti, *Syrians in America*, p. 104 seq; Shipman, "Rites in United States," *Cath. Encycl.*, XIII, 78-86; Shipman, "Greek Catholics in America," *loc. cit.*, VI, 744-752; Shipman, *The Ruthenian Greek Catholics*, p. 12 seq.

[2] Heuser, "Greek Catholics and Latin Priests," *A. E. R.*, IV (1891), 194.

[3] S. Cong. de Prop. Fide, 1 Oct. 1890, *Coll.*, n. 1966, footnote 2; S. Cong. de Prop. Fide. 12 Apr. 1894, *Coll.*, n. 1866; S. Cong. de Prop. Fide, 10 Maii 1892, *A. E. R.*, VII (1892), 66.

[4] S. Cong. de Prop. Fide, 1 Maii 1897, *Coll.*, n. 1966.

In some instances, as this legislation developed, there were points which were similar to the norms and status established for the Italo-Greeks of Lower Italy.[5]

§ 1. Legislation for the Greek-Ruthenian Clergy

The first efforts to arrange for the spiritual care of the Greek Ruthenian Catholics in the United States were promoted by the Greek Ruthenian bishops of Europe. From time to time, they sent priests of their rite to labor among their countrymen.[6] They came with the approval of their respective Ordinaries; and it appears they also had the sanction of the Sacred Congregation of the Propaganda.[7] Although the clergy in question had sufficient authorization, other concomitant circumstances in their coming to this country provoked a situation which was not satisfactory.

An instruction issued by the Holy See to the Greek Ruthenian bishops of Europe, indicates certain complaints of American bishops with reference to the conduct of Ruthenian priests. The Sacred Congregation intimates that the custom has prevailed for some years in the United States and especially in the archdioceses of Philadelphia and St. Paul, which permitted priests of the Greek Ruthenian rite to assume the care of the faithful of their rite in these places. Some of the priests, however, took with them their wives and children which fact caused great scandal to Catholics as well as to non-Catholics. On this account the bishops reasonably feared that the presence of a married clergy would cause great harm to religion and ecclesiastical discipline in their dioceses; moreover, many of these clergymen presumed to exercise the sacred functions without regard for the jurisdiction of the local Ordinaries.[8]

---

5 This may be seen by comparison of certain points in the decree *Ea Semper* (14 Junii 1907, *A. S. S.*, XLI [1908], 3 seq.) for the Greek Ruthenians, and the Constitution *Etsi Pastoralis* (26 Maii 1742, *Coll.*, n. 338) for the Italo-Greeks. (*Stoudion*, IV [1927], 15; Heuser, *loc. cit.*, A. *E. R.*, IV [1891], 200 seq.).

6 Shipman, "Greek Catholics in America," *Cath. Encycl.*, VI, 744-752.

7 Heuser, "Greek Catholics and Latin Priests," *A. E. R.*, IV (1891), 198.

8 S. Cong. de Prop. Fide, 1 Oct. 1890, *Coll.*, n. 1966, footnote 2.

The complaints of the American bishops need no commentary. They are sufficient evidence that certain measures were necessary to remedy the situation. The Congregation of the Propaganda, at this time, Oct. 1, 1890, informed the Greek Ruthenian bishops of the conditions, and issued an instruction with reference to the Ruthenian priests in the United States, and those destined to go there in future.[9]

1. "*Sacerdotes ritus Graeco-Rutheni, qui in status foederatos Americae Septentrionalis proficisci et commorari cupiunt, debent esse coelibes.*"

2. "*Huic S. C. debent in scriptis manifestare quaenam sit dioecesis ad quam pergere exoptant, ut res deducatur ad notitiam Ordinarii eiusdem dioeceseos.*"

3. "*Sistere se debent coram Ordinario illius dioecesis in qua sacrum ministerium exercere vellent, ut ab eo facultates opportunas implorent.*"

4. "*Memorati sacerdotes eorumdem Ordinariorum jurisdictioni subesse debent.*" [10]

This decree represents the initial action on the part of the Holy See to enforce certain regulations relative to Greek-Ruthenian priests emigrating to the United States. It was not a simple matter; prudence and caution were required to legislate satisfactorily for all parties concerned. It was certainly necessary to remove the scandal occasioned by a married clergy, and the maintenance of ecclesiastical discipline demanded the recognition of the rights and jurisdiction of the local Ordinaries. Still any restrictive measures enacted by the Congregation of the Propaganda might be wrongly interpreted by the Greek-Ruthenians as a repression of their ancient customs and laws. This was never the mind of the Holy See, since she has always respected them.[11]

---

9 The notice and content of this instruction was sent to the American bishops, May 10, 1892, in a letter addressed to the Archbishop of Baltimore—Decretum *de Sacerdotibus Ruthenis*, *A. E. R.*, VII (1892), 66.

10 S. Cong. de Prop. Fide, 1 Oct. 1890, *Coll.*, 1966, footnote 2.

11 Scott, *Reunion of the East*, p. 62; Leen, "Eastern Orthodox Church in America," *A. E. R.*, 42 (1910), 53.

The first point of the decree demanded that the Greek-Ruthenian priests who desired to go to the United States in the future, or remain there, must be celibates. This regulation was for them a restriction of their discipline. However, the Holy See did not intend to abolish or ignore the local canon law of the Greek-Ruthenians in force in their native dioceses. It permits married men to be ordained to the priesthood provided they have married before the reception of Holy Orders.[12]

This restriction was necessary and justifiable in the light of peculiar circumstances in this country. The local Ordinaries were cognizant that the immigrant Eastern Catholics belonged to the true fold, although they observed different liturgical rites, and followed particular ecclesiastical laws which had the approval of the Holy See. Nevertheless, in the judgment of the American bishops, the presence of married priests constituted, at least at that time, a grave scandal to Catholics and non-Catholics. With this point in mind, the legislation of the Holy See, which reserved the Greek-Ruthenian missions in the United States to celibate priests of their rite, was

---

12 The impediment which renders null and void a marriage contracted by one in Sacred Orders obtains by special law in the Oriental Churches. The Council of Trullo (692) sanctioned the obligation of celibacy for clerics. A bishop must be a celibate, or if previously married (that is before the reception of Sacred Orders) he must separate from his wife (Can. 12-48). Clerics in major orders may not marry after Ordination (Can. 6); they may, however, continue to live in the conjugal state, if they have married before the reception of Sacred Orders. It seems the connotation of the term "Sacred Orders" differs among the Oriental Churches. Generally speaking, all, Ruthenians excepted, consider deaconship a Sacred Order, but some regard subdeasonship as one of the minor orders. It is clear that among the Italo-Greeks, marriage contracted by a cleric after the reception of priesthood, deaconship, or subdeaconship, is invalid. (Benedict XIV, Const. *Etsi Pastoralis*, 26 Maii 1742, § VII, n. 27, *Coll.*, n. 338). The legislation of the Maronites is similar, but the subdeaconate is not considered a major order. (Synodus Montis Libani [1736], pars II, cap. XI, § 8, n. 9). Among the Ruthenians, the prohibition is restricted with certainty only to the priesthood; doubt exists with reference to the preceding orders. (Synodus Ruthenorum [1720], tit. III, § 8). The Syrians (Synodus Sciarfensis [1888], cap. VI, art. 7, n. 2), and the Copts (Synodus Alex. Copt. [1898], sect. II, cap. 3, art. 7, § 5) approach the Latin discipline and require that all clerics in major orders should be celibates. Cf. S. Cong. de Prop. Fide, 24 Mar. 1858, *Coll.*, n. 1158; Farrugia, *De Matrimonio*, n. 174; Petrovits, *The New Church Law on Matr.*, nn. 272-276; Augustine, *A Commentary on Can. Law*, V, 187 seq.; Cappello, *De Sacramentis*, III, nn. 907-910.

entirely reasonable and expedient. The good of religion demanded the measure, a compelling argument, which far outweighs all objections. It is to be noted also that the decree of the Holy See direct to the Archbishop of Baltimore stated that the Ruthenian bishops of Europe had been advised to recall the married priests to their proper dioceses.[13] The term "celibate priests," as may be seen from a later decree, also embraced priests who were widowers.[14]

The Sacred Congregation of the Propaganda, moreover, took cognizance of all Greek-Ruthenian priests who intended to assume pastoral charges among their people in the United States. Each priest was obliged to give written notice to the Congregation of this intention, and the diocese of his future labors. The Holy See, then conveyed information relative to the cleric and his coming to the American Ordinary. This precaution, no doubt, was taken to assure the admittance only of worthy and celibate priests. The Congregation, as may be inferred, gave no faculties to the priests in question. It is evident, too, that the Greek-Ruthenian Ordinaries in Europe exercised no jurisdiction over their clergy who were missionaries in the United States. They were all placed under the jurisdiction of the local Latin Ordinary to whom they had been sent. Whatever faculties they enjoyed were conferred at his direction. This point, too, emphasizes the effort of the Holy See to maintain the authority and the jurisdiction of the American Ordinaries.[15]

---

13 10 Maii 1892, *A. E. R.*, VII (1892), 66.

14 S. Cong. de Prop. Fide, 12 Aprilis 1894, *Coll.*, n. 1866. This point shall be treated subsequently with reference to the present status of the Greek-Ruthenian priests in the United States. Cf. infra this chapter.

15 Cf. decrees, *supra cit.;* Heuser, "Appointment of a Greek-Ruthenian Bishop in the United States," *A. E. R.*, 37 (1907), 457; *A. E. R.*, 51 (1914), 710; MacKenzie, *Ruthenians*, p. 5. This did not represent a new policy of the Holy See; Italo-Greeks were placed under the jurisdiction of local Latin Ordinaries long ago. Cf. Benedict XIV, Const. *Etsi Pastoralis*, 26 Maii 1742, § IX, n. XIX. Similar instances are not wanting in recent years. Cf. S. Cong. de Prop. Fide, 27 Mar. 1916, art. 2, *A. A. S.*, VIII (1916), 105; *AkKR*, 71 (1894), 231.

§ 2. Past and Present Status of the Other Oriental Priests

The decree of the S. Congregation of the Propaganda addressed to the Archbishop of Baltimore, informed the Ordinaries of the United States of the regulations which governed Greek-Ruthenian priests destined for missionary service in this country. The same decree was extended at this time to all other Oriental priests, irrespective of rite, who intended to labor in the United States.[16] The decree explicitly referred to the clergy of the Greek-Ruthenian rite, who were at that time and are today by far the most numerous of the Oriental priests in this country. The Byzantine rite was also represented by the Greek-Melkite priests from Syria, Greek-Rumanian and Italo-Greek priests; besides, there were also Maronite priests of the Syro-Maronite rite. Since the decree was issued, priests of the Armenian and Syrian (pure) rites have come to the United States.[17]

There is no need to repeat the specific points of this legislation which has already been explained.[18] These regulations established a uniform canonical status for all Oriental priests in America at that period. It is important to notice that the present status of Oriental priests in this country (Ruthenians excepted),[19] who have no Ordinary of their proper rite, remains the same, since the Holy See has not altered or abolished the early decrees. There is, however, a recent letter addressed to the Apostolic Delegate, Washington, D. C., from the Congregation for the Oriental Church, which reaffirms the fact that the Oriental clergy and faithful in places where

---

16 S. Cong. de Prop. Fide, 10 Maii 1892, *A. E. R.*, VII (1892), 66.

17 Cf. Shipman, "Rites in the United States," *Cath. Encycl.*, XIII, 78-86; Shipman, "Greek Catholics in America," *loc. cit.*, VI, 744-752; Scott, *Reunion of the East*, chap. VII, VIII; Hitti, *Syrians in America*, appendix A, p. 125; B, p. 128; *A. E. R.*, VIII (1893), 127; *The Official Catholic Directory*, 1928, p. 656 seq.

18 Cf. supra this chapter.

19 S. Cong. de Prop. Fide pro Negotiis R. O., 17 Aug. 1914, *A. A. S.*, VI (1914), 458 seq.

they have not a proper Ordinary of their rite, are subject to the jurisdiction of the local Latin Ordinary.[20]

§ 3. Oriental Alms Collectors and the Instruction of 1894

The instruction of the Sacred Congregation of the Propaganda on this occasion [21] recalls some unedifying facts. It had become necessary to deprecate and eliminate certain abuses among the Oriental clergy. It happened that some few of their number who had been sent as missionaries to the United States neglected their missions. At any rate some were idle, others collected alms without authorization or regard for local authorities, some even pursued a profitable business or profession.[22] Naturally these instances were a source of scandal to the faithful; neither did they promote the good of religion, nor the esteem of the Catholic clergy. The American bishops complained, too, that when these Oriental priests submitted so-called credentials, the documents were usually written in some Oriental language; consequently, they were generally unintelligible to local authorities. Hence, it was impossible to ascertain whether the persons in question were Catholic or schismatic priests, whether free from censure or not, or whether they might be even simple laymen.

The Congregation of the Propaganda in order to eradicate the abuses in question, prescribed the observvance of the following procedure for all Oriental priests who wished to serve the missions in America.[23]

1. They must first have the permission of the Ordinary *ad quem* in whose territory they are destined to labor.

2. They cannot depart previous to a written declaration made to the Sacred Congregation, stating the diocese to which they wish to go in order to establish a domi-

20 29 Maii 1925; this letter is quoted substantially below in chapter IX, n. 1.

21 12 Aprilis 1894, *Coll.*, n. 1866.

22 Shipman, "Greek Catholics in America," *Cath. Encycl.*, VI, 744-752.

23 12 Aprilis 1894, *Coll.*, n. 1866; Synodus Alex. Coptorum (1898), p. 356, cites this decree.

cile; they must obtain permission in each case from the same Congregation.

3. They must present themselves before the stated Ordinary in America, to whose jurisdiction they must be subject; they must request from him the necessary faculties to exercise the sacred functions, exhibiting at the same time the permission of the Sacred Congregation, and letters of departure approved by their proper Ordinary or by the Apostolic Nuncio or Delegate.

4. The prohibition to collect alms without the proper faculty remains in force; priests who do otherwise are absolutely not to be admitted to exercise the sacred ministry.

The Sacred Congregation again called attention to the regulation which permits only celibate Oriental priests in America (*"qui caelibes aut vidui esse debent"*). Despite the clear legislation of the Holy See, how explain the fact that there are instances of married priests to be found? In the first place, there appears to be no general relaxation or dispensation of the particular regulation for the United States. However, since every Oriental priest must obtain a permission and recommendation from the Congregation for the Oriental Church, before he is permitted to come to the United States, it may be presumed that the Holy See is fully aware of his status. Again, the local Ordinary cannot give faculties to Oriental priests, unless they have documents from the Congregation which permit their entrance to the United States.[24] Hence, if an occasional married priest is admitted to this country, one might conclude, it seems, that the Holy See gives a special dispensation for a particular case. Sometimes, it may be impossible to obtain a sufficient number of celibate priests to supply the Oriental missions; such a situation might warrant a relaxation of the law in some instances.

These norms supplement to some extent previous decrees, but at the same time repeat substantially former

24 S. Cong. de Prop. Fide, 12 Aprilis 1894, *Coll.*, n. 1866.

legislation. Oriental priests in this country and especcially those subject to local Latin ordinaries must be governed by these prescriptions. The Greek-Ruthenian priests are now subject to Ordinaries of their rite; similar legislation is to be found in a special decree.[25] The prohibition to collect alms without proper authorization continues to bind them since no exception has been made.

§ 4. THE ORIENTAL LAITY

The Holy See with characteristic vigilance soon recognized the situation of the Oriental Catholic immigrants in the United States. A decree issued by the Propaganda, May 1, 1897, is confirming evidence of the solicitude and interest of the Church continually manifested towards her spiritual children irrespective of rite.[26] The introduction of this document reflects the constant practice of the Church, which has always protected the liberty of the faithful to follow their proper rite. "*Quocirca Orientalium in America Septentrionali degentium potestatem recognovit proprium exercendi ritum.*"

At this time the Holy See also commended the Oriental faithful to the jurisdiction of the local Latin Ordinaries. This provision is still in force for all Orientals in the United States, except for the Greek-Ruthenians, who are subject to Ordinaries of their own rite.[27] The Holy See has frequently resorted to this practice, and there are other instances at the present day, especially in countries predominantly Latin, where Oriental Catholics are subject to Latin Ordinaries.[28]

These provisions, however, were not adequate, and did not give the Orientals in this country proper facilities to

---

25 S. Cong. de Prop. Fide, 18 Aug. 1914, art. 10, 11, 12., *A. A. S.*, VI (1914), 460; infra this chapter.

26 S. Cong. de Prop. Fide, 1 Maii 1897, *Coll.*, n. 1966.

27 *A.. A. S.*, XVI (1924), 243; S. Cong. de Prop. Fide pro Negotiis R. O., 17 Aug. 1914, *A. A. S.*, VI (1914), 461 seq.

28 This is the status of many Italo-Greeks in Lower Italy (Benedict XIV, Const. *Etsi Pastoralis*, 26 Maii 1742, § IX, n. XIX, *Coll.*, n. 338). The same applies to certain Orientals in Paris (*AkKR*, 71 [1894], 231). In recent times the Greek-Ruthenians of South America have been placed under the jurisdiction of the local Latin ordinaries. Cf. S. Cong. de Prop. Fide pro Negotiis R. O., 27 Mar. 1916, art. 1, *A. A. S.*, VIII (1916), 105.

fulfil their religious duties. This was due mainly to the scarcity of Oriental priests in America which left many of the Eastern Catholics without a priest of their proper rite; consequently, they were destitute of pastoral care. The Sacred Congregation, compelled by this necessity and urged by local bishops, issued the following regulations to promote the spiritual welfare of the Oriental Catholics in the United States.

1. "*Fidelibus Orientalibus ad Am. Septentrionalem confluentibus facultas esto, si libuerit, sese conformandi ritui latino: regrediendum tamen ipsis erit ad ritum proprium simul ac in patriam revenerint.*"

The basis of this concession is found in the legislation of Leo XIII.[29] It assured the Oriental Catholics every opportunity to practice their religion without prejudice to their status as Orientals. Even at the present time there are circumstances and localities in the United States which render it difficult or impossible for an Oriental to follow his rite. This privilege, if exercised, places the Oriental Catholics under the care of a proper pastor who is obliged to regard them as parishioners.

2. "*Orientalibus qui verum et stabile domicilium in Am. Septentrionali constituerint non permittatur transitus ad ritum latinum, nisi obtenta in singulis casibus venia Apostolicae Sedis.*"

The fact that the Holy See permitted the Orientals in the United States to conform to the Latin rite, if they so desired, did not imply a transfer to the Latin rite. The legislation just quoted makes this clear. Orientals in this country who have for a long time, under stress of necessity, conformed to the Latin rite, might readily consider themselves as Latins. In some cases the Latin clergy might even regard their Oriental subjects as Latins and governed by Latin discipline. Although an Oriental has established a permanent domicile in America, he remains, nevertheless, attached to his proper Oriental rite. If he wishes to transfer to the Latin rite,

---

29 Const. *Orientalium Dignitas*, 30 Nov. 1894, n. 9, *Coll.*, n. 1883.

an explicit permission must be obtained from the Holy See. This is the constant practice confirmed by many decrees.[30] The Code does not depart from this legislation.[31]

3. "*In provinciis ecclesiasticis Americae Septentrionalis, in quibus multi sunt fideles Rutheni ritus, Archiepiscopus cuiuscumque provinciae, initis conciliis cum suis suffraganeis, sacerdotem ruthenum coelibatu et idoneitate commendabilem deputet, et, huius defectu, sacerdotem latini ritus ruthenis benevisum, qui super populum et clerum dicti ritus vigilantiam et directionem exerceat, sub omnimoda tamen dependentia Ordinarii loci, qui pro suo arbitrio, facultates ei tribuat quas in Domino expedire iudicaverit.*"

This provision for the Greek-Ruthenians represents a partial recognition of a petition previously submitted to the Holy See by the Greek-Ruthenian clergy. They had requested the erection of a Vicariate Apostolic for their rite in the United States, and also their own Ordinary.[32] The appointment by the local Ordinary of a qualified Greek-Ruthenian priest, or if such a candidate was not available of a suitable Latin priest acceptable to the Ruthenians, endowed with special faculties, would assure better organization and control of the Orientals in question, and would also promote a more exact observance of their rites and customs.[33]

§ 5. The Status of the Greek-Ruthenian Catholics in the United States

The Apostolic letter *Ea Semper,*[34] issued by Pius X in 1907, established a special status for the Greek-Ruthen-

30 S. Cong. S. Officii, 3 Aug. 1639, *Coll.*, n. 96; S. Cong. de Prop. Fide, 8 Mar. 1757, *Coll.*, n. 403; 2 Junii 1760, *Coll.*, n. 429; 6 Oct. 1863, A, a, *Coll.*, n. 1243; Leo XIII, Const. *Orientalium*, 30 Nov. 1894, *Coll.*, n. 1883.

31 Canon 98, § 3; cf. infra chap. VI.

32 S. Cong. de Prop. Fide, 10 Maii 1892, *A. E. R.*, VII (1892), 66; Heuser, "Greek Catholics and Latin Priests," *A. E. R.*, IV (1891), 198.

33 Benedict XIV, Const. *Etsi Pastoralis*, 26 Maii 1742, § IX, n. XXI, *Coll.*, n. 338; Canon 366, § 3; infra chap. V.

34 14 Junii 1907, *Acta Pii* X, V, 57 seq.; *A. S. S.*, XLI (1908), 3 seq. *A. E. R.*, 37 (1907), 457 seq., 513 seq.

ians distinct from other Oriental Catholics in the United States. Their rapid growth in population,[35] together with their particular rites and customs, occasioned many practical difficulties. There were even more regrettable features which aggravated the situation. There appeared to be on the part of some local Latin clergy a lack of zealous co-operation, and a failure to apply previous legislation enacted by the Congregation of the Propaganda to provide for the spiritual welfare of the Oriental faithful.[36] The Oriental clergy, too, were not blameless in this matter; there are indications that some of their number were not examples of zealous missionary endeavor.[37]

These facts together with the suspicious attitude of many Orientals who were fearful of Latin influence, offers some explanation, why many Ruthenian Catholics became apostates or joined schismatic groups. The latter insidiously spread the report during these troublesome times that in America the Ruthenian Catholics were gradually to be latinized.[38] The Holy See, aware of the situation, commissioned the Rt. Reverend Andrew Hobobay, Titular Abbot and Canon of the Greek-Ruthenian diocese of Eperies, Apostolic Visitor to the Greek-Ruthenians in the United States. He began an investigation in 1902 and continued until 1906, when he made his report to the Holy See.[39]

The American Ordinaries at this time inclined to the opinion that the appointment of a Greek-Ruthenian bishop would aid the promotion of the spiritual welfare of his countrymen. A bishop of their own rite could sympathetically appreciate the difficulties of the Greek-

---

35 Estimates showed between 350,000 to 400,000 Greek-Ruthenians in the United States in 1908. Cf. Shipman, "Greek Catholics in America," *Cath. Encycl.*, VI, 744-752.

36 *A. E. R.*, 37 (1907), 459.

37 S. Cong. de Prop. Fide, 12 Aprilis 1894, *Coll.*, n. 1866; Shipman, "Greek Catholics in America," *Cath. Encycl.*, VI, 744-752.

38 Leen, "Eastern Orthodox Church in America," *A. E. R.*, 42 (1910), 531 seq.; Shipman. *loc. cit.*

39 Shipman, *loc. cit.*

Ruthenians in a strange land, and above all fortify them against prevalent dangers to their faith in this country.[40]

A new phase of ecclesiastical legislation began with the publication of the document *Ea Semper.* It provided for the appointment of the first Greek-Ruthenian bishop (titular) in the United States.[41] He was not an Ordinary, but enjoyed merely vicarious jurisdiction delegated according to the discretion of the local Latin Ordinaries.[42] The duties of the Ruthenian bishop had in view the preservation and integrity of the Greek-Ruthenian rite.[43] As a vicar of the local Ordinary, he also assisted in the temporal administration of the Ruthenian missions according to diocesan statutes and direction of the local Ordinary.[44] Provisions were also enacted for the guidance and government of the Ruthenian clergy and people by their bishop under the vigilance of the respective local Latin Ordinaries.[45] The Apostolic Delegate according to the instruction of the Holy See was entrusted with the duty to enforce the observance of the decrees.[46]

The Holy See hoped that these provisions would solve the difficulties of the Greek-Ruthenians in this country. Naturally there was considerable surprise when a petition signed by a number of Ruthenian priests demanded certain changes and modifications. They requested a bishop with ordinary jurisdiction dependent only on the Apostolic Delegate, the admission of a married clergy, the removal of the prohibition for simple priests to administer confirmation, etc.[47] As a matter of fact, the Holy See within a few years made some important changes.

---

40 Litt. Apost. *Ea Semper,* 14 Junii 1907, *A. S. S.,* XLI (1908), 3 seq.

41 *Ibidem; A. E. R.,* 37 (1907), 459, 512.

42 Litt. Apost. *Ea Semper,* art. 2, 3; references to the document will be made in this manner for the remainder of the chapter. The document may be consulted in the following sources: *A. E. R.,* 37 (1907), 513-520; *A. S. S.,* XLI (1908), 3 seq.; *Acta Pii X,* V, 57 seq.

43 Litt. Apost. *Ea Semper,* art. 2.

44 Litt. Apost. *Ea Semper,* art. 3.

45 Litt. Apost. *Ea Semper,* cap. II, III, IV.

46 Litt. Apost. *Ea Semper,* in fine.

47 *Istruzione, Per il Delegato Apostolico degli Stati Uniti su I Ruteni degli Stati Uniti e la Constitutione Ea Semper,* p. 3 seq.

A few years subsequent to the promulgation of the Apostolic letter *Ea Semper,* the Holy See, May 28, 1913,[48] appointed the Rt. Reverend Stephen S. Ortynski, already the Greek-Ruthenian Titular bishop, the first Ordinary of the Greek-Ruthenians in the United States. He was endowed with complete and ordinary jurisdiction over all the clergy, faithful and the affairs of the Greek-Ruthenian rite. The jurisdiction which American Ordinaries had previously exercised over the same subjects now ceased to exist.

This action of the Holy See necessitated certain changes of previous legislation for the Greek-Ruthenian Catholics in the United States. The following year, the Congregation of the Propaganda provided for their new canonical status and also introduced certain other modifications. This legislation is found in the decree *Cum Episcopo* issued August 17, 1914, *ad decenium.*[49] A few months prior to the expected expiration of this decree, the Apostolic Delegate notified the American Ordinaries, that it had been renewed June 21, 1924, for an indefinite period by the S. Congregation for the Oriental Church.[50] This decree which represents the present status of the Greek-Ruthenian Catholics in the United States is divided into four chapters: I. De Episcopo Graeco-Rutheni Ritus; II. De Clero Graeco-Rutheno; III. De Fidelibus Graeco-Ruthenis; IV. De Matrimonio inter Fideles Mixti Ritus.[51]

---

48 Letter of the Ap. Delegate (Washington, D. C.) to the American Ordinaries, 25 August, 1913, *A. E. R.*, 49 (1913), 473.

49 *A. A. S.*, VI (1914), 458 seq.; *A. E. R.*, 51 (1914), 580 seq.; Mechan, ''Greek Ruthenian Church in the United States,'' *A. E. R.*, 51 (1914), 712.

50 Letter of Apostolic Delegate (Washington, D. C., No. 2633-G), Aug. 1924.

51 *Cum Episcopo*, S. Cong. de Prop. Fide pro Negotiis, R. O., 17 Aug. 1914, *A. A. S.*, VI, 458-463. (Subsequent reference to this decree will be made thus: Decr. *Cum Episcopo,* art.—). A year previous, tho Greek-Ruthenians in Canada were given a similar status. Cf. Decr. *Fidelibus Ruthenis,* S. Cong. de Prop. Fide pro Negotiis R. O., 18 Aug. 1913, *A. A. S.*, V, 393-398. (Note subsequent references to this decree. Decr. *Fidelibus Ruthenis,* art.—). The Greek-Ruthenians, as they are usually called in the official documents of the Holy See, inhabit the northern and southern slopes of the Carpathian Mountains. The northern slope constitutes Galicia, now a part of Poland. The territory of the southern slope in part constitutes the republic of Czecko-Slovakia, and the remainder belongs to Hun-

1. *The Bishop of the Greek-Ruthenian rite*

The appointment of the Greek-Ruthenian bishop for the United States is reserved to the Apostolic See.[52] Consequently no intervention or recommendation on the part of the clergy is permitted. This point was made clear in a previous instruction of the Congregation of the Propaganda to the Apostolic Delegate with reference to the Apostolic letter *Ea Semper.* Certain Ruthenian priests petitioned for some modifications of the decree; among these they asked for a voice in the selection of their bishops. The Holy See reminded the petitioners that in their own country the clergy have no voice in the election of the bishops.[53] The Greek-Ruthenian Ordinary and his lawful successors in this country remain under the immediate jurisdiction of the Apostolic See; and they

gary. The people of Galicia prefer to be known as Ukranians, and object to the name Ruthenian. The adoption of the name Ukranian dates back to a nationalist revival of the Ruthenian race in Russia and Galicia in the nineteenth century. Those in Hungary took no part in this movement. Cf. Scott, *Reunion of the East*, p. 27 seq.; Shipman, "Greek Catholics in America," *Cath. Encycl.*, VI, 744-752. It is easy to understand that each group should profess different national sentiments. These facts represent the basis of national groups and factional difficulties, which the above immigrants have also manifested in this country. Naturally these conditions did not always promote harmony even in matters of religious organization. At first the Holy See appointed one bishop (1907) who later became Ordinary (1913) for all Greek-Ruthenian Catholics in the United States. Cf. Litt. Apost. *Ea Semper*, 14 Junii 1907, *A. S. S.*, XLI (1908), 3 seq.; *A. E. R.*, 49 (1913), 473. Evidently this was not the best policy, since the Ordinary naturally came from one group; hence, there was always the danger of offense or dissatisfaction to the other national group. After the death of Bishop Ortynski in 1916, there was no Greek-Ruthenian Ordinary in the United States until 1924. The Holy See then provided a different arrangement, and appointed an Ordinary for each group. The Rt. Reverend Constantine Bohatshewsky, D. D., Titular Bishop of Amisena, was designated Ordinary for all the Ukranian Greek Catholics (Galicia) in the United States. Cf. *A. A. S.*, XVI (1924), 243. He resides in Philadelphia, Pa., and has under his jurisdiction 237,459 laity and 102 priests. Cf. *Official Catholic Directory*, 1928, p. 656 seq.; *Stoudion*, I (1923), 144. In the same year, 1924, the Holy See appointed a second Ordinary of the Greek rite for all Catholics of the Russian, Hungarian (Magyar) and Croatian nationalities in the United States. The Rt. Reverend Basil Takach, D. D., Titular Bishop of Zelensus, is the present Ordinary. Cf. *A. A. S.*, XVI (1924), 243. His official residence is in Munhall, Pa., and he numbers under his jurisdiction 309,046 laity and 139 priests. Cf. *Official Catholic Directory*, 1928, p. 660; *Stoudion*, I (1923), 148.

[52] Decr. *Cum Episcopo*, art. 1; Litt. Apost. *Ea Semper*, art. 1; Decr. *Fidelibus Ruthenis* (Canada), art. 1.

[53] *Istruzione, supra cit.*, p. 7.

will exercise complete and ordinary jurisdiction over the faithful of the Greek-Ruthenian rite, temporarily under the dependence of the Apostolic Delegate.[54]

The canonical status of the Greek-Ruthenian Ordinary in the United States in many respects is identical with that of the local Latin ordinaries. Essentially the obligations and duties are the same.[55] There is at least this important difference: the former exercises a jurisdiction over his subjects which is personal rather than territorial, whilst that of the latter is both territorial and personal. As Ordinary, the Greek Ruthenian bishop is competent to enact particular laws and statutes in harmony with common law for the government of his people. His principal duty by virtue of his office demands the protection of faith and morals of his flock. Special care must be taken to promote the observance of the liturgical rites, and the discipline of the Greek-Ruthenian Church.[56] These duties require that the Greek-Ruthenian Ordinary make frequent and regular episcopal visitations which the Holy See enjoins. In this way he may learn and provide what is necessary for the better progress of the missions. Hence, the Ordinary must question pastors with reference to their parochial duties, especially regarding the care of the sick, the instruction of the young, preaching to the people on days of obligation; records of baptisms, marriages, deaths and the like must be examined. The temporal status of the mission deserves special concern, and the Ordinary is instructed to secure the safe possession of all temporalities of the church. He is admonished in this matter to seek the advice of his consultors and other experts, in order that the church properties may be protected by a secure civil title in accordance with the statutes of the

---

54 Decr. *Cum Episcopo*, art. 2; Litt. Apost. *Ea Semper*, art. 2; Decr. *Fidelibus Ruthenis*, art. 2.

55 Meehan, "The Greek Ruthenian Church in the United States," *A. E. R.*, 51 (1914), 710 seq. The author of this article gives a good summary of the decree *Cum Episcopo* which has been used for frequent reference in this chapter.

56 Decr. *Cum Episcopo*, art. 3; Litt. Apost. *Ea Semper*, art. 2; Decr. *Fidelibus Ruthenis*, art. 3.

respective States.[57] The Apostolic Delegate, Washington, D. C., is delegated as the representative of the Holy See to settle controversies arising between the Ruthenian Ordinary and local Latin Ordinaries; however, a final recourse to the Holy See is always permitted. The recourse either to the Apostolic Delegate or the Holy See is merely *in devolutivo;* that is, the decision of the Ruthenian or Latin Ordinary in a given case which is taken to the Apostolic Delegate stands until reversed by the Delegate. Likewise the decision of the Delegate stands if the case is taken to the Holy See, until the latter changes the former decision of the Delegate.[58] Whenever controversies of a mixed nature affecting the Latins and Orientals are taken to the Holy See, the congregation for the Oriental Church is competent to deal with such cases. This Congregation directly examines cases which may be settled by an administrative or disciplinary process; cases which demand a strict judicial procedure are sent to a tribunal of its own choice.[59]

2. *The Greek-Ruthenian Clergy*

It has always been the desire of the Holy See to have the missions of every country in charge of a native clergy as soon as possible. Already Pius X in the Apostolic letter *Ea Semper* instructed the Greek-Ruthenian bishop of the United States to provide a seminary for the training and education of suitable native candidates of the Greek-Ruthenian rite for the priesthood. In the present decree, *Cum Episcopo,* this obligation is reiterated. Priests and people are urged to contribute to the support of ecclesiastical students. They may be prepared for the mission in other institutions at home or abroad, if this be necessary or advisable in the judgment of the

57 Decr. *Cum Episcopo,* art. 4, 6; Litt. Apost. *Ea Semper,* art. 4, 5; Decr. *Fidelibus Ruthenis,* art. 4, 5; Mackenzie, *Ruthenians,* p. 21; *A. E. R.,* 37 (1907), 461; 51 (1914), 712.

58 Can. 1889, § 1; Decr. *Cum Episcopo,* art. 9; Decr. *Fidelibus Ruthenis,* art. 6; Litt. Apost. *Ea Semper,* art. 6.

59 Can. 257, § 3.

Ordinary.[60] There is special insistance for a capable and zealous clergy endowed with priestly qualifications. It is to be recalled that previous legislation of the *Ea Semper* demanded celibacy as a condition for promotion to Holy Orders of Greek-Ruthenian clerics for the missions in the United States. The decree *Cum Episcopo* is silent about this condition. Since this requirement of celibacy for clerical candidates is neither contrary to the present legislation, nor has it been explicitly revoked, the conclusion seems to follow that the law still obtains. Clerical students, then, who are to be ordained for the Greek-Ruthenian missions in the United States must observe celibacy.[61]

The available native Greek-Ruthenian clergy are not sufficient for present needs. The vast majority have come and continue to come from abroad. The Greek-Ruthenian Ordinaries in this country may request suitable clerics from the Greek-Ruthenian bishops of Galicia and Hungary. The formalities required for admittance of a priest from Europe agree substantially with previous regulations of the Congregation of the Propaganda.[62] 1) The Greek-Ruthenian priest must receive a call for mission service from the Greek-Ruthenian Ordinary in the United States. 2) The cleric must be approved by the Congregation for the Oriental Church. 3) He remains incardinated in the diocese of his origin, but the bishop of origin retains no jurisdiction over him. 4) He is solely under the jurisdiction of the Greek-Ruthenian Ordinary in this country. 5) The priest in question may not return

---

60 At the present time the Greek-Ruthenians have no major seminary in this country. It becomes necessary, therefore, to send their clerical students to other institutions to complete their studies. They may attend local Latin seminaries; this is implied in a former decree. Cf. Litt. Apost. *Ea Semper*, 14 Junii 1907, art. 10, *A. S. S.* XLI (1908), 6.

61 Decr. *Cum Episcopo*, art. 10; Litt. Apost. *Ea Semper*, art. 10; Decr. *Fidelibus Ruthenis*, art. 10; *A. E. R.*, 51 (1914), 713; *A. E. R.*, 37 (1907), 462. Information given by one of the Greek-Ruthenian Ordinaries of this country supports this conclusion. Ecclesiastical students accepted for the diocese must promise to remain celibates and are ordained for the local missions only under that condition. Cf. infra this chapter.

62 Decr. 1 Oct. 1890, *Coll.*, n. 1966, footnote; Decr. 10 Maii 1892, *A. E. R.*, VII (1892), 66; Decr. 12 Aprilis 1894, *Coll.*, n. 1866; Cf. supra chap. IV.

to Europe without the written permission of the Ordinary in the United States. The Ruthenian bishop of Europe who admits clerics without this required permission must notify the Congregation for the Oriental Church. 6) A priest who comes on his own accord without necessary authorization cannot be granted faculties to perform sacred functions or exercise the ministry.[63]

The Holy See in very explicit terms warns that unworthy priests are neither to be sent nor admitted into the United States; if such are found, they are to be dismissed.[64] The Apostolic letter *Ea Semper* described the requisites thus: *sacerdos elegendus sit caelibes, vel saltem viduus et absque liberis, integer vitae, zelo ac pietate praeditus, satis eruditus, lucri non cupidus, et politicis factionibus alienus.*[65] These qualifications need no commentary; however, the question of celibacy offers a difficulty. The later decree *Cum Episcopo* is silent about this point. Since it does not explicitly abrogate the previous law, and contains no statement to the contrary, the conclusion seems to follow that Greek-Ruthenian priests admitted to the United States at the present time must be celibates.[66]

This does not appear entirely conclusive. The Holy See certainly had in mind the legislation of the earlier decrees, which permitted that only celibate Greek-Ruthenian priests could be sent to the United States.[67] As late as 1913 the same restriction is noted for Canada.[68] However, when the decree *Cum Episcopo* was issued (1914) for this country, there is no mention of celibacy as a qualification for Greek-Ruthenian priests to be admitted for mission service. If the decree *Cum Episcopo*

---

63 Decr. *Cum Episcopo*, art. 11, 13; Litt. Apost. *Ea Semper*, art. 11, 13; Decr. *Fidelibus Ruthenis*, art. 12, 14; *A. E. R.*, 51 (1914), 713; *A. E. R.*, 37 (1907), 462.

64 Decr. *Cum Episcopo*, art. 12.

65 Litt. Apost. *Ea Semper*, art. 12.

66 *A. E. R.*, 51 (1914), 713; *A. E. R.*, 37 (1907), 463 seq.

67 S. Cong. de Prop. Fide, 1 Oct. 1890, *Coll.*, n. 1966, footnote; 12 Aprilis 1894, *Coll.*, n. 1866; 10 Maii 1892, *A. E. R.*, VII (1892), 66.

68 S. Cong. de Prop. Fide pro Negotiis R. O., 18 Aug. 1913, art. 11, *A. A. S.*, V (1913), 395.

represents a complete reorganization of the status of the Greek-Ruthenians in the United States, which seems to be the case, it would follow, according to the principle of Canon 22,[69] that the former restriction which permitted only celibate Greek-Ruthenian clergy no longer obtains for this country.

Even if the former legislation retains its force there is a reasonable and natural explanation for the presence of some married Greek-Ruthenian priests in this country. In their native dioceses, the greater part of the secular Greek-Ruthenian priests are married men. Since the American missions must be practically supplied from abroad, it may not be possible in all cases to obtain a celibate priest. The Holy See, with this difficulty in mind, no doubt dispenses from the law in certain cases, otherwise it would be quite impossible at times to supply the Greek-Ruthenian congregations with priests of their proper rite.[70]

The legislation of Pius X, 1907, decreed that all rectors of Greek-Ruthenian missions in the United States are removable *ad nutum Ordinarii.*[71] The subsequent decree confirmed this legislation.[72] The Greek-Ruthenian Ordinary may not, however, remove priests from their mission or transfer them to another without just and serious reasons, as the decree explicitly states.[73] The causes or reasons for removal are not specified. Hence, the general principles must be applied, if a priest's ministry proves ineffective in certain missions, whatever the cause, or if the good of souls demands his services elsewhere, sufficient reason exists in such cases for the Ordinary to proceed with the removal.[74] The rights of the rector are sufficiently protected, since the law permits

---

69 Canon 22. "Lex posterior, a competenti auctoritate lata, obrogat priori, si id expresse edicat, aut si illi directe contraria, aut totam de integra ordinet legis prioris materiam; * * * ."

70 *A. E. R.*, 51 (1914), 713; Cappello, *De Sacramentis*, III, n. 910.

71 Litt. Apost. *Ea Semper*, art. 17.

72 Decr. *Cum Episcopo*, art. 14; Decr. *Fidelibus Ruthenis*, art. 16.

73 *Ibidem.*

74 Can. 2157, 2147; Augustine, *Rights and Duties of Ordinaries*, p. 452, 457; Woywod, *A Practical Commentary*, II, nn. 1988, 1997.

him to have recourse against the decree of removal to the Apostolic Delegate, who must render a decision within three months; recourse to the Holy See is always permitted. The recourse to the Delegate or to the Holy See is *in devolutivo,* that is, the decree of the Ordinary stands until revoked by the Delegate or the Holy See.[75]

The arrangement to provide for the sustenance of the Greek-Ruthenian clergy is somewhat extraordinary. The decree stipulates that the salaries of priests be paid by the Bishop from a common fund derived from all the churches by a proportionate assessment.[76] The stole fees and other similar emoluments of the sacred ministry must be determined by the Greek-Ruthenian Ordinary according to approved customs of the different places.[77] This regulation is in harmony with the legislation of the Third Plenary Council of Baltimore on this point.[78]

Whilst the jurisdiction of the Greek-Ruthenian Ordinary is restricted to the clergy and people of his rite, he is permitted in localities where there is no priest or church for the Ruthenian faithful, to delegate the local Latin priests to administer to the Ruthenian Catholics in the vicinity. This arrangement is to be brought to the notice of the local Latin Ordinary.[79]

3. *The Greek-Ruthenian Laity*

The two final chapters of the decree *Cum Episcopo* are concerned chiefly with the faithful of the Greek-Ruthenian rite; and many definite norms of inter-communication between Latin and Greek-Ruthenian rites are established. Most points of this legislation are not without previous foundation, although certain modifications are noticeable. The Code has embodied not a few of the

---

75 Decr. *Cum Episcopo,* art. 15; Decr. *Fidelibus Ruthenis,* art. 17; Litt. Apost. *Ea Semper,* art. 18; Canon 1889, § 1.

76 Decr. *Cum Episcopo,* art. 16; Decr. *Fidelibus Ruthenis,* art. 18; Litt. Apost. *Ea Semper,* art. 19.

77 Decr. *Cum Episcopo,* art. 17; Decr. *Fidelibus Ruthenis,* art. 19.

78 *Acta et Decreta,* n. 294.

79 Decr. *Cum Episcopo,* art. 18; *Fidelibus Ruthenis,* art. 22-23.

principles found in this decree, which now determine the relations between the different Catholic rites.[80]

The Greek-Ruthenian faithful are bound to frequent and to support their own proper churches; moreover, they must observe the prescriptions of their rite. In localities where there are neither churches nor priests of the Greek-Ruthenian rite, or if great distance constitutes a grave inconvenience for the faithful to reach their proper church, they must hear Mass in a church of another Catholic rite,[81] and also receive the Sacraments from a priest of another rite.[82] Practically the same concessions are already found in the legislation of Leo XIII, with reference to all Oriental Catholics.[83]

The frequent or even continuous attendance of Latin or other Catholic churches implies no change of rite whatsoever.[84] The transfer to another rite requires the permission of the S. Congregation for the Oriental Church. Neither is it granted without serious and reasonable cause, nor without consultation with the Greek-Ruthenian Ordinary.[85]

The Greek-Ruthenian Catholics in the United States, in order to avoid grave inconveniences, may with the permission of their proper Ordinary observe the feasts and fasts according to the custom of the place where they live. In these cases it is their privilege to conform to

80 Points of the decree which are treated in relation to the Code are to be found in subsequent chapters; for the present a mere mention of such matter will suffice.

81 Canon 1249.

82 Decr. *Cum Episcopo*, art. 19; Litt. Apost. *Ea Semper*, art. 21; Decr. *Fidelibus Ruthenis*, art. 24; Cf. the following chapters regarding the reception of the Sacraments in another rite: *Baptism*, chap. VII; *Confirmation*, chap. VIII; *Holy Communion, Paschal Communion, Holy Viaticum*, chap. IX; *Penance*, chap. X; *Extreme Unction*, chap. XI; *Certain Principles with reference to the Marriages of Orientals*, chap. XII, § 4.

83 Const. *Orientalium Dignitas*, 30 Nov. 1894, n. 2, *Coll.*, n. 1883; S. Cong. de Prop. Fide, 1 Maii 1897, *Coll.*, n. 1966.

84 Latin priests are forbidden to persuade or force the Greek-Ruthenians to change their rite under threat of penalty. Cf. Decr. *Cum Episcopo*, art. 21. The Code retains the prohibition, but does not mention the penalty. Cf. Canon 98, § 2; infra chap. VI.

85 Decr. *Cum Episcopo*, art. 20; Decr. *Fidelibus Ruthenis*, art. 25; Canon 98.

the calender of the Latin Church.[86] Again the Holy See insists that such observance absolutely implies no change of rite. The faithful are not exempt from attendance at Mass on days of obligation in the churches of their own rite, if there is one in the locality.[87]

4. *Marriages between the Faithful of Different Rites*

There is no prohibition for Catholics of different rites to intermarry. When the husband and wife adhere to different rites, inconveniences may arise, e. g., the observance of different feasts and fasts. In order to avoid these difficulties, the law permits the wife to join the rite of the husband, and with the dissolution of the marriage bond, she may again resume her native rite.[88] There appears to be no obligation for the woman to change her rite even whilst the marriage perdures.[89] When the Greek-Ruthenians contract marriage among themselves or with persons of different rites, the form prescribed by the decree *Ne Temere* must be observed, and the marriage is to be celebrated before the pastor of the bride. Dispensations which may be necessary when persons of mixed rites marry, are to be requested and given by the Ordinary of the bride.[90] Since the promulgation of the Code, Greek-Ruthenians who contract marriage with Latins, must observe the form prescribed by the Code.[91]

If husband and wife belong to different rites, and if the wife chooses to follow her proper rite during the marriage—which is her privilege, each depends upon the

86 This faculty is especially happy to prevent difficulties and inconveniences in a Latin Catholic country, since it must be noted that most Orientals follow their particular Church Calendar, and observe different feasts and fasts. The Maronites, however, follow the Gregorian calendar. Cf. Benedict XIV, Const. *Allatae Sunt*, 26 Julii 1755, nn. 44-46, *Coll.*, n. 395; Zitelli-Solieri, *Apparatus Juris Eccl.*, nn. 1176-1177.

87 Decr. *Cum Episcopo*, art. 27; Decr. *Fidelibus Ruthenis*, art. 33; Litt. Apost. *Ea Semper*, art. 26.

88 Decr. *Cum Episcopo*, art. 28, 29; Decr. *Fidelibus Ruthenis*, art. 34, 35.

89 The Code has embodied this law, and its distinctions are somewhat clearer. Cf. Canon 98, § 4; infra chap. VI.

90 Decr. *Cum Episcopo*, art. 30, 31; Decr. *Fidelibus Ruthenis*, art. 37, 38, 39; cf. infra chap. XII, nn. 3, 4, 5.

91 Canons 1099, § 1, n. 3; 1094 seq. Cf. infra chap. XII, § 4.

pastoral care of the pastor of his or her rite. This regulation has some important consequences, e. g., the celebration of the funeral services and the right to the emoluments belong to the pastor of the rite of the deceased.[92]

All the children born of lawful marriage of parents of mixed rites, are to be baptized according to the rite of the father, and come under the jurisdiction of the father's pastor. Children who are baptized under stress of necessity according to different rite, do not change their status as indicated above. The illegitimate child, the law decrees, follows the rite of the mother.[93]

These regulations governing the present status of husband, wife, and children in marriages of mixed rites among the Greek-Ruthenian Catholics of the United States, have introduced radical changes, and modified or abrogated much of the former legislation which was contained in the Apostolic Letter *Ea Semper.*[94]

---

92 Decr. *Cum Episcopo,* art. 26; Decr. *Fidelibus Ruthenis,* art. 32; Litt. Apost. *Ea Semper,* art. 33.

93 Decr. *Cum Episcopo,* art. 32, 33, 34; Decr. *Fidelibus Ruthenis,* art. 39, 40, 41. Cf. infra chap. VI, VII.

94 Cf. Litt. Apost. *Ea Semper,* art. 27-36; cf. infra chap. VI, VII; *A. E. R.,* 51 (1914), 716.

CHAPTER V

THE ORIENTAL CHURCHES AND THE DISCIPLINE OF THE LATIN CHURCH

The initial Canon of the Code indicates the attitude of the supreme legislator towards the Oriental Churches in the matter of ecclesiastical discipline. The Holy See officially recognizes that they have and retain their proper discipline which has been their privilege since time immemorial. When many of the Oriental groups, at least in part, returned to unity at the Council of Ferrara-Florence,[1] they were permitted to retain their ancient rites and customs.[2] Since that date, the Roman Pontiffs have consistently provided that the venerable Oriental rites should suffer no injury.[3] The Church has not changed her policy in recent years. The Code promulgated for the Latin Church does not interfere with the discipline of the Eastern churches. A juridical axiom presumes laws to be territorial, unless it is evident that they have a personal force.[4] The ecclesiastical discipline of the Oriental groups seems more properly to be of a personal character. Laws are said to be personal which directly and immediately affect those for whom they have been enacted independent of any territory; hence, personal laws bind those obligated wherever they may be located. Laws of this nature need not be territorial; it suffices that they are intended for a complete society. There are complete communities of a personal nature

---

1 Fortescue, *The Orthodox Eastern Church*, p. 208.

2 Eugene IV, Const. *Laetentur Coeli* (in Conc. Florent.), 6 Julii 1439, *Fontes*, n. 59.

3 Clement VIII, Const. *Magnus Dominus*, 23 Dec. 1595, *Bullarium Romanum*, X, 239; Paul V, Breve, 10 Dec. 1615, *Bullarium Romanum*, XII, 341; Benedict XIV, Const. *Etsi Pastoralis*, 26 Maii 1742, § IX, n. I seq., *Coll.*, n. 338; Benedict XIV, Const. *Allatae Sunt*, 26 Julii 1755, nn. 3-17, *Coll.*, n. 395; Leo XIII, Const. *Orientalium Dignitas*, 30 Nov. 1894, *Coll.*, n. 1883.

4 Canon 8, § 2.

which *de jure* have no proper territory. It appears that the legislation of such a society is personal rather than territorial.[5] Maroto[6] observes that the dioceses of the Oriental rites, whether in the Orient or in North America, are to be considered personal rather than territorial.[7]

An Oriental is always considered a member of his proper rite, unless he has lawfully changed to another with the permission of the Holy See.[8] Adherence to any rite, supposes as a consequence, subjection to its particular discipline; this fact also indicates the personal force of Oriental legislation. The status of the Greek-Ruthenian Catholics in the United States illustrates these points. They are living in various parts of the country, still juridically they are subject to one of the two Greek-Ruthenian Ordinaries. One has jurisdiction over all subjects from Galicia; the other over all subjects from Podocarpathia.[9] The jurisdiction of the Greek-Ruthenian Ordinaries is personal, and extends to their respective subjects in the United States. They govern their people in harmony with the liturgical norms of the Greek-Ruthenian rite; their disciplinary laws must be modified according to particular decrees which prevail in the United States.[10]

The uniform and comprehensive Code of ecclesiastical discipline which regulates the faithful of the Latin Church is a fortunate characteristic. This identity of discipline is in marked contrast to the Oriental Churches which have no uniform Code. The various rites have different and particular ecclesiastical laws. It is true that there are many points where Latin and Oriental legislation agree; points of divergence are also numerous.[11]

---

5 Maroto, *Institutiones Juris Canonici*, I, n. 183; Suarez, *De Legibus*, lib. I, cap. 6, n. 11.

6 *Op. cit.*, n. 183, footnote 2.

7 Mansella (*De Imped. Matr. Diriment. et Processu Judiciali*, p. 175, seq.) cites similar examples.

8 Canon 98, § 3.

9 *A. A. S.*, XVI (1924), 243; cf. supra chap. IV, footnote 50.

10 S. Cong. de Prop. Fide Pro Negotiis R. O., 17 Aug. 1914, *A. A. S.*, VI, 458 seq.

11 Cappello, *Jus Pontificium*, VII (1927), 55 seq.

The divine constitution of the Church postulates uniformity of disciplines in matters which pertain to the natural, divine positive, and apostolic law. In the early centuries before Christendom was divided by the pernicious influences of schism and heresy, some similar ecclesiastical laws governed the Churches of the East and West. Such enactments had a common origin in the first eight Ecumenical Councils.[12]

Canonists sometimes characterize the Oriental discipline as a *jus sui generis*.[13] This statement is based upon the fact that the different rites have their proper ecclesiastical discipline. It is quite impossible for the lawgiver to provide for all legal contingencies, and to foresee all difficulties; however, a regrettable feature of Oriental legislation seems to be that it is not sufficiently complete and extensive to embrace even some of the more practical juridical cases of frequent occurrence.

The distinction made in the first Canon, which exempts the Oriental Church from the discipline of the Latin Church is not recent. The opinion has been advanced since the early part of the seventeenth century, that the faithful of the Oriental rites were not bound by the pontifical decrees of the Latin Church.[14] Missionaries of that period submitted the difficulty to the Sacred Congregation of the Propaganda. A special commission of theologians and canonists examined the question; their response, given July 4, 1631, maintained that the subjects of the Oriental Patriarchates should not be considered bound by papal constitutions, except in the following instances: 1. When the constitutions treated matters of faith. 2. When the Pope explicitly mentioned and extended the law to the Orientals. 3. When the nature of the law implicitly embraced the Orientals, e. g., the appeal from the Pope to a general council.[15]

---

12 Cicognani, *Commentarium ad Lib I Cod.*, p. 9; Maroto, *op. cit.*, I, n. 198, a.

13 Cicognani, *op. cit.*, p. 9; Maroto, *op. cit.*, n. 173.

14 Azor, *Instit. Morales*, pars I, lib. V, cap. 11, sec. 7.

15 Benedict XIV, Const. *Allatae Sunt*, 26 Julii 1755, n. 44, *Coll.*, n. 395, footnote. Ayrinhac, *General Leg. of the New Code*, n. 78.

The resolution of the above Commission has enjoyed considerable weight. Roman Pontiffs have referred to it, and followed its conclusions in particular instances.[16] A recent application is found in the response of the S. Congregation of the Council, which declared that the discipline of the decree *Ne Temere,* relative to the form of marriage, did not embrace the Orientals.[17] The decrees for the Greek-Ruthenians in the United States[18] and Canada[19] are in practice an acceptance of the same policy.[20]

§ 1. The Code in Relation to Orientals

The first Canon expressly defines that the legislation of the Code affects merely the Latin Church, and applies to the Oriental Churches only in matters which of their nature must concern them.

"Licet in Codice juris Canonici Ecclesiae quoque Orientalis disciplina saepe referatur, ipse tamen unam respicit Latinam Ecclesiam, neque Orientalem obligat, nisi de iis agatur, quae ex ipsa rei natura etiam Orientalem afficiunt."

The interpretation and application of this Canon offers legal difficulties and doubts. The extent of the legislation of the Code to the Orientals is all embraced in the phrase, "*quae ex ipsa natura rei etiam (ecclesiam) Orientalem afficiunt.*" The statement is sufficiently comprehensive to include all possible cases, but it is very often difficult to become definite and practical. The norms followed

16 Benedict XIV, Const. *Allatae Sunt,* 26 Julii 1755, n. 44, *Coll.,* n. 395; S. Cong. de Prop. Fide, 8 Nov. 1882, *Coll.,* n. 1578; S. Cong. de Prop. Fide, 6 Aug. 1885, *Coll.,* n. 1640.

17 S. Cong. Conc., 1 Feb. 1908, ad Iam, *A. S. S.,* XLI (1908), 80, 108.

18 Pius X, Litt. Apost. *Ea Semper,* 14 Junii 1907, *A. S. S.,* XLI (1908), 3 seq.; S. Cong. de Prop. Fide pro Negotiis R. O., 17 Aug. 1914, *A. A. S.,* VI (1914), 458 seq.

19 S. Cong. de Prop. Fide pro Negotiis R. O., 18 Aug. 1913, *A. A. S.,* V, (1913), 393.

20 It is important to note that the Constitutions of the Holy See directed to one of the various Oriental rites, does not bind the other rites, unless there is an expressed extension. Cf. Benedict XIV, Const. *Etsi Pastoralis,* 26 Maii 1742, § VIII, n. XXIV, *Coll.,* n. 338; Papp-Szilagyi, *Enchiridion Juris Eccl. Orient. Cath.,* § § 23, 55; Maroto, *op. cit.,* I, n. 198.

by the Holy See previous to the Code must be invoked to determine the legislation which *natura rei* affects the Orientals.

Blat [21] advises a careful notice of the Canons: 1. Which are an expression of the divine law, natural or positive. 2. Which implicitly refer to and include the Oriental Church. Canons which expressly mention the various rites will be easily recognized.

Natural Law. Since the natural law is not subject to change, it follows that all men must necessarily be governed by its precepts. The Church cannot tamper with the natural law, although as a perfect society, she may interpret and declare obligations which arise from its precepts.[22] It is obvious that the canons of the Code which follow from the natural law are already *ex natura rei* universal obligatory norms of action; e. g., Canon 1068, § 1, antecedent and perpetual impotency, either on the part of the man or woman * * *, prevents marriage by the very law of nature. Canon 1399 gives instances of books prohibited by the natural law.

Divine Positive Law. Divine positive law consists of a group of ordinances enacted by God, and made known to man through revelation.[23] Hence, these laws are to be found in the inspired sources of Sacred Scripture and Tradition. Divine positive law may enunciate truths known as dogmas, and also promulgate disciplinary precepts.[24] The latter may be divided into the moral, ceremonial, and judicial. The moral precepts are principles of nautral law confirmed by Christ as the Divine Lawgiver; e. g., the unity and indissolubility of marriage.[25] New moral principles were given by Christ, such as the obligation to administer and to receive the Sacraments.[26] The ceremonial or liturgical precepts prescribe the essential elements of the Holy Sacrifice and the Sacraments.

---

21 *Commentarium*, Liber I, n. 50.
22 Neuberger, *Canon 6*, p. 68.
23 Slater, "Law, Divine," *Cath. Encycl.*, IX, 71.
24 Neuberger, *op. cit.*, p. 68 seq.
25 Maroto, *op. cit.*, I. n. 17.
26 Maroto, *op. cit.*, I, n. 17.

Finally the judicial precepts reflect the constitution of the Church, and the essential principles of ecclesiastical government established by Christ.[27]

The conclusion follows that all Canons of the Code which are declarations of divine positive law bind all Catholics alike, whether they are an expression of a dogmatic truth or a disciplinary decree.[28] Canons that contain such fundamental laws must be accepted *natura rei* by the Orientals; e. g., Canon 100, § 1, the Catholic Church and the Apostolic See have the nature of a moral person by divine institution; Canon 107, by reason of divine institution a distinction exists between clergy and laity; Canon 108, § 3, the divinely constituted hierarchy of orders consists of bishops, priests, and ministers; by reason of jurisdiction, the Supreme Pontiff and subordinate bishops; Canon 732, the Sacraments of Baptism, Confirmation, and Orders which imprint a character, cannot be repeated;[29] Canon 911, the Church has authority to grant indulgences.

In matters of faith and Catholic doctrine there is no exception of person. All Catholics must accept the dogmatic Canons defined by the Church.[30] Doctrinal points which are to be found especially in decrees of the Roman Pontiffs, the instructions of the Holy Office, the Sacred Congregation of the Propaganda, the Congregation for the Oriental Church, and the Sacred Poenitentiary are of the same tenor. The judgment of the Holy See as manifested in the condemnation of theories and propositions *contra fidem et mores* must be accepted by all.[31] The

27 Neuberger, *op. cit.*, p. 69; Wernz, *Jus Decretalium*, I, n. 87.

28 Cicognani, *op. cit.*, pp. 9, 10; Maroto, *op. cit.*, I, n. 173.

29 Cf. Canons which define the Sacraments and indicate their essential matter and form.

30 E. g., Eugene IV, Const. *Laetentur Coeli* (in Con. Florent), 6 Julii 1439, *Fontes*, n. 51; Eugene IV, Const. *Exultate Deo* (in Conc. Florent.), 22 Nov. 1439, *Fontes*, n. 52; Eugene IV, Const. *Cantate Domino* (in Conc. Florent.), 4 Feb. 1441, *Fontes*, n. 54; Pius IX, Litt. Apost. *Ineffabilis Deus*, 8 Dec. 1854, *Acta Pii* IX, I, 597, 619.

31 E. g., Pius IX, Syllabus errorum (1864), *Fontes*, n. 543.

prohibition of books and magazines opposed to Catholic faith and Christian morality is a frequent case.[32]

There are Canons of the Code which are not strictly expressions of the divine law, but follow as deductions therefrom. Canons which declare such obligations bind all, irrespectively of rite. The duty to receive the Holy Viaticum in danger of death is a declaration of the divine law, a consequence of the divine positive precept to partake of the Holy Eucharist.[33] The obligation for the pastor to say the *Missa pro populo,* is a similar example of the application of this principle. Although a bishop is bound by divine law to offer Mass for his flock, hypothetically speaking, the pastor has an obligation to celebrate the *Missa pro populo ex jure divino.* This is stated in an instruction addressed to the Apostolic Delegates in the Orient.[34] Canon 228, § 2, states that from the judgment of the Roman Pontiff, there is no appeal to an Ecumenical Council. By divine institution, the Vicar of Christ is the Supreme authority in the Church in matters of faith and morals. It follows, then, that his judgment as that of a divinely appointed teacher permits no appeal. The same reasoning applies to Canon 1257, which declares that it is solely the duty of the Holy See

---

32 Cf. Canon 1399 for examples of forbidden books, etc. Maroto, *op. cit.,* I, n. 168; Cicognani, *op. cit.,* p. 10. Recently the Congregation for the Oriental Church was asked whether the Orientals are also bound by the decrees of the Holy Office relative to the condemnation of books and periodicals. At this time special mention was made regarding the prohibition and penalties imposed against the "Action Française." Cf. Cong. S. Officii, 3 Feb. 1928, *A. A. S.,* XX (1928), 76. The Congregation for the Oriental Church declared that the decrees mentioned above affect the faithful of every rite and all are bound in the same way, since the decrees are more than disciplinary and directly refer to matters of doctrine. The Church desires by such enactments to maintain and to protect faith and morals; for this purpose the Code in Canon 1396 provides and sanctions that books condemned by the Holy See are to be considered prohibited in every place and in whatsoever translation. Cf. S. Cong. pro Ecclesia Orientali, 26 Maii 1928, *A. A. S.,* XX (1928), 195.

33 Gasparri, *De SS. Eucharistia,* II, n. 1147; canons 864, 866, § 3.

34 S. Cong. de Prop. Fide, 8 Nov. 1882, *Coll.,* n. 1578; Gasparri, *op. cit.,* I, nn. 496-502. The Code speaks of this obligation in Canons 339, § 1, and 466. The determination of this law is left to the Church; hence, the Oriental bishops or priests are not bound to celebrate the *Missa pro populo* on days prescribed in the Code. They observe the laws of their respective rites in this matter. Cf. S. Cong. de Prop. Fide, 23 Martii 1863, *Coll. Lac.,* II, 560, n. 49.

to regulate the liturgy and approve the liturgical books of the Church.[35] The *lex orandi* must conform to the *lex credendi.*

Express Mention of the Different Rites. The Canons of the Code which explicitly refer to the various rites are not infrequent. It is clear that in such instances, the Orientals must be governed in accordance with the legislation found in the common law. The list of Canons quoted below furnishes the chief examples in which the legislation of the Code expressly embraces the Oriental Catholics:

Canon 98 provides for the determination of rite, and the transfer from one rite to another.

Canon 106, n. 4, in the matter of precedence, the diversity of rites is not considered.

Canon 257 constitutes and defines competency of the Congregation for the Oriental Church.

Canon 366, § 3, where a diversity of rites demands, the ordinary may appoint a Vicar General.

Canon 542, n. 2, without a written permission of the Congregation for the Oriental Church, an Oriental Catholic cannot licitly enter a religious order of the Latin Church. (Cf. Canon 2411).

Canon 622, § 4, Oriental religious of whatsoever order or dignity, must have a recent and authentic rescript from the Congregation for the Oriental Church, before the Latin Ordinary may permit them to collect alms in his territory * * * .

Canon 733, in the confection and administration of the Sacraments, the rites and ceremonies of the approved liturgical books of the Church must be followed. All must conform to their proper rite, save in the exceptions admitted by law in Canons 851, § 2 and 866.

Canon 756, children must be baptized in the rite of their parents. If one of the parents is a Latin, and the

35 Benedict XIV, Const. *Allatae Sunt,* 26 Julii 1755, n. 27, *Coll.,* n. 395.

other an Oriental, the children must be baptized in the rite of the father, unless particular law rules otherwise. If only one of the parents is a Catholic, the children must be baptized in the rite of the Catholic parent.

Canon 782, § 5, Oriental priests, who enjoy the faculty to confer the Sacrament of Confirmation together with Baptism on infants of their rite, are forbidden to confirm infants of the Latin rite.

Canon 804, § 1, Oriental priests who are strangers, wishing to celebrate Mass, must exhibit an authentic and valid *celebret* obtained from the Oriental Congregation.

Canon 811, § 1, the priest who is to celebrate Mass shall wear the cassock and the sacred vestments prescribed by the rubrics of his rite; Canon 816, the Oriental priest must everywhere celebrate Mass according to his proper rite, with leavened or unleavened bread; Canon 818, in harmony with the rubrics of his liturgical books; Canon 819, in the proper liturgical language; Canon 820, a priest may celebrate Mass only on days permitted by his rite; Canon 823, § 2, if the altar of the proper rite is lacking, he may celebrate on the consecrated altar of another Catholic rite.

Canon 851, the priest shall distribute Holy Communion either with unleavened or leavened bread according to his proper rite. When necessity urges and if no priest of another rite is present, it is lawful for an Oriental priest who uses leavened bread to administer the Eucharist in unleavened bread; likewise a Latin or Oriental who uses unleavened bread, may administer Holy Communion in the leavened form; each one, however, must observe the rubrics of his proper rite.

Canon 866, the faithful, irrespective of rite, may for devotional motives, receive Holy Communion consecrated according to any rite; they are urged to fulfill the paschal precept in their proper rite; except in cases of necessity Holy Viaticum is to be received in one's own rite.

Canon 881, § 1, approved Latin confessors may validly and licitly absolve Catholics of the Oriental rites.

Canon 905, the faithful may confess to any approved priest, even if he is of another rite, if they desire.

Canon 955, § 2, and 961, Latin bishops require an Apostolic indult to ordain licitly subjects of the Oriental rites.

Canon 1004, if anyone has received certain orders in an Oriental rite and obtains Apostolic indult to be promoted to higher orders in the Latin rite, the subject must first receive the orders of the Latin rite which are not conferred in the Oriental rite.

Canon 1006, § 5, when Latin bishops ordain Oriental clerics with an Apostolic indult, or vice versa, the ordination days prescribed by the Code must be followed.

Canon 1097, § 2, marriage of Catholics of mixed rites is to be celebrated in the rite of the bridegroom and before his pastor, unless a particular law rules otherwise.

Canon 1099, § 1, n. 3, Orientals who contract marriage with Latins must observe the form prescribed by the Code.

Canon 1249, the precept to hear Mass is fulfilled if one is present at the Sacrifice celebrated in any Catholic rite in accordance with the prescriptions indicated by the Code.

Canon 1399, editions of the original text and ancient versions of the Sacred Scriptures, even of the Oriental Church, published by non-Catholics are forbidden by law; the same holds for translations into any language.

The Orientals too are affected by certain penalties enumerated by the Code, e. g., against heretics and schismatics, Canons 2314 and 2317; against affiliation with forbidden societies, Canon 2335; contra sollicitantes, Canon 904.[36]

The Orientals are not deprived of the spiritual favors granted to the Church in general. The Sacred Poenitentiary has declared that all Orientals may gain the in-

36 Cf. infra chap. X, § 2 with reference to penalties which apply to the Orientals.

dulgences conceded by the Roman Pontiff in a universal decree.[37]

§ 2. Instances of Latin legislation which may affect Orientals

Commentators indicate other cases in which Orientals may be bound by Latin legislation. They maintain that laws which are strictly territorial or *leges reales,* oblige them. Suppose the case of an Oriental who licitly elects to be buried from a Latin church, it follows that the legislation on ecclesiastical sepulture in the Code must be observed.[38] Laws enacted to promote public order or to remove scandal, bind all persons in the territory. A diocesan synod might prohibit carnivals or public dances under church auspices by threatening a penalty. Such a prohibition affects the Orientals in the territory. The avoidance of scandal and the good of religion demand *ex natura rei,* that all observe the law.[39] Laws which determine certain solemn acts would also bind the Orientals. This would apply for certain judicial acts of Orientals before a Latin tribunal.[40]

§ 3. Latin Legislation as a Source of Oriental Discipline

Canonists of the Eastern and Western Church maintain that in cases where particular Oriental legislation has not provided for certain contingencies, in practice the legal gap may be bridged by invoking the principles of the Latin Code as a subsidiary source.[41] After the reunion with the Holy See, the Oriental Church has adopted many points from the Latin legislation in order to provide for the utility of the Church, and the circumstances of the time. Many of the Tridentine enactments

37 Resp. 7 Julii 1917, *A. A. S.*, IX, 399; cf. infra chap. X, § 3.
38 Cicognani, *op. cit.*, p. 13; Maroto, *op. cit.*, n. 198, c.
39 *Ibidem.*
40 Maroto, *loc. cit.;* Cicognani, *loc. cit.*
41 Papp-Szilagyi, *Enchiridion Juris Eccl. Orient.*, §§ 23, 55; Cicognani, *op. cit.*, p. 14; Maroto, *op. cit.*, I, n. 173.

have been adopted by the Orientals. Examples of legislation thus appropriated are the election of Vicars Capitular during the vacancy of the diocese, cathedral chapters, and the celebration of diocesan synods. The legislation of the Western Church may supply deficiencies of the Oriental Codex only in so far as such legislation is not prejudicial to the Eastern rites. Hence to the same extent, the present Latin Code may be considered an auxiliary font of Oriental legislation.[42] This seems especially true of the principles in the fourth book of the Code, *De Processibus.* The many norms of judicial procedure therein contained are based upon the principles of natural equity and justice, Roman law, and finally the Church has also added elements which facilitate the process of justice. Although the norms of judicial procedure given in the Code are strictly proper to the Latin Church, generally speaking, they are not opposed to the rites and customs of the Orientals. In times past the Holy See has provided the Orientals with norms of judicial procedure for certain cases which were similar to those of the Latin church.[43]

§ 4. The Orientals in the United States

Since the Code exempts the Orientals from the discipline of the Latin church, save in matters which of their nature pertain to them,[44] do the Oriental Catholics who have acquired a domicile in the United States enjoy the same exemption? In the first place, it must be determined whether the Oriental who abandons the residence of his native land and establishes a domicile among Latins, as in the United States, still remains a member of his rite.

The Code clearly states that no one may transfer to another rite, or, after a legitimate transfer, resume his

42 *Ibidem.*

43 E. g., Instr. S. Cong. S. Officii, 20 Junii 1883 (ad Episcopos Rituum Orient.), *Coll.*, nn. 1588, 1587.

44 Canon 1.

native rite, without the permission of the Holy See.[45] This principle was also constantly maintained before the Code.[46] The various decrees for the Orientals in the United States [47] all indicate that the Oriental who establishes a domicile or quasi domicile in this country, remains a member of his rite. The legislation for Canada [48] and South America [49] is of the same tenor. The Orientals necessarily remain affiliated with their proper rite regardless of their place of residence. This fact forces the conclusion that they are also governed by a particular discipline proper to their respective rite. The notion of an Oriental Church implies, not only proper liturgical rites, but also a proper canonical discipline.[50] If an Oriental leaves his native land, and acquires a domicile in the United States, this fact does not change his rite, nor exempt him from his proper ecclesiastical legislation. The existing bond of rite presupposes its logical derivatives, a proper liturgy and a canonical discipline. This seems equitable; a Latin who establishes a domicile in the Orient, continues to be bound by the legislation of the Code. The fact of domicile does not exempt him from the observance of the common discipline of the Latin Church, so long as he remains a member of the Latin Church. Therefore, it appears reasonable that the Orientals in the United States must be bound to the liturgical and canonical legislation proper to their respective rite.

---

45 Canon 98, § 3.

46 S. Cong. S. Officii, 3 Aug. 1639, *Coll.*, n. 96; S. Cong. de Prop. Fide, 2 Junii 1760, *Coll.*, n. 429; Benedict XIV, Const. *Praeclaris*, 18 Mar. 1746, *Coll.*, n. 356; S. Cong. de Prop. Fide, 6 Oct. 1863, A, a, *Coll.*, n. 1243; Leo XIII, Const. *Orientalium*, 30 Nov. 1894, n. 7, *Coll.*, n. 1883.

47 S. Cong. de Prop. Fide, 1 Maii 1897, n. 2, *Coll.*, n. 1966; S. Cong. de Prop. Fide, 14 Junii 1907, art. 22, 23, *A. S. S.*, XLI (1908), 8; S. Cong. de Prop. Fide pro Negotiis R. O., 17 Aug. 1914, art. 20, *A. A. S.*, VI (1914), 462.

48 S. Cong. de Prop. Fide pro Negotiis R. O., 18 Aug. 1913, art. 25, 26, *A. A. S.*, V (1913), 397.

49 S. Cong. de Prop. Fide pro Negotiis R. O., 27 Mar. 1916, art. 5, 6, 7, *A. A. S.*, VIII (1916), 106.

50 The same is not true of the Western Church; there are different liturgical rites: the Ambrosian, Gallican, Mozarabic, and Roman; but in matters of discipline, all are subject to the common law of the Code.

§ 5. The Orientals under the jurisdiction of Latin Ordinaries

There are in the United States, members of several Oriental rites, some well represented in numbers, scattered throughout the various dioceses of the country.[51] Orientals who have no proper Ordinary are under the jurisdiction of the respective Latin Ordinary in whose diocese they have their domicile.[52] The determination and extent of the jurisdiction of Latin Ordinaries over Orientals in the United States offers some practical difficulties.[53] It has already been shown that although Orientals may acquire a domicile in this country, they are not subject to the discipline of the Code, except within the limits provided by the first Canon. It may be stated as a general principle, that the jurisdiction conceded to the Latin Ordinaries over Oriental subjects, cannot be exercised in prejudice to the Oriental rites or discipline.

In many instances the jurisdiction of the Latin Ordinary is quite evident; e. g., he alone grants faculties at his discretion to Oriental priests subject to him.[54] Since the Oriental faithful are committed to his pastoral care, it follows that the Ordinary may establish churches and missions, and appoint priests to take charge of such congregations.[55] There is no express provision, but as a consequence, it is within the power of the Ordinary to transfer or remove Oriental priests from their charges,

---

51 Scott, *The Reunion of the East*, p. 31 seq.; Shipman, "Greek Catholics in America," *Cath. Encycl.*, VI, 744-752; Shipman, "Rites in the United States," *Cath. Encycl.*, XIII, 78-86.

52 S. Cong. de Prop. Fide, 1 Maii 1897, *Coll.*, n. 1966; S. Cong. pro Eccl. Orient. (ad Delegatum Apost., Washington, D. C.), 29 Maii 1925.

53 The same difficulty does not exist with reference to the Greek-Ruthenians. They are subject to their own Ordinaries who exercise complete and independent jurisdiction. Hence, it is easier for them to observe their proper liturgical rite and canonical discipline; the latter are also governed by particular decrees with references to their status in the United States. Cf. Decr. S. Cong. de Prop. Fide pro Negotiis R. O., 17 Aug. 1914, *A. A. S.*, VI (1914), 458 seq.

54 S. Cong. de Prop. Fide, 12 Aprilis 1894, *Coll.*, n. 1866; S. Cong. de Prop. Fide, 1 Oct. 1892, *Coll.*, n. 1966, footnote; *A. E. R.*, VII (1892), 66.

55 S. Cong. de Prop. Fide, 1 Maii 1897, *Coll.*, n. 1966.

if the utility of the Church, and the good of religion demands. Such a procedure must follow the principles of equity and justice.[56]

The acquisition and protection of Church properties of the Oriental parishes must be governed by local legislation. The Church in such matters follows the prescriptions of the civil law proper to the territory, as long as there is no opposition to divine positive or canonical norms.[57] Since the civil laws may vary in different States, the diocesan norms will also vary to conform to the particular state legislation. The Third Council of Baltimore calls attention to this point and stresses the obligation to follow the civil code.[58] This legislation is properly territorial and applies to all.[59] It is evidently the mind of the Holy See that the Orientals should comply with local legislation in these matters. The decree *Cum Episcopo* admonishes the Greek-Ruthenian Ordinary to use all diligence for the security of Church temporalities; caution must be exercised to abide by the civil laws of the various States.[60]

It is interesting to note that Benedict XIV held that all pastors irrespective of rite must present the *cathedraticum.* The conditions require that they be pastors and subject to the local Ordinary. The opinion is based upon a decision of the Congregation of the Council.[61] These necessary conditions may be verified in some Oriental congregations of the United States.

---

56 The legislation provided for the Greek-Ruthenians in the United States suggests a possible norm of action in this matter. All Greek-Ruthenian priests who have the care of souls are removable *ad nutum* of the Greek-Ruthenian Ordinary. A priest who has been moved may appeal against the decree of the Ordinary, *in devolutivo,* to the Apostolic Delegate. The Delegate shall take action within three months; however, the right to have recourse to the Holy See, also *in devolutivo,* remains intact. Cf. Decr. S. Cong. de Prop. Fide pro Negotiis R. O., 17 Aug. 1914, art. 14, 15. *A. A. S.,* VI (1914), 461; supra chap. IV, § 5.

57 Canon 1529.

58 *Acta et Decreta III Plen. Conc. Balt.,* n. 270.

59 Maroto, *Institutiones Juris Can.,* I, n. 198; Cicognani, *Commentarium ad Lib. I Cod.,* p. 13.

60 S. Cong. de Prop. Fide pro Negotiis R. O., 17 Aug. 1914, art. 5, *A. A. S.,* VI (1914), 459.

61 8 Feb. 1738, *Thesaurus* VIII, 23; Canon 1504; Doheny, *Church Property: Modes of Acquisition,* p. 57, footnote 7.

The jurisdiction which the Latin Ordinary possesses over Oriental Catholics is conceded by the Congregation for the Oriental Church.[62] Its competency extends to all Oriental subjects irrespective of residence. The Congregation is competent in all affairs, whatsoever their nature, which pertain to the rites or discipline of the Oriental Churches. Questions of a mixed character are also reserved to its jurisdiction; e. g., the marriage between a Latin and an Oriental; celebration of Mass by an Oriental in a Latin Church. Briefly the Congregation for the Oriental Church exercises cumulative jurisdiction of all the other Congregations combined over the Oriental Churches, save in matters which are reserved to the Holy Office.[63] The Congregation also decides controversies which pertain to Oriental affairs, but only in an administrative or disciplinary manner; causes which demand a formal judicial procedure are given to a tribunal of its choice, or the Congregation may constitute a competent tribunal for the case in hand.[64]

Hence the Latin Ordinary who has cases relative to his Oriental subjects, which demand the intervention of the Holy See, must submit such questions to the Sacred Congregation for the Oriental Church. Suppose there is need of dispensations from certain matrimonial impediments, the Ordinary must request such dispensations from the above Congregation, or obtain the necessary faculties to dispense Oriental subjects.[65] If an Oriental subject who is bound by his particular law, requests permission to conform to laws of the Latin Church in the matter of fast and abstinence, because of the practical difficulties to observe the Oriental discipline in a Latin territory, the Latin Ordinary could not grant such a

---

62 Benedetti, *Schema Facultatum pro Cong. Eccl. Orientali* (sub praelo); Pius IX, Const. *Romani Pontificis*, 6 Jan. 1862, *Coll.*, n. 1223; Pius X, Const. *Sapienti Concilii*, 29 Junii 1908, *A. A. S.*, I (1909), 7 seq; Benedict XV, Const. *Dei Providentia*, 1 Maii 1917, *A. A. S.*, IX (1917), 529.

63 Canon 247.

64 Canon 257; Ayrinhac, *Constitution of Church According to Code*, n. 55; Wernz-Vidal, *Jus Canonicum*, II, n. 500, II, n. 500.

65 Cf. infra chap. XII, § 5.

permission, unless he has the necessary faculties from the Oriental Congregation.[66]

§ 6. A Vicar General for the Oriental Rites

Where members of different Oriental rites are living in Latin dioceses, and are under the jurisdiction of the local Latin Ordinaries, it is often difficult to provide for their proper and particular ecclesiastical government. In some localities certain Oriental groups are sufficiently numerous and fortunate to have a church and pastor of their own rite; in such cases, it is possible for them to observe their proper liturgical and canonical discipline; in other places, they depend upon the infrequent administration of an Oriental priest, or possibly are entirely under the pastoral care of the local Latin pastor.

The practice of the Holy See suggests the appointment of a Vicar General to aid in the government of the Orientals in a Latin diocese. Benedict XIV [67] provided that the Latin Ordinaries of Lower Italy, who had Italo-Greek subjects, should appoint a vicar acceptable to the Orientals and one well versed in their laws and customs. The Latin priest was not excluded from the office, but the Italo-Greek priest was to be preferred. A similar direction was given to the Latin Ordinaries of the United States for the government of the Greek-Ruthenians [68] previous to the appointment of their own Ordinaries.

66 Benedict XIV, Const. *Allatae Sunt*, 26 Julii 1755, nn. 2, 47, *Coll.*, n. 395. The Congregation of the Propaganda some thirty years ago granted to the Oriental faithful in the United States the faculty to conform to the Latin rite (Decr. S. Cong. de Prop. Fide, 1 Maii 1897, n. 1, *Coll.*, n. 1966). The decree is not specific, and it is not clear whether this concession would include the permission to conform to the laws of the Latin Church with reference to fast and abstinence. Since no exception is made, the general faculty apparently includes this particular concession. The fact that Orientals must conform to the Latin rite under stress of necessity is considered more or less odious; however, even the Orientals in the United States are free to conform to their proper discipline if they so desire. It might be noted that the Greek-Ruthenians may, with the permission of their Ordinary, conform to the feasts and fasts according to the customs of the place. (S. Cong. de Prop. Fide pro Negotiis R. O., 17 Aug. 1914, art. 27, *A. A. S.*, VI (1914), 462).

67 Const. *Etsi Pastoralis*, 26 Maii 1742, § IX, n. XXI, *Coll.*, n. 338.

68 S. Cong. de Prop. Fide, 1 Maii 1897, n. 3, *Coll.*, n. 1966.

The Code admits the same law: "*Unus (Vicarius Generalis) tantum constituatur, nisi vel rituum diversitas vel amplitudo dioecesis aliud exigat.* * * *"[69] Since the Canon admits more than one Vicar General if the diversity of rites demands, it does not seem to exclude the possibility of having several, for the different Oriental rites in the diocese. A glance at the history of the law insists that the Vicar General for the Orientals be acceptable to all, and familiar with their respective laws and customs. If there are several Oriental rites represented in a diocese, it could hardly be expected that one man be well versed in all Oriental codes, since each rite has its proper discipline. Again it would be doubtful whether a Vicar General of one rite would be acceptable to all other groups.

The advantage of this provision is obvious. In dioceses where the Eastern Catholics are numerous, and canonical questions relative to their discipline are frequent, a Vicar General familiar with their liturgy and legislation may expedite and execute their proper ecclesiastical discipline. He can especially direct the proper procedure in matrimonial cases, and in controversies which involve Orientals.

---

69 Canon 366, § 3; Dugan, *The Judiciary Department of the Diocesan Curia*, p. 25.

CHAPTER VI

THE DETERMINATION OF PERSONS ACCORDING TO RITE.

The various rites observed in the Catholic Church may be divided into two general classes, the Latin and the Oriental. All of the rites of the Latin Church are governed by the legislation of the Code. The Oriental rites, the Armenian, the Antiochene, Alexandrian, Chaldean and Byzantine,[1] together with their many modifications, however, have their particular hierarchical constitution, government and discipline.[2]

The Code defines in many instances the mutual relations between the Latin and the Oriental rites based upon the Pontifical laws and decrees of the past, and also effects some innovations.[3] The purpose of Canon 98 is to determine juridically to which rite a person adheres, and as a consequence, to which ecclesiastical discipline he is bound.[4] Hence the norms of this canon define the relations of physical persons to the Code.[5] The prescriptions enumerated are general principles which indicate the rite, or the transfer from one rite to another, or the mutual relations of the Latin and Oriental Catholics.[6]

Canon 98, § 1. *"Inter varios Catholicos ritus ad illum quis pertinet, cuius caeremoniis baptizatus fuit, nisi forte baptismus a ritus alieni ministro vel fraude collatus fuit, vel ob gravem necessitatem, cum sacerdos proprii ritus praesto esse non potuit, vel ex dispensatione Apostolica,*

---

1 Benedict XIV, Const. *Allatae Sunt*, 26 Julii 1755, n. 3, *Coll.*, n. 395; Fortescue, *The Mass*, p. 108.

2 Ayrinhac, *General Legislation in New Code of Can. Law*, n. 209.

3 Chelodi, *Jus de Personis*, n. 96.

4 Blat, *Commentarium*, Liber II, n. 23.

5 Maroto, *Institutiones Juris Can.*, I, n. 456.

6 Blat, *op. cit.*, Liber II, nn. 23-27; Woywod, *A Practical Commentary*, I, n. 75; Chelodi, *Jus de Personis*, n. 96; Maroto, *op. cit.*, I, nn. 456-457; Ayrinhac, *op. cit.*, nn. 209-211; Vermeersch-Creusen, *Epitome*, I, n. 191.

cum facultas data fuit ut quis certo quodam ritu baptizaretur, quin tamen eidem adscriptus maneret."

These norms represent a summary of the legislation enacted by the Holy See at various times to promote and to protect the Oriental rites. Each group depends mostly upon a natural growth through the acquisition of souls by the Sacrament of Baptism. Hence it is logical that its ceremonies should ordinarily indicate the rite of the person baptized.[7]

The valid reception of Baptism makes one a member of the Church of Christ.[8] It does not seem quite correct to state that the mere reception of the Sacrament determines the rite of the person.[9] The Canon legislates that the ceremonies of Baptism, proper to the different rites, determine the particular rite of which the recipient of the Sacrament is a member.[10] In order that the ceremonies of Baptism may designate the lawful rite of the person, it presupposes the observance of Canon 756: Children are to be baptized in the rite of the parents; in the event that the parents are of different rites, the rite of the father is preferred, unless a particular law rules otherwise; if one party is a non-Catholic, the rite of the Catholic party always has the preference.[11] However, this is not sufficient to protect the rights of the child or its parents. The Church realizes that cases and circumstances may arise when this rule becomes difficult or impossible. When Baptism is conferred according to another rite on account of (a) fraud, (b) necessity, (c) or an Apostolic dispensation without obligation to remain a member of the rite in which one is baptized, the

---

7 Benedict XIV, Const. *Etsi Pastoralis*, 26 Maii 1742, § II, n. XI, *Coll.*, n. 338; Heiner, *Benedicti XIV Papae Opera Inedita*, cap. I, n. 1.

8 Canon 87.

9 Chelodi, *Jus de Personis*, n. 96; Vermeersch-Creusen, *Epitome*, I, n. 191.

10 Wernz-Vidal, *Jus Canonicum*, II, n. 21; Maroto, *op. cit.*, n. 457; *Conf. Bulletin of the Archd. of New York*, V (1927), 106.

11 Cf. infra chap. VII.

Code provides that a person is considered a member of the rite in which he should have been baptized.[12]

Fraud. Solicitude for the Oriental groups has resulted in protective measures against fraud. Benedict XIV reprimanded the Greek-Melkites who at times followed the Latin rite. It seems that parents had their children baptized by the Latin missionaries, since Greek-Melkite priests were lacking. Many persons thus baptized when they attained adult age observed the Latin rite. This fact provoked a controversy regarding the rite of the persons baptized under the circumstances above mentioned. It did not appear reasonable that they should be considered Latins. Some, no doubt, were satisfied to remain members of the Latin Church. The Holy See decided that the persons in question should declare before an authorized delegate the rite they wished to follow. Once the selection was made, they were not free to abandon it. This measure removed all suspicion that the Holy See or the Latin missionaries had forced the Greek-Melkites to remain Latins, since they were baptized in the Latin rite under the stress of necessity.[13] A similar decree was later given for the Greek-Ruthenians in Europe to guard against illicit ministrations of the sacraments by priests of another rite.[14] The obvious conclusion follows that Baptism fraudulently conferred by a minister of another rite is illicit. According to law, it neither changes the rite nor affects the status of the person who is the victim of such deception.[15]

Necessity. The Church has always provided for extreme conditions. She does not demand the impossible and she is willing to dispense from her laws when the spiritual welfare of the individual requires it. The Church has ruled that a person must always adhere to the

---

[12] Pont. Comm. Interp. Cod., 16 Oct. 1919, Ad Dub. 11, *A. A. S.*, XI, 478; Woywod, *op. cit.*, I, n. 75; Vermeersch-Creusen, *Epitome*, I, n. 191.

[13] Benedict XIV, ep. encycl. *Demandatum*, 24 Dec. 1743, nn. 16-19; Benedict XIV, Const. *Praeclaris*, 18 Mar. 1746, *Coll.*, n. 356; Heiner, *op. cit.*, cap. I, nn. 6-10.

[14] S. Cong. de Prop. Fide, 6 Oct. 1863, C, a, d, *Coll.*, n. 1243.

[15] Blat, *op. cit.*, Liber II, n. 24; Canon 98, § 3.

rite of his parents according to the prescriptions of Canon 756. Imminent danger of death, unreasonable delay of Baptism, a long journey or grave impending difficulties to reach a church, or to procure the proper priest may all be classed as cases of necessity which lawfully permit the reception of Baptism in another rite.[16]

Cases of necessity may occur frequently in the United States among the Oriental Catholics. Often there are a few scattered families in a Latin parish. Even in a constituted mission or station where an Oriental priest calls at intervals, Baptism might often have to be deferred too long, not to mention instances where there is danger of death. If such conditions prevail, the mind of the Church indicates that the Orientals must receive the proper sacramental administrations from the Latin pastor in the vicinity.[17] Prudence would dictate that a Latin pastor should assure his Oriental subjects that they cannot be latinized, that an Oriental must remain attached to his rite, and may not transfer to another without permission of the Holy See.[18] If the Latin pastor neglects his pastoral obligation to provide for the spiritual needs of the Orientals in the above cases, there is the constant danger of proselytizing on the part of heretical or schismatic ministers. They will readily administer Baptism to those presented. Such a *communicatio in sacris* has been strictly forbidden by the Holy Office, and it has only permitted Baptism by a schismatic or a heretic in extreme necessity and when no Catholic person is present.[19]

Apostolic dispensation. Finally the Holy See sometimes allows a person to receive Baptism in another rite without obligation of adhering to the rite in which it

16 Benedict XIV, Const. *Etsi Pastoralis*, 26 Maii 1742, § II, n. XI, *Coll.*, 338; S. Cong. de Prop. Fide, 6 Oct. 1863, C, a, d, *Coll.*, n. 1243.

17 S. Cong. de Prop. Fide, 1 Maii 1897, *Coll.*, n. 1966; Leo XIII, Const. *Orientalium*, 30 Nov. 1894, n. 9, *Coll.*, n. 1883; Synodus Alex. Coptorum, sect. II, cap. I, art. V, n. X; Synodus Sciarfensis Syrorum, cap. I, art. IX, n. 6; S. Cong. de Prop. Fide pro Negotiis R. O., 17 Aug. 1914, art. 19, 20, *A. A. S.*, VI (1914), 461.

18 S. Cong. de Prop. Fide pro Negotiis R. O., 17 Aug. 1914, art. 20, 21, *A. A. S.*, VI (1914), 462; Canon 98, § 1, § 2, § 3.

19 S. C. S. Officii, 20 Aug. 1671, *Coll.*, n. 198.

was conferred. This demands a dispensation from the Holy See in every case, since the Canon does not provide for any exceptions.[20]

Canon 98, § 2. *"Clerici nulla modo inducere praesumant sive Latinos ad Orientalem, sive Orientales ad Latinum ritum assumendum."*

Whatever may be the duties and obligations of ecclesiastics towards persons of another rite, they are strictly prohibited to induce them to change their rite. There must be no effort to persuade anyone by threats or promises to relinquish his proper rite. When Benedict XIV issued his encyclical *Demandatum* in order to prevent the abuses of the Latin missionaries who were accused of latinizing their Oriental subjects, severe penalties were established. The Pontiff threatened the missionaries, who evidently were religious, with privation of the active and passive vote in their elections, and inability for office or degree in their order or congregation.[21] Again the same Pontiff declared in another Constitution, that no one was to prevail upon an Oriental to transfer from the Byzantine to the Latin rite. This was strictly forbidden, and Benedict XIV approved the penalties annexed to the violation of this law.[22] These penalties, the Pope avers, are in harmony with the decrees issued by Urban VIII for the Greek-Ruthenians.[23] Pope Urban insisted that it was unlawful for the Uniate Greek-Ruthenians, whether clerics, religious, or laymen, to change to the Latin rite without the permission of the Holy See. Bishops and prelates were not to presume to concede a transfer of rite to any subject under pain of nullity of the act.[24] When Leo XIII issued his Constitution, the legislation was even more severe. The prohibitions and

---

20 Benedict XIV, Const. *Etsi Pastoralis*, 26 Maii 1742, § II, n. XI, *Coll.*, n. 338.

21 Benedict XIV, ep. encycl. *Demandatum*, 24 Dec. 1743, nn. 15-19, *Fontes*, n. 338; Antoine, *Theologia Moralis*, IV, 444; Fortescue, *The Uniate Eastern Churches*, pp. 34-35; Heiner, *op. cit.*, pp. 3-4.

22 Benedict XIV, Const. *Allatae Sunt*, 26 Julii 1755, n. 21, *Coll.*, n. 395.

23 Heiner, *op. cit.*, pp. 4-5.

24 S. Cong. de Prop. Fide, 7 Feb. 1624, Heiner, *op. cit.*, p. 4; Decr. S. Cong. de Prop. Fide, 7 Julii 1624, Heiner, *op. cit.*, p. 5.

penalties extended to any Latin missionary, secular or religious, who induced by co-operation or counsel, an Oriental to transfer to the Latin rite. Its violation was punished by *suspensio ipso facto a divinis,* privation and exclusion from office, besides the penalties enumerated by Benedict XIV.[25] The decrees which provided for the Orientals in the United States and elsewhere are of the same tenor.[26] With the promulgation of the Code, the spirit of the law retains its force. Ecclesiastics are strictly forbidden to force a person to change his rite. The law extends to both the Latin and the Oriental clergy. There is this important difference: the Code makes no mention of ecclesiastical penalty attached to the violation of the law.[27] Hence, it seems one must apply the rule of Canon 6, n. 5,[28] and it appears logical to conclude that the penalties enforced by Benedict XIV and Leo XIII no longer obtain.[29]

Canon 98, § 3. *"Nemini licet sine venia Apostolicae Sedis ad alium ritum transire, aut post legitimum transitum, ad pristinum reverti."*

A person is a member of the rite in which he has been lawfully baptized, or should have been, according to norms of Canon 98, § 1, and Canon 756. Positive law demands, moreover, that no one may transfer from one

---

25 Leo XIII, Const. *Orientalium,* 30 Nov. 1894, n. 1, *Coll.,* n. 1883; Benedict XIV, Const. *Demandatum,* 24 Dec. 1743, § 15, *Fontes,* n. 338.

26 S. Cong. de Prop. Fide, 6 Oct. 1863, A, c. *Coll.,* n. 1243; Pius X, Litt. Apost. *Ea Semper,* 14 Junii 1907, art. 21, *A. S. S.,* XLI (1908), 8; S. Cong. de Prop. Fide pro Negotiis R. O., 17 Aug. 1914, art. 21, *A. A. S.,* VI (1914), 462.

27 Augustine, *A Commentary on the New Code,* II, 22.

28 "Quod ad poenas attinet, quarum in Codice nulla fit mentio, spirituales sint vel temporales, medicinales, vel ut vocant vindicativae, latae vel ferendae sententiae, eae tamquam abrogatae habeantur."

29 Neuberger, *Canon 6,* p. 50 seq. p. 46. The penalties sanctioned in the above Constitutions inflicted against Latin missionaries in the Orient who endeavor to latinize Orientals, were enacted to protect the Oriental rites. If these penalties constitute a part of the particular legislation of the Eastern Churches, it does not seem that they would be abrogated by the norms of the Code, since it does not affect the Oriental Church. (Can. 1). Therefore, the principle of Canon 6, n. 5, would not abrogate the penalties mentioned by the Holy See. Cf. Benedetti, *Schema Facultatum S. Cong. pro Eccl. Orientali.* Even if this assumption is correct, a reasonable doubt arises whether the penalties in question still obtain. Consequently, they could hardly be enforced.

rite to another, or after a legitimate change, revert to the first without permission from the Holy See. If anyone on his own accord, or by an authority inferior to the Holy See, has transferred to another rite, the transfer would be invalid. *De jure* it cannot be said that such a person has changed his rite.[30]

This law of the Code is well fortified by past legislation. Urban VIII forbade the Greek-Ruthenians, whether laymen, ecclesiastics, secular or religious, and especially the monks of St. Basil the Great, to transfer to the Latin rite without authorization of the Apostolic See. Special emphasis is placed upon the condition that only the Holy See may permit such a transfer, but no Greek-Ruthenian Ordinary.[31] Many other decisions of the Holy See insist upon this permission.[32] It is to be noted that no departure from the above regulations is evident in the decrees for the Orientals in the United States,[33] Canada,[34] nor South America.[35]

The provisions of Benedict XIV for the Italo-Greeks admit of some exception, but there is constant insistence upon the general rule. If a lay person of the Byzantine rite wished to transfer to the Latin rite, the case of the individual was left to the prudent judgment of the bishop. The Ordinary, however, was not authorized to allow groups or communities to transfer to the Latin rite without the intervention of the Holy See.[36] This particular provision is opposed to Canon 98, § 3, hence,

---

30 *AkKR*, LXXI (1894), 225; Antoine, *Theologia Moralis*, IV, 443 seq.; Blat, *op. cit.*, Liber II, n. 25.

31 S. Cong. de Prop. Fide, 7 Feb. 1624, Heiner, *op. cit.*, p. 4; 7 Julii 1624, Heiner, *op. cit.*, p. 5.

32 S. C. S. Officii, 3 Aug. 1639, *Coll.*, n. 96; S. Cong. de Prop. Fide, 8 Mar. 1757, *Coll.*, n. 403; S. Cong. de Prop. Fide, 2 Junii 1760, *Coll.*, n. 429; Benedict XIV, Const. *Praeclaris*, 18 Mar. 1746, *Coll.*, n. 356; S. Cong. de Prop. Fide, 6 Oct. 1863, A, a, *Coll.*, n. 1243.

33 Pius X, Litt. Apost. *Ea Semper*, 14 Junii 1907, art. 21, 22, 23, *A. S. S.*, XLI (1908), 8; S. Cong. de prop. Fide pro Negotiis R. O., 17 Aug. 1914, art. 20, *A. A. S.*, VI (1914), 462.

34 S. Cong. de Prop. Fide pro Negotiis R. O., 18 Aug. 1913, art. 26, *A. A. S.*, V (1913), 397.

35 S. Cong. de Prop. Fide pro Negotiis R. O., 27 Mar. 1916, art. 6, 7, *A. A. S.*, VIII (1916), 106.

36 Benedict XIV, Const. *Etsi Pastoralis*, 26 Maii 1742, § II, n. XIII, XIV, *Coll.*, n. 338.

it seems to be abrogated; again, there is no specific mention that it still obtains. There are various decrees which permit the Oriental Catholics to conform to the Latin rite in certain points of discipline, especially where they are without their own priests or churches. Whilst the Oriental Catholics in such circumstances may receive all the sacred ministrations of the Church, there is no change of rite implied.[37] The Code embodies these concessions and at the same time upholds the principle that there is no change of rite unless there is explicit permission from the Holy See.

There is one apparent difficulty suggested by Canon 98, § 3. The Congregation of the Propaganda ruled in 1838, that a heretic or schismatic Oriental returning to the fold may choose the Oriental rite which he preferred.[38] The same Congregation declared that this privilege was not abrogated by Leo XIII.[39] Is this privilege abolished by the Code? It does not seem so. In a strict sense the Code is only placing the conditions for a lawful change from one Catholic rite to another. This protects each Catholic group and assures its continuity. The law is intended to govern those already in the fold. Surely nothing should interfere with the choice of the separated Orientals upon their return. If they prefer this or that Oriental rite, they possibly have good reasons. The *bonum fidei* outweighs any objections. Vermeersch is of the opinion that this privilege still obtains.[40]

Before the Code, it was permissible to transfer from one Oriental rite to another in certain cases without the permission of the Holy See. For instance, when two Oriental rites were both using unleavened bread as the matter for the Holy Eucharist, a person might change from one rite to the other with only the consent of the

37 Leo XIII, Const. *Orientalium*, 30 Nov. 1894, n. 2, *Coll.*, n. 1883; Pius X, Const. *Tradita ab Antiquis*, 14 Sept. 1912, n. VI, *Fontes*, n. 698; S. Cong. de Prop. Fide, 1 Maii 1897, nn. 1, 2, *Coll.*, n. 1966.

38 S. Cong. de Prop. Fide, 20 Nov. 1838, *Coll.*, n. 878; cf. also footnote 1.

39 S. Cong. de Prop. Fide, 4 Feb. 1896, footnote 2, *Coll.*, n. 1883; Leo XIII, Const. *Orientalium*, 30 Nov. 1894, n. 11, *Coll.*, n. 1883.

40 Vermeersch-Creusen, *Epitome*, I, n. 191.

Ordinaries concerned. Such a transfer was possible from the Syro-Maronite to the Armenian rite. A similar transfer was permitted, also, if both rites used leavened bread. The present law apparently abolishes the above provision, since Canon 98, § 3, explicitly states no one may change rite or transfer to another without permission from the Holy See.[41]

The present law demands that if one has obtained a lawful transfer to another rite, he cannot resume his former rite without the consent of the Holy See.[42] This is to prevent a mixture of rites and at the same time to foster the liturgy and discipline proper to each group. If a person were permitted to follow any rite without restriction, such freedom would not be conducive to good order.

Canon 98, § 4. *"Integrum est mulieri diversi ritus ad ritum viri, in matrimonio ineundo vel eo durante, transire; matrimonio autem soluto, resumendi proprii ritus libera est potestas, nisi jure particulari aliud cautum sit."*

This law is not entirely new. The Church ordinarily has given preference to the rite of the husband. This is no doubt the recognition of his position as head of the family and authority of the household. Whenever persons of mixed rites marry, the law permits the wife, if she wishes, to transfer to the rite of her husband. She is free to do so at the time of, or during, the marriage. When the union is dissolved, the woman may again resume her native rite. Such provisions foster greater harmony in the family circle, and make for uniformity in the fulfillment of religious obligations in points of discipline; e. g., the observance of the same holydays of obligation, the same laws of fasts and ab-

---

41 S. Cong. de Prop. Fide, 20 Nov. 1838, *Coll.*, n. 878.

42 Leo XIII, Const. *Orientalium*, 30 Nov. 1894, n. 7, *Coll.*, n. 1883; S. Cong. de Prop. Fide pro Negotiis R. O., 18 Aug. 1913, art. 26, *A. A. S.*, V (1913), 397; S. Cong. de Prop. Fide pro Negotiis R. O., 27 Mar. 1916, art. 7, *A. A. S.*, VIII (1916), 106.

stinence. The law, however, does not make it obligatory that the wife transfer to the rite of her husband.[43]

Although it is lawful for a woman who has joined the rite of her husband to resume her proper rite when the marriage is dissolved, it would not always seem expedient to do so immediately. A practical case might occur where the husband dies and leaves a number of children who have only begun their religious education. The law demands, with but few exceptions, that the children must adhere to the rite of the father. If the mother makes use of her privilege immediately, this becomes a more difficult and complicated affair.[44] In many cases it might result in a disregard of the law. Prudence seems to dictate some delay, at least until the children have been educated in the customs and practices of their rite. The letter of the law, however, does not hinder the woman from resuming her native rite as soon as the marriage is dissolved.

The woman may also resume her proper rite should the marriage be dissolved by a declaration of nullity, or an Apostolic dispensation; e. g., *super matrimonium ratum et non consummatum.*[45] Whenever the wife chooses to follow the rite of her husband in accordance with the norm of this Canon, the text indicates, that she is not free to resume her native rite until after the dissolution of the marriage. Among the Italo-Greeks a woman who has transferred to the rite of her husband is not permitted to resume her own rite when the union is dissolved.[46]

It may be of interest to consider the sources of this legislation. In 1595, Clement VIII established certain norms for the Italo-Greeks when persons of mixed rites married. It is to be noted that the Latin rite was preferred. A Latin husband or wife must adhere to his or her rite, whilst a Greek wife or husband must observe

---

43 S. Cong. de Prop. Fide, 25 Julii 1887, ad 3, *Coll.*, n. 1678.

44 Cf. supra infra chap. VII.

45 Blat, *op. cit.*, Liber II, n. 26.

46 Benedict XIV, Const. *Etsi Pastoralis*, 26 Maii 1742, § VIII, n. VII, VIII, IX, Coll., 338; *AkKR*, LXXI (1894), 222 seq.

the Latin rite. If this was not advisable, they were free to follow their proper rite.[47] The same norms were retained by Benedict XIV.[48] The prescriptions of Leo XIII which gave preference to the rite of the husband, were subsequently embodied by the Code with a mere change of the wording.[49]

The Apostolic letter *Ea Semper* for the Greek-Ruthenians in this country gave regulations similar to those of the Italo-Greeks. The Latin husband or wife was not permitted to change his or her rite; however, a Ruthenian husband or wife was permitted to join the rite of the Latin spouse, or both parties were free to follow their own rite.[50] Subsequent decrees have altered these regulations. Since the Code affected no change, the present regulations for the Greek-Ruthenians in this matter are in harmony with the common law.[51] All other Orientals in case of marriages of mixed rites conform to the Code, unless particular law rules otherwise, as the Canon allows.[52]

Where husband and wife belong to different rites, and the latter as the law permits, elects to adhere to her native rite, she remains subject to the proper pastor of her rite and she is dependent upon him for the sacramental and other ministrations which are reserved to the pastor.[53]

---

47 "Maritus Latinus uxoris Graecae ritum non sequatur. Latina uxor non sequatur ritum mariti Graeci. Graeca vero uxor sequatur ritum mariti Latini. Quod si id fieri non possit, quisque conjugem in suo ritu, Catholico tamen, manere permittatur." Clement VIII, Const. *Sanctissimus*, 31 Aug. 1595, *Coll.*, n. 176, footnote 1; Decr. S. C. S. Officii, 13 Feb. 1669, *Coll.*, n. 176.

48 Benedict XIV, Const. *Etsi Pastoralis*, 26 Maii 1742, § VIII, n. VII, VIII, IX, X; Heiner, *Benedicti XIV Papae Opera Inedita*, pp. 5-6.

49 Leo XIII, Const. *Orientalium*, 30 Nov. 1894, n. 8, *Coll.*, n. 1883.

50 Pius X, Litt. Apost. 14 Junii 1907, art. 27, 28, 29, 30, 31, *A. S. S.*, XLI (1908), 9.

51 S. Cong. de Prop. Fide pro Negotiis R. O., 17 Aug. 1914, art. 28, 29, *A. A. S.*, VI, 463.

52 Canon 98, § 4.

53 S. Cong. de Prop. Fide pro Negotiis R. O., 18 Aug. 1914, art. 26, *A. A. S.*, VI (1914), 462.

Canon 98, § 5. *"Mos, quamvis duiturnus, sacrae Synaxis ritu alieno suscipiendae non secumfert ritus mutationem."*

The historical development of this privilege is to be found in the Constitution *"Tradita ab Antiquis"* of Pius X.[54] The faithful were forbidden generally to receive Communion promiscuously in another rite, although concessions to the contrary are also evident as the Pope recalls. But such faculties were not always and everywhere in use.

It is to be noticed that Benedict XIV forbade the Latins in Lower Italy to receive Communion from the Greek priest *sub specie fermentati;* he permitted the Greeks, destitute of their proper priest, to communicate *in azymo* from Latin priests.[55] The same rules were later extended to the Greek Melkites [56] and Copts.[57] The general custom demanded, if possible, the reception of Holy Communion in one's proper rite. It was considered lawful to communicate otherwise only in cases of extreme necessity.[58]

After the interruption of the Vatican Council, discipline was relaxed not only for extreme cases, but also to encourage a more frequent reception of the Sacrament. If there was neither church nor priest of their rite in the locality, Latins and Orientals were free to approach the Holy Table of another Catholic rite.[59] Leo XIII in his epochal Constitution for the Orientals made generous concessions. The faithful were permitted to communicate in another rite when they had no proper priest or church, or if a great distance to their church constituted a grave inconvenience. *"Idque fixum resideat, eum qui*

---

54 14 Sept. 1912, *Fontes*, n. 698; cf. infra chap. IX, §§ 3, 6.

55 Benedict XIV, Const. *Etsi Pastoralis*, 26 Maii 1742.

56 Benedict XIV, Const. *Demandatum*, 24 Dec. 1743, § 18, *Fontes*, 338.

57 Benedict XIV, Inst. *Eo Quamvis*, 4 Maii 1745, § 12 seq., *Fontes*, n. 357.

58 Pius X, Const. *loc. cit.;* S. Cong. de Prop. Fide, 6 Oct. 1863, C, d, *Coll.*, n. 1243.

59 Pius X, Const. *loc. cit.;* S. Cong. de Prop. Fide, 18 Aug. 1893, *Coll.*, n. 1846.

alieno ritu vel diu communicaverit, non propter ea consendum mutasse rituum."[60]

Pius X, the eminent advocate of frequent communion, granted the faculty to Latins and Orientals to communicate *sive in azymo sive in fermentato.* The reception was restricted to a church and from priests of a Catholic rite. This privilege did not imply a change or transfer of rite. "*Unusquisque in nativo ritu permanebit, etiamsi consuetudinem diu tenuerit communicandi ritu alieno.*"[61] The principle of the Code is merely a restatement and recognition of the concessions of Pius X and Leo XIII.[62]

---

60 Leo XIII, Const. *Orientalium,* 30 Nov. 1894, n. 2, *Coll.,* n. 1883; S. Cong. de Prop. Fide, 14 Feb. 1896, *Coll.,* n. 1883 (Note).

61 Pius X, Const. *Tradita ob Antiquis,* 14 Sept. 1912, n. VI, *Fontes,* 698, *A. A. S.,* IV, 616.

62 The question of devotional Communion, Paschal Communion and Holy Viaticum will be discussed in subsequent articles. Cf. Canon 866; infra chap. IX, § 6.

CHAPTER VII

THE RITE OF BAPTISM

The Code legislates that the ceremonies of Baptism determine the rite of the person baptized; one becomes a member of the rite in which he has been baptized, or should have been, under ordinary circumstances.[1] Some rule, however, is needed to determine according to which Catholic rite Baptism is to be conferred. The selection of the rite is neither left to the individual, nor to the parents, in case of infants. The purpose of Canon 756 is to establish juridically the rite in which a person is to be baptized under the various circumstances which may arise. This depends generally on the rite of the parents; if each parent belongs to a different rite, the law establishes certain preferences.

Canon 756, § 1. *"Proles ritu parentum baptizari debet."*

It is a duty for parents to provide for the spiritual welfare of their offspring, and it is natural that children should follow the rite of their elders. The law is, therefore, a statement of the duties and rights of the parents. This prescription is quite an easy matter when both parents belong to the same rite. The law presupposes this fact in most cases.[2]

Oriental parents may be forced by circumstances to have their children baptized by a priest of the Latin rite, or even by a minister of a different Oriental rite, ordinarily not entitled to baptize the children in question. In many localities of the United States, Oriental Catholics have neither their proper Churches nor priests.

---

1 Canon 98, § 1; cf. supra chap. VI.

2 Benedict XIV, Const. *Etsi Pastoralis*, 26 Maii 1742, § II, n. VI, VIII, *Coll.*, n. 338; Benedict XIV, ep. encycl. *Demandatum*, 24 Dec. 1743, § 17, *Fontes*, n. 338.

Although this case may occur frequently, the Code solves any difficulty which might arise. Whenever necessity of this nature prevails, parents may have their children baptized lawfully by a priest of another rite. Even if the child is baptized illicitly or fraudulently by a minister of a different rite, there is likewise no change of rite possible.[3] Again, danger of death or a prolonged delay of Baptism are instances which do not admit the postponement of the Sacrament. In fact it becomes a serious matter for parents to have the Sacrament administered at the earliest opportunity. In such cases, it matters not according to which rite Baptism is conferred; the child remains a member of the rite of the parents.[4] A response of the Pontifical Commission for the Authentic Interpretation of the Code makes this quite clear. The following doubt was proposed: "*Utrum qui ad preces parentum, contra praescriptum Can.* 756, *a ritus alieno ministro baptizati sint, pertineant ad ritum in quo sunt baptizati, vel ad ritum in quo, juxta Can.* 756, *baptizati debuissent.*" Resp. "*Prout casus exponitur, negative* ad 1am. partem; *affirmative,* ad 2am. partem."[5]

The Code makes no provision for the rite of the children should the parents themselves lawfully change to another. In the time of Benedict XIV, it was decreed that if both parents changed their rite, the children who had not attained the use of reason, followed the condition of the parents; if only one or the other changed, the children must adhere to the rite of the father.[6] The above regulation of Benedict XIV seems to offer a solution for similar cases which might occur after the promulgation of the Code. It appears to be within the natural right of the parents to determine the rite of their children below the age of reason. Of course the sup-

---

3 Canon 98, § 1; cf. supra chap. VI.

4 Woywod, *A Practical Commentary,* I, n. 650; Cappello, *De Sacramentis,* I, p. I, n. 176; cf. supra chap. VI.

5 16 Oct. 1919, *A. A. S.,* XI, 478.

6 Benedict XIV, Const. *Praeclaris,* 18 Martii 1746, *Coll.,* n. 356; Benedict XIV, ep. encycl. *Demandatum,* 24 Dec. 1743, § 17, *Fontes,* n. 338; Heiner, *Benedicti XIV Papae Opera Inedita,* cap. I, nn. 6-10; Chelodi, *Jus de Personis,* n. 96, footnote 7.

position applies only in the transfer from one Catholic rite to another.

Canon 756, §2. "*Si alter parentum pertineat ad ritum Latinum, alter ad Orientalem, proles ritu patris baptizetur, nisi aliud jure speciali cautum sit.*"

There is evident preference for the rite of the father in cases where the parents adhere to mixed Catholic rites. This is a general rule recognized by the Oriental Catholics.[7] If Baptism is conferred in cases of necessity by a priest not of the father's rite, this does not change the provision of the law; the child is considered a member of its father's rite, even if it baptized illicitly by a minister of another rite.

A difficulty arises when persons of mixed Catholic rites intermarry. Although the wife has joined the rite of her husband, which Canon 98, § 4 permits, she remains free in most instances to resume her former rite at the dissolution of the marriage. Granted that the children of such a marriage must follow the rite of their father, may the children below the age of reason after the death of their father, join the rite of their mother if she returns to her native rite? A regulation of Benedict XIV, quoted above, might be interpreted to favor an affirmative conclusion. It must be noted, however, that the Pontiff did not mention the exact case. He states that when both parents change their rites, children below the age of reason must follow the rite of their elders. If only one parent changed to another rite, the children must follow the rite of their father.[8] It does not seem probable from the text of the Code that children below the age of reason in the case proposed are permitted to follow the rite of their mother if she becomes a widow. The Code declares explicitly, if parents belong to mixed rites, the children follow the rite of the father, unless particular law

7 Synodus Alex. Coptorum (1898), sect. II, cap. I, art. V, n. XXV; Synodus Sciarfensis (1888), cap. I, art. IX, n. 12.

8 Benedict XIV, ep. encycl. *Demandatum*, 24 Dec. 1743, §§ 16, 17; *Fontes*, n. 338; *Conference Bulletin of the Archdiocese of New York*, V, n. 4, p. 109 seq.

provides otherwise. Therefore, it appears, that beyond the exception admitted by law, although a woman is free to resume her native rite after the death of her spouse, the obligation remains to educate the children according to the rite of their father.[9]

The Code does not interfere with particular law; hence, it must be recognized. An outstanding exception exists among the Italo-Greeks; their particular legislation established by the Holy See seems to favor the Latin rite. In a marriage between an Italo-Greek husband and a Latin wife, although the father's rite is given preference, still the law provides that in certain cases with the consent of the husband, the children may be baptized lawfully according to the Latin rite of their mother.[10] This law must be followed if the above circumstances are verified. When the Apostolic Letter *Ea Semper* was issued for the Greek-Ruthenians in the United States, this same exception applied.[11] Subsequent legislation has changed this provision of the decree.[12]

An unusual regulation prevails among the Greek-Ruthenians of Galicia. If one of the parents belongs to the Latin rite, and the other to the Greek-Ruthenian, the children are to be baptized and educated according to sex in the rite of their parent. Children of the clergy, however, must all follow the rite of the father.[13]

Among the Greek-Ruthenians in the United States, if the parents belong to mixed Catholic rites, the children must follow the rite of the father. This regulation is

---

9 Cf. supra chap. VI, explanation of Canon 98, § 4.

10 Benedict XIV, Const. *Etsi Pastoralis,* 26 Maii 1742, § II, n. X, *Coll.,* n. 338. It must be noted that a child thus baptized is subject to the jurisdiction of the Latin pastor, since it was lawfully baptized as a Latin. Hence, if there is question of ecclesiastical burial, the pastor has the right to conduct the obsequies, unless the child after the age of reason licitly elected to be buried from a church of another rite. It seems to follow that the pastor has the same right and duty to administer Extreme Unction, or to assist at marriages. Cf. Benedict XIV, loc. cit. § II, n. XI, XII, *Coll.,* n. 338.

11 Pius X, Litt. Apost. *Ea Semper,* 14 Junii 1907, art. 34, 35, *A. S. S.,* XLI (1908), 10.

12 Cf. infra this chapter.

13 S. C. de Prop. Fide, 6 Oct. 1863, D, c, d, *Coll.,* n. 1243.

found in the decree *Cum Episcopo;* [14] similar norms have been given for Greek-Ruthenians in other countries.[15] These recent provisions have been adopted in the present law of the Code. It is also to be noted that in all cases where a child is not baptized by a priest of the father's rite, the minister who conferred Baptism on account of necessity or otherwise, must transmit a record of the Baptism to the proper pastor and must indicate the rite of the child.[16]

Canon 756, § 3. *"Si unus tantum sit Catholicus, proles hujus ritu baptizanda est."*

The Church at all times has strictly prohibited the marriages of Catholics with infidels and with members of heretical or schismatical sects. If in such a union there exists a danger of perversion for the Catholic party, it is forbidden by divine law itself.[17] The Church sometimes for very grave reasons grants a dispensation to contract a mixed marriage, but only when certain conditions are verified. Among these conditions, the Church demands that the non-Catholic party must remove all danger of perversion to the Catholic party, and both must promise that all children shall be baptized and educated in the Catholic faith.[18] When an Oriental Catholic is a party to a mixed marriage, the same promises are exacted.[19] This is evident from their particular legisla-

---

14 S. C. de Prop. Fide pro Negotiis R. O., 17 Aug. 1914, art. 32, 33, *A. A. S.*, VI (1914), 403.

15 S. Cong. de Prop. Fide pro Negotiis R. O., 18 Aug. 1913, art. 39, 40, *A. A. S.*, (1913), V, 398; S. Cong. de Prop. Fide pro Negotiis R. O., 27 Mar. 1916, art. 18, 19. A. A. S., VIII (1916), 107.

16 Cf. decrees supra, *loc. cit.*

17 Canons 1071, 1060.

18 Canons 1061, 1071; *Rituale Romanum,* cap. I, tit. II, n. 27; Woywod, *A Practical Commentary,* I, nn. 1039-42; nn. 1055-57; Vlaming, *Praelectiones Juris Matr.*, I, n. 218.

19 Cappello, *De Sacramentis,* III, n. 900, 906; Papp-Szilagyi, *Enchiridion Juris Eccl. Orient. Cath.*, § 102, p. 257; Zhisman, *Das Eherecht der Orientalischen Kirche,* pp. 544-545.

tion,[20] and from many instructions of the Holy See.[21]

These conditions are founded upon the divine law, hence, only the rights of the Catholic party are considered in these matters. In cases of mixed marriages, there arises, therefore, a grave obligation to procure the Catholic Baptism and education of the children by reason of the divine law.[22]

---

20 Synodus Alex. Coptorum (1898), sect. II, cap. II, art. VIII, § 5, n. 3, IV. Synodus Sciarfensis Syrorum (1888), cap. I, art. XV, § 7, n. 5. Synodus Montis Libani (1736), pars II, cap. XI, n. 7, VII, *Coll. Lac.*, II, 165.

21 Benedict XIV, ep. encycl. *Inter Omnigenos,* 2 Feb. 1744, § 6. *Coll.*, n. 345; S. Cong. S. Off. (Instr. ad Omnes Episcopos Ritus Orient.), 12 Dec. 1888, nn. 1-12, *Fontes,* n. 1112; *Coll.,* n. 1696; Instr. S. Cong. de Prop. Fide (Ad Ep. Gr-Rumenos),—1858, *Coll.,* n. 1154.

22 Pius VIII, Litt. Ap. *Litteras altero,* 25 Mar. 1830, *Fontes,* n. 482; S. Cong. S. Officii, 16 Sept. 1824, *Fontes,* n. 866 ad 5; Vlaming, *Praelectiones Juris Matr.,* I, n. 224; Petrovits, *The New Church Law on Matr.,* nn. 193, 246; Wernz-Vidal, *Jus Canonicum,* V, n. 177; Chelodi, *Jus Matr.,* n. 60. The Code is silent about the rite of Baptism for illegitimate children. Juridically, their father is not recognized; it seems, therefore, reasonable to conclude that an illegitimate child follows the rite of its mother. Cf. Chelodi, *Jus de Personis,* n. 96, footnote 3. There are several decrees which support this conclusion. Cf. S. Cong. de Prop. Fide, 6 Oct. 1863, D, c, *Coll.,* n. 1243; S. Cong. de Prop. Fide pro Negotiis R. O., 27 Mar. 1916, art. 20, *A. A. S.,* VIII (1916), 107; S. Cong. de Prop. Fide pro Negotiis R. O., 17 Aug. 1914, art. 34, *A. A. S.,* VI (1914), 463.

CHAPTER VIII

THE SACRAMENT OF CONFIRMATION

§ 1. The Minister of Confirmation among the Orientals

The Council of Trent declared that the bishop alone is the ordinary minister of Confirmation.[1] The Code restates this doctrine,[2] which the Church has defined at various times.[3] The extraordinary minister of Confirmation, continues the Code, is a priest to whom this faculty has been conceded by common law or special indult of the Holy See.[4]

The priests of the Latin rite who are competent by indult to administer Confirmation, confirm validly only the faithful of the Latin rite, unless otherwise expressly provided.[5] Since this is a delegated faculty, the priest who is delegated, has only such power as is granted him. He must observe the limits of his delegation as to place, time, manner and persons, or other restrictions made by competent authority.[6] These restrictions are evident in

---

1 Conc. Trident., *sess.* VII, *de confirmatione*, can. 3, Denzinger-Bannwart, *Enchiridion Symbolorum*, n. 873; *sess.* XXIII, *de ordine*, can. 7, Denzinger-Bannwart, *op. cit.*, n. 970; Wernz, *Jus Decretalium*, III, n. 733.

2 Canon 782, § 1.

3 C. 2, D. XCV; c. un., X, *de sacra unctione*, I, 15; Innocent IV, ep. *Sub Catholicae*, 6 Mar. 1254, § 3, *Fontes*, n. 34; Clement VI, ep. *Super Quibusdam*, 29 Sept. 1351, *Fontes*, n. 42; Eugene IV, Const. *Exultate Deo* (in Conc. Florent.), 22 Nov. 1439, § 11, *Fontes*, n. 52; Van Espen, *Compendium Jus Ecclesiasticum*, I, pars II, tit. III, cap. II, n. 8 seq.

4 Canon 782, § 2; cf. references supra; The Code grants this faculty by law to the following: "Hac facultate ipso jure gaudent praeter S. R. E. Cardinales ad normam Canon 239, § 1, n. 23, Abbas vel Praelatus nullius, Vicarius et Praefectus Apostolicus, qui tamen ea valide uti nequeunt, nisi intra fines sui territorii et durante munere tantum." Cf. Canons 782, § 3; 294, § 2.

5 Canon 782, § 4.

6 Wernz, *Jus Decretalium*, III, n. 733; Woywod, *A Practical Commentary*, I, n. 683.

cases where Latin priests have enjoyed the faculty to confer Confirmation.[7]

The Church demands another condition for the valid administration of Confirmation by the extraordinary minister. The priest, whether Latin or Oriental, who enjoys, by law or indult, the privilege to confirm must use Holy Chrism consecrated by a bishop.[8] It is beyond the scope of this article to discuss the theoretical question whether the Roman Pontiff could delegate a priest to consecrate the Holy Chrism required for this Sacrament. The fact remains that the Holy See has demanded in many pronouncements that it be consecrated by one in episcopal orders.[9]

The early practice of the Church, which is still retained by many of the Oriental rites, permits the administration of Confirmation immediately after Baptism, although it is a sacrament absolutely distinct.[10] Among the Orientals with few exceptions the priest is the extraordinary minister. This faculty he enjoys by express or at least by tacit delegation on the part of the Holy See. An ancient custom vindicates this privilege of certain Oriental priests.[11] The reunion Council of Florence (1439), says nothing which expressly reprobates it.[12] Hence, this fact might be regarded as a tacit delegation.

---

7 Benedict XIV, Const. *Cum Ad*, 9 Jan. 1741, *Fontes*, n. 305; Benedict XIV, ep. encycl. *Demandatum*, 24 Dec. 1743, § 14, *Fontes*, n. 338; Augustine, *A Commentary on Canon Law*, IV, 101-102; "Rites and Ceremonies of the Sacraments," *Homiletic and Pastoral Review*, XXVIII (1928), 402-408.

8 Canon 781, § 1; Wernz, *op. cit.*, III, n. 735.

9 Benedict XIV, *De Synodo Dioecesana*, lib. VII, cap. 7, n. 4 seq; lib. VII, cap. 8, n. 1 seq; Innocent XIII, Const. *Cum Ad*, 13 Sept. 1721, *Fontes*, n. 279; Benedict XIV, Const. *Eo Quavis*, 4 Maii 1745, § 8, *Fontes*, n. 357; S. Cong. de Prop. Fide, 4 Maii 1774, *Coll.*, n. 503; Synodus Sciarfensis (1888), cap. V, art. III, n. 4; Synodus Ruthenorum (1720), tit. III, § II; Woywod, *A Practical Commentary*, I, n. 681; Blat, *Commentarium*, Liber III, p. I, n. 73.

10 Wernz, *op. cit.*, III, n. 732; Antoine, *Theologia Moralis*, V, 80 seq.; Synodus Sciarfensis, *loc. cit.*, nn. 1-4; Synodus Ruthenorum (1720), *loc. cit.*; Denzinger, *Ritus Orientalium*, I, 61.

11 Benedict XIV, *De Synodo Dioecesana*, lib. VII, cap. 9, n. 1 seq.; Antoine, *Theologia Moralis*, V, 95.

12 Eugene IV, Const. *Laetentur Coeli* (In Conc. Florent.), 6 Julii 1439, § 9, *Fontes*, n. 51; Eugene IV, Const. *Exultate Deo* (in Conc. Florent.), 22 Nov. 1439, § 11, *Fontes*, n. 52.

The more recent Synods of the Oriental rites mention the custom that the priest confirms after Baptism. *Ab immemorabili* he is considered the delegated minister to confer this sacrament, although there is some restriction to administer Confirmation after private Baptism.[13] When such Synods have the approval of the Holy See, it seems that the custom is given express sanction.

It is well to notice that in some instances the Holy See has acted differently. The privilege of certain Oriental priests to confirm has been expressly withdrawn. Hence the presumption that they are tacitly delegated ceases for the specified groups. As a consequence, they no longer enjoy the faculty to administer Confirmation, since they are interdicted by supreme authority.[14] Nicholas IV forbade the priests of Bulgaria to confirm, Innocent IV, the priest in the kingdom of Cyprus, and Clement VIII, the Italo-Greek priests of Lower Italy.[15] The Maronites departed from the general custom of the Orientals in the Synod of 1736, later approved by Benedict XIV. The Synod decreed that simple priests are not to presume to administer Confirmation.[16] Here there is positive evidence that the Syro-Maronite priests do not enjoy the delegated faculty, as the extraordinary ministers of Confirmation.[17] Benedict XIV enforced the enactment of his predecessor, Clement VIII, among the Italo-Greek priests in Lower Italy. They were forbidden to administer Confirmation. The Sacrament was to be conferred by the Latin bishops in the vicinity.[18] When the Cardinals of the Sacred Congregation of the Propagation for the Affairs of the Oriental Church assembled in plenary session, November 17, 1917, they decided to

---

13 Synodus Sciarfensis, cap. V, art. III, nn. 3-4; Synodus Alex. Coptorum, sect. II, cap. III, art. III, nn. 4-5.

14 Antoine, *Theologia Moralis*, V, 96, 97; Cappello, *Jus Pontificium*, VII (1927), n. 8, p. 59.

15 Benedict XIV, *De Synodo Dioecesana*, lib. VII, cap. IX, nn. 4, 5; Clement VIII, Const. *Sanctissimus Dominus*, 31 Aug. 1595, *Fontes*, n. 179.

16 Synodus Montis Libani (1736), pars II, cap. II, n. 15; cap. III, n. 2, *Coll. Lac.*, II, 121, 123.

17 Benedict XIV, *De Synodo Dioecesana*, lib. VII, cap. IX, n. 5.

18 Benedict XIV, *Etsi Pastoralis*, 26 Maii 1742, § III, n. 1, *Coll.*, n. 338.

restore to the Italo-Greek priests the faculty to administer Confirmation. This resolution was approved by Benedict XV in a private audience to the Secretary of the above Congregation.[19]

A practical question may now be raised. Do the Greek-Ruthenian priests in the United States enjoy the delegated faculty to administer Confirmation at the present time? When the Apostolic Letter *Ea Semper* was issued for the Ruthenians in the United States, this faculty was explicitly withdrawn: *"Presbyteris Ruthenis in America commorantibus penitus interdicitur, ne baptizatos Sacra Chrismate consignent: et si secus fecerint, sciant se invalide egisse."* [20]

This restriction was opposed to the custom of their native land where the Greek-Ruthenian priests enjoy the delegated faculty to confirm.[21] A subsequent decree, *Cum Episcopo,* for the same Orientals in the United States presents a difficulty with reference to this point. There was no explicit revocation of the prohibition which forbade the Greek-Ruthenian priests to administer Confirmation. The matter was passed over in silence.[22] Since the first regulation is neither contrary to any ruling in the second decree, nor expressly revoked, strictly speaking, it seems one would be forced to conclude that the prohibition in the Apostolic letter *Ea Semper* still obtains.

It seems doubtful whether this is the mind of the Holy See. The legislation of the decree *Cum Episcopo* might represent a total rearrangement of the status of the Greek-Ruthenians in the United States, more in conformity with their rite and discipline in their native land. If this is the mind of the legislator, the previous prohibition should be considered abolished.[23] There is reason to believe, it seems, that the second decree, *Cum*

---

19 Acta S. Cong. de Prop. Fide pro Negotiis R. O., 17 Nov. 1917.

20 Pius X, Ap. Litt. *Ea Semper,* 14 Junii 1907, art. 14, *A. S. S.,* XLI (1908), 7.

21 Synodus Ruthenorum (1720), *loc. cit.,* tit. III, § II.

22 S. Cong. de Prop. Fide pro Negotiis R. O., 17 Aug. 1914, *A. A. S.,* VI (1914), 458-463.

23 Canon 22; Neuberger, *Canon 6,* p. 29 seq.

Episcopo, represents a complete revision of the previous status. A year before this decree for the Ruthenians in the United States, a similar one was issued for Canada, and there is no prohibition for Ruthenian priests to administer the Sacrament of Confirmation.[24] In 1916, another decree for the same Orientals in South America was issued, and no restriction is evident.[25] With these facts in mind, one would hesitate to maintain that the Greek-Ruthenian priests in the United States do not enjoy the faculty to confirm their subjects.[26]

After the publication of the decree *Ea Semper,* the Greek-Ruthenian clergy sent a plea to the Holy See with reference to the prohibition that priests may not administer the sacrament of Confirmation; the Holy See was asked to revoke this law.[27] The plea later met with a favorable response, and the Holy See revoked the prohibition, and permitted the Greek-Ruthenian priests in the United States to administer Confirmation as they had done in the past according to the custom of their rite.[28]

The Code explicitly forbids the Oriental priests to confirm children of the Latin rite, although they might baptize them lawfully, when certain extreme circumstances are verified.

"Nefas est presbyteris ritus Orientalis, qui facultate vel privilegio gaudent Confirmationem una cum Baptismo infantibus sui ritus conferendi, eandem ministrare infantibus Latini ritus." [29]

---

24 S. Cong. de Prop. Fide pro Negotiis R. O., 17 Aug. 1913, *A. A. S.*, V (1913), 393-399.

25 Decr. S. Cong. de Prop. Fide pro Negotiis R. O., 27 Mar. 1916, *A. A. S.*, VIII (1916), 105-107.

26 Augustine, *A Commentary on Canon Law,* IV, 104-105.

27 Cf. *Istruzione,* S. Cong. de Prop. Fide, Mar. 1908, to the Apost. Delegate of the United States, n. 6.

28 This information was given by the Rt. Rev. C. Bohachevsky, D. D., Ordinary for the Greek-Ruthenians from Galicia in the United States. The document of the Holy See which revoked the prohibition of the *Ea Semper* was lost, it seems, during the long vacancy of the Ruthenian diocese from 1916-1924. This testimony is sufficient evidence that the Greek-Ruthenian priests lawfully administer the sacrament of Confirmation.

29 Canon 782, § 5.

Does the Oriental priest act validly if he confirms Latin infants despite the restriction? The law apparently contains no invalidating clause, and hence there is no positive reason to say that his administration of the Sacrament is null in such cases. The Church, however, has at different times made very severe prohibitions against Oriental priests who presume to confirm Latins whom they baptize. The practice is strictly forbidden by the Holy See, and Oriental bishops are reminded that they must absolutely restrain their clergy in this matter.[30]

Authors do not agree as to the force of the clause *nefas est.* Blat maintains the words signify a divine prohibition. This supposes a necessary faculty which is wanting to Oriental priests in so far as they are extraordinary ministers.[31] In other words, he seems to intimate that their faculty is so restricted that they cannot confirm validly subjects of the Latin rite. The Code explicitly states that Latin priests, who by indult, have the faculty to confirm, may administer the Sacrament validly only to the faithful of the Latin rite, unless the indult expressly provides otherwise.[32] Is the restrictive clause *nefas est* equivalent to the prohibition given to the Latin priests which makes their administration invalid if they exceed their faculty? Blat seems to think so since he holds that the reason is the same in both cases, namely, a divine prohibition. According to this opinion, Confirmation given to Latins by Oriental priests would be invalid.

Vermeersch holds that the nullity of Confirmation administered to Latins by Oriental priests is not apparent. He favors the opinion that the restrictive clause *nefas est* expresses a mere prohibition.[33] Decrees of the Holy See seem to favor such a conclusion. Instruc-

---

30 S. Cong. de Prop. Fide, 5 Julii 1886, Coll., n. 1660; S. Cong. de Prop. Fide, 6 Oct. 1863, C, a, *Coll.*, n. 1243; Augustine, *A Commentary on Canon Law*, IV, 104.

31 Blat, *op. cit.*, Liber III, n. 76, § 2.

32 Canon 782, § 4.

33 Vermeersch, *Periodica*, XII (1924), 11-13.

tions issued to the Ruthenian priests and others strictly forbid them to confirm Latins whom they happen to baptize,[34] but do not state positively that it is invalid.

In 1886, the Congregation of the Propaganda was asked whether or not certain persons who were confirmed by schismatic priests must again be confirmed absolutely or conditionally. The reply is based upon a response of the Holy Office.[35] After an examination of the question, it was not deemed expedient in the case proposed to repeat the Sacrament. The following observations are important: If the person in question is to be promoted to Orders, if the person himself or his parents request the Sacrament, it is to be given *sub conditione et sub secreto.* Again, if after investigation, it is found that an instrument was used for the anointing in the administration of the Sacrament, it is to be repeated, provided the above suppositions are verified. Vermeersch observes the Holy See implicitly seems to favor the validity of Confirmation given by schismatic priests without the instrument in question.[36]

It is to be noted that the Holy See has never positively stated that the prohibition of uniate Oriental priests to administer Confirmation to Latins is under pain of invalidity. Neither has she pronounced positively against the same administration of schismatical priests. If one considers these facts, it certainly appears more probable that Oriental priests who enjoy the faculty to confirm, administer validly to Latins, but illicitly.[37] Synods among the Orientals stress the same law as contained in the above decrees.[38]

---

34 S. Cong. S. Officii, 1782, *Coll.*, n. 552; S. Cong. de Prop. Fide, 6 Oct. 1863, C, a, *Coll.*, n. 1243; S. Cong. de Prop. Fide, 5 Julii 1886, ad Iam, *Coll.*, n. 1660.

35 S. C. S. Officii, 14 Jan. 1885, *Coll.*, n. 1630.

36 Canon 781, § 2.

37 Vermeersch, *Periodica*, XII (1924), 11-13; Prümmer, *Manuale*, n. 284; Cappello, *Jus Pontificium*, VII (1927), n. 8, p. 59; Cappello, *De Sacramentis*, I, n. 206.

38 Synodus Sciarfensis, cap. III, art. IX, n. 6; Synodus Ruthenorum, tit. III, § 1.

Another difficulty may be proposed. May Oriental priests who enjoy the faculty to confirm, administer the Sacrament to children of other Oriental rites whom they baptize? The Holy See answered this question by making a distinction. Oriental priests who confirm by virtue of tacit privilege may confirm validly not only children of their own rite, but also those of other rites wherein exists the same privilege.[39]

§ 2. The Subject of Confirmation among the Orientals

Since many of the Oriental rites administer Confirmation immediately after Baptism, the question naturally presents itself, who is a suitable subject for Confirmation? Any baptized person, not yet confirmed, may validly receive the Sacrament. For a licit reception, adults must be in a state of grace, well instructed in their religion, and have the proper intention.[40] Baptized infants, before they attain the use of reason, are fit subjects for Confirmation. They may not receive this Sacrament licitly, except among the Oriental rites where this custom obtains.[41] This practice differs widely from the Latin church. At the present time, Confirmation is usually conferred around the seventh year; in extreme cases such as danger of death, or other grave and just causes, it may be administered at an earlier age.[42]

In Spain and Latin American countries, legitimate custom, it appears, permits the Confirmation of children generally before they attain the use of reason.[43] This practice is an exception to the prevalent ecclesiastical law of the Latin Church, and her mind on this subject is

---

39 S. C. S. Officii, 22 Aprilis 1896, *Coll.*, n. 1926; Augustine, *op. cit.*, IV, 113-115.

40 Wernz, *Jus Decretalium*, III, n. 734.

41 Wernz, *op. cit.*, III, n. 734; Synodus Sciarfensis, cap. V, art. III, n. 4; Synodus Ruthenorum, tit. III, § 2; Benedict XIV, *De Synodo Dioecesana*, lib. VII, cap. IX, n. 1 seq.

42 Canon 788; Benedict XIV, *De Synodo Dioecesana*, lib. VII, cap. X, n. 1 seq.; Blat, *op. cit.*, Liber III, n. 83.

43 Conc. Plen. Amer. Lat. (1899), n. 520; Wernz, *Jus Decretalium*, III, n. 734; Blat, *op. cit.*, Liber III, n. 83.

expressed in many pronouncements.[44] The Maronites are among the Orientals who conform to the practice of the Latin Church, and prescribe that children should have reached the age of reason before this Sacrament is conferred.[45]

§ 3. The reception of Holy Communion by Infants after Confirmation among the Orientals

The Council of Trent declared that children, prior to the dawn of reason, are not obligated by any necessity to receive the Holy Eucharist. Through Baptism they are already constituted in the state of grace, which they cannot forfeit at such an early age. However, the Council did not condemn that ancient custom which was observed in some places.[46] For a long time, the practice prevailed both in the Eastern and in the Western churches that infants after Baptism were confirmed, and also partook of the Holy Eucharist.[47] This custom gradually disappeared in the West during the twelfth and thirteenth centuries.[48] Cappello observes that it is not so common in the East today, and is gradually falling into disuse. No doubt, this is brought about through greater respect towards the Sacrament. In some few regions the custom still obtains.[49] Where it still exists the infant partakes of the Holy Eucharist under the species of wine.[50] When the Holy See was asked to forbid the practice in the Coptic Church, it refused to introduce innovations and sustained their ancient custom.[51]

---

44 Benedict XIV, Instr. *Eo Quamvis Tempore*, 4 Maii 1745, § 6 *Coll.*, n. 351; Leo XIII, Litt. Apost. *Abrogata*, 22 Junii 1897, *Coll.*, n. 1973; S. C. S. Officii, 11 Dec. 1850, n. 12, *Coll.*, n. 1054; S. Cong. de Prop. Fide, 4 Maii 1774, *Coll.*, n. 503.

45 Synodus, Montis Libani, pars II, cap. III, n. 8, *Coll. Lac.*, II, 126.

46 Conc. Trident., *sess.* XXI, can. 4, Denzinger-Bannwart, *op. cit.*, nn. 933, 937; Gasparri, *De Eucharistia*, II, n. 1121.

47 Benedict XIV, *De Synodo Dioecesana*, lib. VII, cap. XII, n. 1 seq.; Antoine, *Theologia Moralis*, V, 75.

48 Wernz, *Jus Decretalium*, III, n. 738; Canon 854, § 1.

49 Cappello, *De Curia Romana*, I, 244; Denzinger, *Ritus Orientalium*, I, 39.

50 Gasparri, *op. cit.*, II, n. 1122.

51 S. C. S. Officii, 14 Junii 1741, *Coll.*, n. 326.

Benedict XIV tolerated the custom among the Italo-Greeks. He insisted that it contains nothing opposed to orthodox faith and sound morals, so long as the Greeks firmly believe that such communion for infants is not necessary for salvation, and that Baptism may be validly and licitly administered without it.[52] The Pontiff demanded the necessary reverence and respect to the Holy Eucharist in its administration to infants. Some of the Synods among the Orientals mention the above custom. It prevails among the Greek-Ruthenians [53] and Coptic rites.[54] Others have abolished it and strictly forbid the reception of the Holy Eucharist by infants; this is the case among the Syrians (*puri*) [55] and the Maronites.[56]

---

52 Heiner, *Benedicti XIV Papae Opera Inedita*, cap. V, 213; Const. *Etsi Pastoralis*, 26 Maii 1742, § II, n. VII, *Coll.*, n. 338; Laemmer, *In Decreta Conc. Ruth. Zamosciensis Animadversiones*, § 21.

53 Synodus Ruthenorum, tit. III, § 1; Synodus Montis Libani (1736), pars II, cap. 12, n. 13.

54 Synodus Alex. Coptorum, sect. II, cap. III, art. IV, n. 6.

55 Synodus Sciarfensis, cap. V, art. II, nn. 5, 19; cap. V, art. IV, § I, n. III.

56 Synodus Montis Libani, pars II, cap. II, n. 19, *Coll. Lac.*, II, 122.

CHAPTER IX

THE CELEBRATION OF MASS AND THE HOLY EUCHARIST

§ 1. The Credentials of a Strange Priest Wishing to Celebrate Mass

The Church has often insisted that only worthy priests are to be admitted to the celebration of the Holy Sacrifice. Prudent and wholesome legislation demanded of traveling and unknown clerics authentic letters of recommendation from their Ordinary or religious Superior, before they were permitted to perform ecclesiastical functions outside of their proper churches. Vestiges of such regulations are already evident in the Canons of the Council of Chalcedon (451),[1] and the Decretals record similar enactments;[2] later, the Council of Trent provided some very definite and strict measures.[3] The Code does not deviate greatly from past legislation in this important matter of discipline.

Canon 804, § 1. "*Sacerdos extraneus ecclesiae in qua celebrare postulat, exhibens authenticas et adhuc validas litteras commendatitias sui Ordinarii, si sit saecularis, vel sui Superioris, si religiosus, vel Sacrae Congregationis pro Ecclesia Orientali, si sit ritus Orientalis, ad missae celebrationem admittatur, nisi interim aliquid eum commisisse constet, cur a Missae celebratione repelli debeat.*"

---

1 C. 7, D. LXXI; Motry, *Diocesan Faculties*, p. 50.

2 C. 3, X, *de clericis peregrinis*, I, 22; Gasparri, *De SS. Eucharistia*, I, nn. 362-367.

3 Conc. Trident., *sess.* XXIII, *de reform.*, cap. XVI, "Nullus praeterea clericus peregrinus sine commendatitiis sui Ordinarii litteris, ab ullo episcopo ad divina celebranda, et sacramenta administranda admittatur." Cf. *Canones et Decreta Conc. Trident.*, p. 163; Wernz, *Jus Decretalium.*, III, nn. 531-535.

The term "*sacerdos extraneus ecclesiae,*" does not refer merely to extra-diocesan priests. In a strict sense it applies, also, to any priest who wishes to celebrate Mass in a church to which he is not attached. *Per se* the letter of recommendation is necessary, and may be demanded whenever the conditions mentioned above are verified.[4] The mere fact that a priest is not incardinated in the diocese wherein he actually resides does not make him an *extraneus*. Urgent missionary needs or other important reasons, may require the services of the priest in a another diocese. In such cases he becomes subject to the jurisdiction of the local Ordinary by reason of his newly acquired domicile or quasi-domicile.[5]

The letter of recommendation and identity issued by the various authorities is ordinarily called *a celebret.*[6] This document gives testimony of the bearer's rank, and certifies that he is free from ecclesiastical censure; it is likewise a testimonial of the priest's good standing in his diocese.[7] The *celebret* is authentic if it is signed by the proper authority, and if it has the official seal.[8] Together with this authenticity, the *celebret* must still be in force, "*adhuc litterae validae.*" Its nature is of a temporary character, wherefore, it is valid only for the period issued. The period is not determined by the Canon, but is left to the prudent judgment of the authority who issues the document. With the expiration of the stipulated time, the document is no longer admitted. The *celebret* is also *ipso facto* invalid should the bearer render himself unworthy to celebrate Mass.[9] One could not refuse, however, to admit the validity of a *celebret* from knowledge gained solely through the Sacrament of Penance.[10]

---

4 Motry, *Diocesan Faculties*, p. 48 seq.

5 Canons 91, 92; Wernz-Vidal, *Jus Canonicum*, II, nn. 9-11.

6 Augustine, *A Commentary on Canon Law*, IV, 129; Woywod, *A Practical Commentary*, I, nn. 699, 700.

7 Wernz, *Jus Decretalium*, III, n. 532; Motry, *op. cit.*, p. 53.

8 Vermeersch-Creusen, *Epitome*, II, n. 76; Canon 1813.

9 Augustine, *op. cit.*, IV, 131; Motry, *op. cit.*, pp. 49, 52.

10 S. C. S. Officii, 18 Nov. 1682, Denzinger, *Enchiridion Symbolorum*, n. 1220.

A priest who is a member of an Oriental rite must obtain this document from the Sacred Congregation for the Oriental Church.[11] Historical facts indicate that this regulation is not arbitrary. In times past it has happened that certain Oriental priests have exhibited *celebrets* issued and signed by their Ordinaries; however, the documents were written in some Oriental language, and unintelligible to most Latin pastors and bishops. Frequently the bearers were imposters; in many instances not even clerics, nor priests in good standing, who had left their diocese without the authorization of their Ordinary. These men prepared their own *celebrets.* The documents, written in Arabic, Armenian, or Syriac, were shown to the Latin pastors who, without further ado, admitted the bearers to the celebration of Mass. Many of these men were unworthy, and positively debarred by ecclesiastical law from offering the Holy Sacrifice. There were serious abuses in this matter even in the United States.[12] In order to eliminate these evils and scandals, the Holy See ruled that an Oriental priest must obtain his *celebret* from the Congregation for the Oriental Church. The law is now embodied in the Code.

The present purpose demands merely a discussion of the law in its application to the Oriental priests in the United States. It does not seem that they are governed only by the Code; particular decrees issued for this country must also be considered.[13] A twofold division is advisable, and each group will be considered separately. 1. The Greek-Ruthenian priests who have their proper

---

11 Augustine is of the opinion that this applies only if the Oriental priest expects to celebrate Mass in a church of a different rite and diocese; otherwise it would be difficult to understand why Orientals are subject to more rigorous treatment than the Latins. Cf. Augustine, *A Commentary on Canon Law,* IV, 129; Woywod, *op. cit.,* I, n. 701. The inference of the above author does not seem to militate against the spirit of the law. As long as the priest remains within his diocese and celebrates Mass in churches of his own rite, his Ordinary may envoke the penalties of the law to prevent any abuse.

12 S. Cong. de Prop. Fide, 12 Aprilis 1894, *Coll.,* n. 1866.

13 S. Cong. de Prop. Fide, 1 Oct. 1890, *Coll.,* n. 1966, footnote; 12 Apr. 1894, *Coll.,* n. 1866; 10 Maii 1892, *A. E. R.,* VII (1892), 66; S. Cong. de Prop. Fide pro Negotiis R. O., 17 Aug. 1914, *A. A. S.,* VI (1914), 458 seq.

Ordinaries. 2. Priests of other Oriental rites who are under the jurisdiction of the respective local Latin Ordinaries.

1. *Greek-Ruthenian Priests*

The decree *Cum Episcopo* invested the Greek-Ruthenian bishop in the United States with complete and ordinary jurisdiction over the clergy and the people of his rite.[14] In order to provide sufficient clergy, the Ruthenian Ordinaries may secure priests from the bishops of Galicia and Podocarpathia to labor in this country. They must be approved by the Oriental Congregation. If a Greek-Ruthenian priest comes to the United States on his own accord, and without the proper credentials of the Sacred Congregation, he is strictly forbidden to exercise priestly faculties, neither may they be granted to him by the local Greek-Ruthenian Ordinary. However, if the priest has testimonial letters from the Sacred Congregation, and if he is accepted by the Greek-Ruthenian Ordinary, he is immediately under his jurisdiction. The local Ordinary concedes faculties to say Mass and to administer the Sacraments according to his discretion.[15] This later fact seems to furnish sufficient basis to conclude that the Greek-Ruthenian Ordinaries in the United States may issue the required *celebret* or letter of recommendation to their priests to celebrate Mass outside of their own churches.[16] Reason points to the fact that the Ruthenian bishop in the United States is best qualified to give letters of recommendation, since he should know whether his subjects are free from ecclesiastical censure, and worthy of the *celebret*.[17]

---

14 S. Cong. de Prop. Fide pro Negotiis R. O., 17 Aug. 1914, *A. A. S.*, VI, 458; supra chap. IV, § 5, n. 2.

15 Decr. *supra cit.*, art. 11, *A. A. S.*, VI, 460; S. Cong. de Prop. Fide, 12 Aprilis 1894, *Coll.*, n. 1866.

16 Augustine, *op. cit.*, IV, 130; Woywod, *op. cit.*, I, n. 701.

17 A letter to the Apostolic Delegate from the Oriental Congregation, with reference to the other Oriental priests in America subject to Latin bishops, indicates by way of deduction that Oriental priests who have their own Ordinary in America, are subject to him in everything and for everything. This should include the concession of the *celebret*. Cf. letter to the Apostolic Delegate, May 29, 1925, which is quoted in this chapter, § 2.

The case is different if one presupposes a Ruthenian priest who wishes merely to visit the United States, or to transact a matter of business. His intention is not to remain or to labor as a missionary under the jurisdiction of a Greek-Ruthenian Ordinary. In this instance the priest must obtain his celebret from the Congregation for the Oriental Church. Similar regulations have also been issued for Latin priests of Italy. If they desire to go to America or the Phillipine Islands, they must obtain letters from the Consistorial Congregation. In Spain and Portugal, the Papal Legates issue these letters to emigrating clergy.[18]

2. *The Other Oriental Priests*

All Oriental priests laboring among their people in this country who have not their own Ordinaries are under the jurisdiction of the local Latin Ordinaries. It is important to notice that the Holy See does not permit an Oriental priest to come to America to engage in mission service without the permission of the Ordinaries *a quo* and *ad quem.* The priest must make known to the Congregation for the Oriental Church, the diocese in which he intends to labor and to establish a domicile. After these preliminaries, the Sacred Congregation issues a letter of recommendation to the emigrating priest, however, it confers no faculties. The priest in question must obtain the necessary faculties to exercise the sacred ministry from the local Ordinary in whose diocese he is to labor.[19] With these regulations in mind, it seems correct to assume that the local Latin Ordinary may issue the *celebret* to Oriental priests who are subject to his jurisdiction, and who have a domicile in his diocese. The fact that all the faculties which they enjoy depend upon the will of the Ordinary should not exclude the concession of a *celebret.*

---

[18] S. Cong. Consist., 30 Dec. 1918, *A. A. S.*, XI (1919), 41; Woywod, *op. cit.*, I, n. 702; Ferreres, *Casus Conscientiae*, II, nn. 876-881.

[19] S. Cong. de Prop. Fide, 10 Maii 1892, A. E. R., VII (1892), 66. S. Cong. de Prop. Fide, 12 Aprilis 1894, *Coll.*, n. 1866; Cf. supra chap. IV, §§ 1, 2, 3.

A letter in recent years to the Apostolic Delegate in Washington, D. C., from the Sacred Congregation for the Oriental Church apparently approves this conclusion. The Sacred Congregation had been requested to extend the *celebret* of a certain Syrian priest for the diocese of Brooklyn, which favor it granted with certain limitations. The Congregation, however, made some important observations. It declared that the priest mentioned above, as well as other Orientals, who have not their own Ordinary in America, are subject in everything and for everything to the Ordinary of the place. Now it seems reasonable to assume from this declaration, that the Latin Ordinary may grant the *celebret* to the Oriental priests under his jurisdiction, as long as they remain his subjects. This gives the Oriental priests in question the same status in this matter, as the Latin priests who obtain their *celebrets* from their proper Ordinary.[20]

The case is entirely different, if the Oriental priest is without a domicile in America, and if he is not subject to the jurisdiction of the Latin Ordinary. Suppose the Oriental priest is a visitor or a special agent, it is obvious that his *celebret* and credentials must be obtained from the Congregation for the Oriental Church.

§ 2. The Credentials of Alms' Collectors and the Celebration of Holy Mass

The Third Council of Baltimore decreed that priests from abroad who came to collect alms without proper authorization may not celebrate Mass even once without

---

[20] The pertinent content of the letter referred to in the text follows: "* * * Quanto poi al Rev. ——— ——— di rito Siro posso assiculare la S. V. che e stata accordata una proroga del suo Celebret per la sola diocesi di Brooklyn e per la durata di un anno. *Quindi egli come tutti gli altri Orientali che non abbiano un proprio Ordinario in America deve in tutto e per tutto stare soggetto all'Ordinario del luogo nel quale risiede, ne potra ivi o altrove esercitare facolta eventualmente accordate dal suo Patriarca o Ordinario, i quali fuori del rispettivo territorio non hanno alcuna giurisdizione sul Clero e sui fedeli salvo nei casi provvisti dal Diritto Comune.* Di cio dia pure conferma quando le torni opportuno ai Vescovi che ne la richiedano a scanso di equivoci e di abusi che sono sempre tanto spiacevoli in cose si gravi e delicate." S. Cong. pro Ecclesia Orientali (ad Delegatum Apostolicum, Washington, D. C.), 29 maggio, 1925.

the permission of the local Ordinary.[21] This particular law is not opposed to the Code; hence, its force obtains.[22] The Code provides expressly that all particular norms enacted by the local Ordinary, relative to the admission of strange priests to celebrate Mass, must be observed by all.[23] Of course it is presupposed that any local regulations are not opposed to the common law of the Code, otherwise such measures would have no legal force.[24]

The question arises whether this law of the Council may be extended to Oriental priests from abroad whose sole purpose is to gather funds. The regulation of the Council of Baltimore has been enacted to prevent abuses and scandals. Public order and the *bonum commune* demand that such evils be eradicated. The purpose of the law is frustrated, unless all are held to observe it. Since there is question of scandal and serious abuse, which tend to the detriment of the Church and religion, *natura rei* Orientals are bound by the decree.[25]

There are other laws with reference to Oriental collectors which must be considered. The Code explicitly legislates for religious. Without an authentic and recent rescript of the Oriental Congregation, the Ordinaries of the Latin rite must not permit any Oriental religious of whatsoever order or dignity to collect money in their territory, nor may they send subjects to the Oriental dioceses for a similar purpose.[26]

This regulation refers only to religious, therefore, it cannot be extended to secular Oriental priests. Another Canon of the Code also forbids the collection of alms for pious purposes by all private persons, whether laymen or clerics, without the authorization of the Holy See or the

---

21 *Acta et Decreta*, n. 295; Woywod, *A Practical Commentary on Canon Law*, I, n. 701.

22 Canon 6, n. 1.

23 Canon 804, § 3. "Peculiares hac de re normae, salvis huius canonicis praescriptis, ab Ordinario loci datae, servandae sunt ab omnibus. * * *"

24 Motry, *op. cit.*, p. 49.

25 Maroto, *Institutiones Juris Canonici*, n. 198, cf. Cicongani, *Commentarium ad Lib. Ium Codicis*, p. 13 seq.

26 Canon 622, § 4.

local Ordinary.[27] However, since this is purely a disciplinary law, it is doubtful whether *per se* it embraces the Orientals; but they are bound, nevertheless, by similar laws.[28] There is a special decree which affects Oriental alms' collectors in America. It prescribes that they must have the authorization of the Sacred Congregation for the Oriental Church. If, then, any Oriental priest appears without this permission and approval of his cause, the local Latin Ordinaries are absolutely forbidden to permit such a priest to exercise the sacred ministry.[29]

The decree makes no distinction, whether the priests be secular or religious; it states simply and clearly that all Oriental collectors of alms, must have the approval and permission of the Holy See, otherwise the local Ordinary is strictly prohibited to allow them to perform the sacred functions. There is no possible escape from the law for the Oriental collectors from abroad. If they expect to celebrate Mass, they must have the necessary authentic and recent documents from the Sacred Congregation for the Oriental Church. Although an Oriental has permission or a rescript from the Holy See to collect alms in this country, the local Ordinary has a right to see the document and to decide upon its validity.[30]

An Oriental priest who solicits alms and ignores the requirements of the law has no complaint, if he is refused permission to say Mass. The very fact that he lacks authorization casts suspicion upon him and the worthiness of his cause. The measure is a reasonable one, and necessary to prevent a repetition of the abuses and scandals that have occurred in the past.[31]

---

27 Canon 1503; Doheny, *Church Property: Modes of Acquisition,* p. 50 seq.

28 S. Cong. de Prop. Fide, 24 Sept. 1882, *Coll.,* n. 1575.

29 S. Cong. de Prop. Fide, 12 Apr. 1894, *Coll.,* n. 1866.

30 Canon 51; Doheny, *op. cit.,* p. 51.

31 S. Cong. de Prop. Fide, 12 Aprilis 1894, *Coll.,* n. 1866. Oriental Priests in the United States subject to Latin Ordinaries, or to Ordinaries of their own rite, who are rectors of missions or congregations are not forbidden to collect alms for church purposes from their own people. As rectors, they act in an official capacity, and not as private persons. Cf. Doheny, *op. cit.,* p. 51. However, if an Oriental rector solicits funds from persons who do not belong to his congregation, he must follow local regulations and also have the necessary authorization from the Holy See. Cf. the decree cited above in this footnote.

Only very recently abuses in this matter have come to the notice of the Congregation for the Oriental Church. It appears that certain persons calling themselves Orientals, or even alleging false names and declaring that they belong to the Oriental clergy, have been traveling in Italy and other regions collecting alms and Mass stipends. These individuals are accustomed to exhibit spurious documents in order to establish their pretended identity and the so-called permission to gather funds. The Congregation stated that no one had the required faculty to collect alms and Mass stipends. In order to stop this fraud and above all to protect the good repute of the Oriental clergy, the Holy See warned that Ordinaries should be watchful, lest, pastors, religious Superiors, and the faithful are deceived by the unauthorized collectors; furthermore, if they have given Mass stipends to the impostors there remains a grave obligation to have them satisfied.[32]

---

32 S Cong. pro Ecclesia Orientali, Aprilis 1928, *A. A. S.*, XX (1928), 107; Maii 1928, *A. A. S.*, XX (1928), 161. The transmitting or the sending of Mass stipends to Oriental priests in the Orient, offers a practical difficulty. (The remarks which follow are taken from Keller, *Mass Stipends*, p. 129). The decree *Cum plures* prescribed that stipends may be sent to Oriental priests abroad through the Apostolic Delegate in the Orient; however, they may not be sent directly to lay people, Oriental priests, or even to a titular bishop in that country. It was permissible to send stipends immediately to an Ordinary in the East, but the sender was obliged to inform the Apostolic Delegate in the Orient to whom and how many stipends were sent. Cf. S. C. Cong. de Prop. Fide, 15 Julii 1908, *A. S. S.*, XLI, 400. Blat, *Commentarium*, Liber III, p. I, n. 132. If the decree *Cum plures* legislates primarily for the Eastern Churches, its prescriptions are still in force by virtue of the first Canon, since the Code does not, generally speaking, abrogate the legislation of the Eastern Churches. If the decree applies directly to the Latin Church, it no longer obtains, because the Code has made different provisions. Although both opinions are probable, in practice a doubtful law is not binding. The decree according to Keller (*op. cit., loc. cit.*) is at most only a doubtful one. One could, therefore, send stipends directly to priests in the Orient. It may be noted that a person may offer the usual manual stipends to Oriental priests in the United States. The mere giving of stipends directly to a priest known to the donor is not the same as transmitting or sending them to the Orient. Cf. Keller, *op. cit.*, p. 130.

§ 3. The Matter of the Holy Eucharist: Unleavened and Leavened Bread

The caption of this article recalls one of the many discussions which preceded the Eastern Schism. The final rupture occurred under Michael Cerularius, who, in 1053, renewed and consummated the schism. He was especially indignant that the Latin Church used unleavened bread for the Consecration of the Holy Eucharist.[33] Cerularius and his followers questioned the validity of unleavened bread as the suitable matter for the Sacrament. The Reunion Council of Florence condemned their error, and defined as an article of faith: "*Item in azymo sive in fermentato pane triticeo, corpus Christi veraciter confici; sacerdotesque in altero ipsorum Domini corpus conficere debere, unumquemque scilicet juxta suae Ecclesiae sive Occidentalis sive Orientalis consuetudinem.*"[34] The Council neither proscribed the custom of the East nor of the West; the declaration safeguards the practices of the various rites, but all must profess that either leavened or unleavened bread is valid matter for the consecration of the Holy Eucharist.

The present purpose does not demand a discussion of the question, whether Christ consecrated with leavened or unleavened bread at the Last Supper. The Church has declared that both are valid matter, and hence, it is merely a point of discipline which decides the licit matter of the respective rites. The Code restates the disciplinary portion of the decree of the Council of Florence: "*In Missae celebratione sacerdos, secundem proprium ritum, debet panem azymum vel fermentatum adhibere ubicumque Sacrum litet.*"[35]

Considerable diversity exists among the Orientals; the Armenians and Maronites, like the Latins, consecrate

---

33 Fortescue, *The Orthodox Eastern Church,* 177 seq.; Jugie, *Theologia Dogmatica Christianorum Orientalium,* art. V, p. 311 seq.

34 Eugene IV, Const. *Lactentur Coeli,* 6 Jul. 1439, § 4, *Fontes,* n. 51.

35 Canon 816; Benedict XIV, Const. *Etsi Pastoralis,* 26 Maii 1742, § I, n. II, *Coll.,* n. 338; Benedict XIV, Const. *Allatae Sunt,* 26 Julii 1755, n. 22, *Coll.,* n. 395; Tanquerey, *Synopsis Theologicae Dogmaticae,* III, 416-420; Gasparri, *De SS. Eucharistia,* II, n. 803.

with unleavened bread;[36] the various Byzantine rites, together with the Chaldean, Syrian, and Coptic rites use leavened bread.[37] The rite of each Church must be observed. It is gravely forbidden for Latin or Oriental priests who according to their rite must consecrate with unleavened bread to use leavened bread. The same prohibition holds for Oriental priests who must use leavened bread for the Holy Eucharist; they cannot lawfully consecrate with unleavened bread. This conclusion follows from the declaration of the Council of Florence and other pronouncements of the Holy See. The Church does not permit a mixture of rite; the Code, therefore, merely reaffirms her mind and practice which has been defined for centuries.[38]

The Code, no doubt, has settled the question which was formerly disputed by theologians, whether a Latin priest in the Orient could licitly celebrate Mass with leavened bread, or whether a Greek among Latins could lawfully use unleavened bread. St. Alphonsus and others responded affirmatively, and asserted this to be the more common and probable opinion.[39] Gasparri espoused a contrary teaching; he based his opinion on the papal constitutions which insist that a priest must celebrate according to his rite, whenever he says Mass.[40] The words of the Canon, "*ubicumque (sacerdos) Sacrum litet,*" certainly seem to indicate that Gasparri's opinion

---

36 Benedict XIV, Const. *Allatae Sunt*, 26 Julii 1755, n. 23, *Coll.*, n. 395; Synodus Montis Libani (1736), pars II, cap. XII, n. 7, *Coll. Lac.*, II, 190.

37 S. Cong. de Prop. Fide, 20 Nov. 1838, *Coll.*, n. 878; Benedict XIV Const. *Allatae Sunt*, 26 Julii 1755, n. 21, *Coll.*, n. 395; Bona, *Rerum Liturgicarum*, lib. I, cap. XXIII, n. 1; Augustine, *A Commentary on Canon Law*, IV, 572-3; Antoine, *Theologia Moralis*, V, 147 seq. Among the Orientals who use unleavened bread may be included the Chaldeans in Malabar, and the Greeks of Grottaferrata. Cf. *AkKR.*, VIII (1862), 173, n. 5.

38 *Missale Romanum, De Defectibus*, cap. III, n. 3; Benedict XIV, Const. *Etsi Pastoralis*, 26 Maii 1742, § VI, n. X, *Coll.*, n. 338; Pius V, Const. *Providentia*, 20 Aug. 1566, § 1, *Fontes*, n. 113; Gasparri, *op. cit.*, II, n. 804; Antoine, *Theologia Moralis*, V, 154; Pius X, Const. *Tradita ab Antiquis*, 14 Sept. 1912, n. 1, *A. A. S.*, IV (1912), 615.

39 *Theologia Moralis*, lib. VI, n. 203.

40 Gasparri, *op. cit.*, II, n. 805.

has been approved. In view of this, the teaching of St. Alphonsus cannot be sustained.[41]

In extreme necessity may a Latin or Oriental priest who must use unleavened bread for the Holy Sacrifice, consecrate with leavened bread in order to administer the Holy Viaticum? In the same circumstances may the Oriental priest who must use leavened bread, consecrate with unleavened bread? Renowned theologians answer in the negative. They reply that the common good, on account of which the Church has strictly decreed that everyone must observe his own rite, prevails over the private good of the individual.[42] Since this is an ecclesiastical law, is it not reasonable to suppose that it does not bind when extreme necessity exists, or when there is conflict with a divine precept? A divine precept urges the reception of Holy Viaticum in danger of death. Cappello seems to think that it is lawful for a Latin priest to celebrate with leavened bread or a Greek priest with unleavened bread in such circumstances.[43] The above opinion is based upon the milder discipline of the Code in reference to the administration of the Holy Eucharist of another rite.[44] In practice one must conclude that an apostolic indult is necessary for a priest whose rite demands unleavened bread to consecrate with leavened bread, or vice versa. Gasparri remarks that this faculty is never given *per modum actus,* but is sometimes granted for a time, even without a transfer to another rite.[45]

§ 4. The Place for the Celebration of Holy Mass

No doubt there are in the United States, localities where the Oriental priests have not their own churches. When such circumstances prevail, it becomes very difficult to observe their respective rites. The question now

---

41 Cappello, *De Sacramentis,* I, n. 282.
42 St. Alphonsus, *op. cit.,* lib. VI, n. 203.
43 Cappello, *De Sacramentis,* I, n. 281; Woywod, *A Practical Commentary.* I, n. 718.
44 Canon 851.
45 Gasparri, *op. cit.,* II, n. 804.

arises: may an Oriental priest celebrate Mass in a Latin church, or upon an altar of the Latin rite? The Church itself offers no difficulty so long as it is a Catholic edifice.[46]

A more practical question and one immediately connected with the Holy Sacrifice, concerns the proper altar which the Code and liturgical laws prescribe. Generally speaking, the present law does not deviate from past legislation, which permitted the celebration of Mass upon any consecrated Catholic altar of another rite, when an altar of the rite of the minister was lacking. The celebrant, however, must always celebrate Mass according to his rite.[47]

Canon 823, § 2. "*Deficiente altari proprii ritus, sacerdoti fas est ritu proprio celebrari in altari consecrato alius ritus Catholici, non autem super Graecorum antimensiis.*"

As a general rule, the Oriental churches have but a single consecrated altar.[48] This custom obtained at one time both in the East and in the West. Mass was celebrated on this altar only once a day. Although this practice has long ago passed in the West, in the Orient it is still much in evidence.[49] Exceptions, however, are noticeable,[50] especially among the Maronites who follow quite closely the Latin Church in this matter.[51]

---

46 Canon 823, § 1; S. C. Officii, 5 Junii 1889, *Coll.*, n. 1707; S. C. Officii, 1 Dec. 1757, *Coll.*, n. 408, S. Cong. de Prop. Fide, 12 Mar. 1809, *Coll.*, n. 697; Benedict XIV, Const. *Praeclaris*, 18 Mar. 1746, *Coll.*, n. 356; Wernz, *Jus Decretalium*, III, n. 447, scholion; Gasparri, *De SS. Eucharistia*, I, n. 279; Augustine, *A Commentary on Canon Law*, IV, 173.

47 Gasparri, *op. cit.*, II, n. 805.

48 Gasparri, *op. cit.*, I, nn. 287, 290.

49 Bona, *Rerum Liturgicarum*, lib. I, cap. XIV, n. 3; Assemanus, *Bibliotheca Orientalis*, II, 184; III, p. I, 248; Benedict XIV, Const. *Allatae Sunt*, 26 Julii 1755, n. 37, *Coll.*, n. 395; Benedict XIV, Const. *Demandatum*, 24 Dec. 1743, § § 8, 9, *Fontes*, n. 338.

50 Synodus Alex. Coptorum (1898), sect. II, cap. III, art. IV, pars II, IV, n. XI, p. 113.

51 Zitelli-Solieri, *Apparatus Juris Eccl.*, n. 1174; Synodus Montis Libani (1736), pars II, cap. XIII, n. 17; The Maronites, however, make an exception: "In altari autem, in quo Episcopus missam celebravit, nullus alius sacerdos ea die celebrare praesumat, nisi prius licentiam obtinuerit." Cf. *ibidem, loc. cit.*

The custom of the Oriental Church of a single altar, and only one Mass thereon the same day, becomes intelligible if one recalls that the custom of concelebration still obtains in the Eastern rites. It is no longer permissible in the Latin Church, except in the Ordination Mass of priests and in the Consecration Mass of bishops.[52] In the Oriental rites its use is more frequent especially on major liturgical days. The bishop or ranking priest is the leading celebrant, and together with him they concelebrate the Holy Sacrifice. This custom not only has the approval of the Holy See but she commends its observance.[53] In recent times some of the Orientals have departed from the ancient custom and now permit more than one Mass on the same altar the same day to satisfy the piety of the people. But the Holy Sacrifice is repeated by different celebrants.[54]

In order to accommodate priests who wish to say Mass, the Orientals of the Byzantine rite have chapels or oratories with extra altars adjoining the churches, called *parecclesiae,* where the sacred liturgy may be celebrated privately by one priest on days when they do not have

---

52 Canon 803.

53 Gasparri, *op. cit.,* I, n. 360; Benedict XIV, *Allatae Sunt,* 26 Julii 1755, n. 38, *Coll.,* n. 395; Benedict XIV, ep. encycl. *Demandatum,* 24 Dec. 1743, § 9, *Fontes,* n. 338; Synodus Alex. Coptorum (1898), *loc. cit.,* n. XII; Synodus Montis Libani (1736), pars II, cap. XIII, n. 18.

54 Synodus Sciarfensis (1888), cap. V, art. V, § 7, n. 1, p. 111. Synodus Alex. Coptorum, *loc. cit.,* n. I, p. 113. Canon 806 forbids a Latin priest to say more than one Mass a day, with the exception of Christmas and All Souls day, when he may say three Masses, otherwise an Apostolic indult or permission of the Ordinary is necessary. If, according to the the prudent judgment of the Ordinary, a considerable number of people must omit Mass on days of obligation for lack of priests, he may grant faculties for his priests to binate. Generally speaking, such privileges are not known among the Orientals. It would not be in harmony with their rite. The privilege of the Latin Church in this regard has never been introduced or permitted by the Holy See. Cf. Wernz, *Jus Decretalium,* III, n. 543, footnote 174; Gasparri, *op. cit.,* I, n. 374; Synodus Montis Libani (1736), *loc. cit., Coll. Lac.,* II, 221; Synodus Sciarfensis, *loc. cit.,* § 7, n. 1, p. 112; Synodus Alex. Coptorum, *loc. cit.,* n. XI, p. 113; Benedict XIV, Const. *In Superiori,* 29 Dec. 1755, Fontes, n. 437. When the Holy See was asked whether the Oriental priests enjoyed the privilege of celebrating three Masses on All Souls day, as did priests of the Latin rite, the response was in the negative. Cf. S. Cong. de Prop. Fide pro Negotiis R. O., 22 Mar. 1916, *A. A. S.,* VIII, 104.

concelebration.[55] Gasparri remarks that today there are to be found in the Byzantine Churches not only altars for Greeks, but often, also, a Latin altar for the Latins.[56] In this country one cannot expect to find the Oriental churches equipped with Latin altars. The occasion to celebrate on the consecrated altar of another rite would be extremely rare for a Latin priest amongst us. If possible, one is always bound to celebrate in a church and upon an altar of one's own rite. The privilege granted by the Canon to say Mass on a consecrated altar of another rite is lawful only when an altar of the priest's rite is lacking. There are other conditions which must also be verified. The Latin priest must celebrate according to his rite, which presupposes that he has a Roman Missal, the necessary vestments, sacred vessels, leavened bread, etc., without which a lawful celebration becomes impossible.[57]

The Church does not favor the indiscriminate use of the church or altar of another rite. But a legitimate cause is sufficient to admit Oriental priests into Latin churches where they may celebrate Mass and administer the sacraments to their people. Benedict XIV remarks that this was done openly in Rome. Armenian, Coptic, Melkite, and Greek priests officiated in Latin temples. The Pontiff required that they have all things necessary to carry out the sacred liturgy according to their respective rites. He admonished them further to be on their guard lest the novelty of their rites excite the admiration of the curious.[58] The same Pope also permitted the Greek priests of Lower Italy to accept the portable altar consecrated by Latin bishops. This, however, was not obligatory. They could also use the Greek *antimension.*[59]

55 Zitelli-Solieri, *op. cit.*, nn. 1175, 1174; Gasparri, *op. cit.*, I, n. 287; Benedict XIV, Const. *Allatae Sunt*, 26 Julii 1755, nn. 39, 40, *Coll.*, n. 395; Bona, *op. cit.*, lib. I, cap. XX, n. 2 seq.

56 Gasparri, *op. cit.*, I, n. 287; Bliley, *Altars According to the Code*, p. 16.

57 Canons 811, § 1, 816, 818, 819, 820, 823; Cappello, *De Sacramentis*, I, nn. 814-816; Gasparri, *op. cit.*, I, n. 352.

58 Benedict XIV, Const. *Allatae Sunt*, 26 Julii 1755, nn. 35, 40, *Coll.*, 395; Gasparri, *op. cit.*, I, n. 352.

59 Benedict XIV, Const. *Etsi Pastoralis*, 26 Maii 1742, § VI, n. XVII, *Coll.*, n. 338; Heiner, *Benedicti XIV Papae Opera Inedita*, cap. III, n. 5.

In this country the Oriental priests may be forced to use a Latin altar quite frequently. In many localities they have not their own churches. Since they are lacking an altar of their own rite, it is lawful to use any Catholic consecrated altar. In the Latin church the term "*altare consecratum*" may be taken in a broad sense, which embraces both the fixed and portable altar.[60] Hence, any altar where a Latin priest may say Mass, may be used by the Oriental priest when it is impossible to have an altar of his own rite. A licit celebration demands, also, the proper vestments, sacred vessels, leavened or unleavened bread; in fact everything necessary to officiate according to the rite of the minister.[61]

The Code forbids Latin priests to celebrate Mass on the *antimension* of the Byzantine or Greek rites.[62] The antimension consists of a piece of linen or silk, ordinarily ten inches wide and fourteen inches long. It is richly decorated with religious images and inscriptions; it also contains relics of the saints, and is solemnly consecrated by the bishop. Where the Byzantine priest has no consecrated altar, the *antimension* is sufficient for the celebration of Mass. It must be used, however, even when the altar is consecrated.[63] It is restricted to the Orientals that follow the Byzantine rite.

The Church has rarely given an indult to Latin priests to use the *antimension* for the celebration of Holy Mass. Benedict XIV granted to Latin priests in certain mis-

---

60 They are both called consecrated by the Code: "Ut Missae sacrificium super illud celebrari possit, altare debet esse, secunuum liturgicas leges, consecratum; idest vel totum, si agatur de immobili, vel ara tantum portabilis, si de mobili." Cf. Canon 1199, § 1.

61 Canons 811, § 1, 816, 819, 820; Benedict XIV, Const. *Allatae Sunt*, 26 Julii 1755, n. 35, *Coll.*, n. 395; Cappello, *op. cit.*, I, nn. 814-816; Antoine, *Theologia Moralis*, V, 185 seq.

62 S. C. S. Officii, 7 Junii 1726; *Coll.*, n. 306; Benedict XIV, Const. *Etsi Pastoralis*, 26 Maii 1742, § VI, nn. XIX, VIII, *Coll.*, n. 338; Heiner, *Benedicti XIV Papae Opera Inedita*, cap. III, n. 6.

63 Bliley, *Altars According to the Code*, p. 16; *A. E. R.*, III (1890), 90-91; Braun, *Der Christliche Altar*, I, 519 seq.; Renaudot, *Liturgiarum Orientalium Collectio*, I, 164-165, 311; Nilles, *Symbolae*, II, 861, footnote 1.

sionary regions of Russia the faculty to say Mass on the Greek *antimension* on account of the scarcity of Latin churches in those parts.[64]

§ 5. The Minister of Holy Communion

The Code clearly indicates that the Church does not favor a mixture of rites. From the preceding article it is evident that the minister of the Holy Sacrifice must consecrate according to his respective rite with leavened or unleavened bread. *Per se* when the priest administers Holy Communion the same prescriptions apply.[65] However, in this case the present law admits a reasonable exception. It permits a priest to administer the Holy Eucharist consecrated according to a different rite under certain conditions, even if there is a difference in the use of unfermented or fermented bread.

Canon 851, § 2. *"Ubi vero necessitas urgeat nec sacerdos diversi ritus adsit, licet sacerdoti Orientali qui fermentato utitur, ministrare Eucharistiam in azymo, vicissim Latino aut Orientali qui utitur azymo, ministrare in fermentato; at suum quisque ritum ministrare servare debet."*

This is comparatively a recent concession. The discipline of the past was not so liberal; several pronouncements of the Holy See declared that it was not only illicit, but they strictly forbade priests to administer the Holy Eucharist consecrated according to another rite, if there was a diversity in the use of leavened or unleavened bread.[66]

The law of the Code is identical with a previous concession of Pius X.[67] In the first place it should be noted

---

64 Benedict XIV, Const. *Imposito Nobis*, 29 Mar. 1751, § § 8, 9; *Fontes*, n. 410. This historical data is also presented, *ibidem*, § § 1-7; Gasparri, *op. cit.*, I, n. 352.

65 Canon 851, § 1.

66 Const. *Etsi Pastoralis*, 26 Maii 1742, § VI, nn. X, XI, *Coll.*, n. 338. Pius V, Const. *Providentia*, 20 Aug. 1566, § 1, *Fontes*, n. 113. Benedict XIV, Const. *Allatae Sunt*, 26 Julii 1755, § § 23, 34, *Coll.*, n. 395; S. Cong. de Prop. Fide, 24 Sept. 1863, *Coll.*, n. 1242; 30 Aprilis 1866, ad 2am, *Coll.*, n. 1288; Zitelli-Solieri, *Apparatus Juris Eccl.*, n. 1188.

67 *Tradita ab Antiquis*, 14 Sept. 1912, n. II, III, *A. A. S.*, IV (1912), 615.

that Latin and Oriental priests who consecrate with unleavened bread, are not restricted by the present Canon to administer the Holy Eucharist consecrated according to another rite, so long as the matter of the Sacrament remains the same. Likewise, the Oriental priests who use leavened bread are not prohibited to administer the Holy Eucharist consecrated according to another Oriental rite which also uses leavened bread. There is one phrase which offers a difficulty, *"ubi vero necessitas urgeat."* What degree of necessity makes it lawful for a Latin priest to administer Holy Communion consecrated with leavened bread, or a Greek to administer the Sacrament consecrated with unleavened bread? Woywod maintains that if a person must omit an ordinary devotional Communion it is not sufficient for a priest to make use of the Canon. One must not, however, demand extreme necessity as urges in danger of death, since the law positively provides for such a case.[68] Necessity apparently urges if the Paschal precept must be fulfilled, or a long interval has elapsed since a person's previous Communion, or one is about to submit to a serious operation, or begin a perilous journey. Such cases, it seems, would certainly permit a priest to administer the Holy Eucharist consecrated according to another rite, although there is a difference in the use of fermented or unfermented bread, provided that the proper liturgical minister is not present.[69] There are certain commentators who are inclined to a more lenient interpretation, or perhaps they do not stress the element of necessity mentioned by the Canon.[70] Woywod remarks, that these commentators apparently confuse the privilege granted to the people to receive Holy Communion in any Catholic rite, with the conditions which licitly permit a priest to ad-

68 Canon 866, § 3.

69 Woywod, *A Practical Commentary,* I, n. 748.

70 Blat, *Commentarium,* Liber III, n. 168; Vermeersch, *Theologia Moralis,* III, n. 422; Augustine, *Commentary on the Code of Canon Law,* IV, 222.

minister the Sacrament consecrated in a rite which differs in the use of leavened or unleavened bread.[71] Since the words of the Canon stress the element of necessity, it must be the mind of the legislator to prevent indiscriminate mixing of rites. Hence, it is proper to demand a serious reason to make use of the privilege.

One must not forget, however, that the Church urges frequent reception of the Holy Eucharist.[72] Suppose a case, where a number of devotional communicants are in a Latin church and it is the scheduled time for the distribution of Holy Communion, but the priest in charge is attending a sick call. May not an Oriental priest, a visitor, who consecrates with leavened bread, administer the Holy Eucharist consecrated in the Latin rite to the waiting congregation? If there is considerable delay some will be unable to receive for the day. Here is an occasion of necessity to satisfy devotional communicants which the Church desires. It does not appear opposed, therefore, to the mind of the legislator to permit the Oriental priest to distribute Holy Communion in the present case. Since the Church counsels frequent Communion, the lawgiver wished to provide for all reasonable contingencies; this fact offers another reason, apparently within the spirit of the Canon, to permit the Oriental priest to administer Holy Communion in the proposed instance. If the degree of necessity is too severely insisted upon the law would be useless for practical purposes.[73]

Another point of the law insists that when a priest distributes Holy Communion in accordance with this Canon, he must always observe the liturgical prescriptions of his rite in giving Holy Communion.[74]

---

71 *Op. cit.*, I, n. 748.

72 Canon 863.

73 Vermeersch, *Theologia Moralis*, III, n. 422.

74 Pius X, Const. *Tradita ab Antiquis*, 14 Sept. 1912, n. II, *A. A. S.*, IV, 615.

§ 6. The Reception of Holy Communion in the Different Rites

1. *Devotional Communion*

The practical unrestricted access to Holy Communion in any Catholic rite, as permitted today, was unknown until comparatively recent times. Prior to the mitigated legislation of Pope Pius X in 1912,[75] and the present relaxation of the Code, positive law demanded that everyone must receive the Holy Eucharist consecrated with leavened or unleavened bread according to the proper rite of the communicant.[76] The official documents of the Holy See clearly indicate that such was the mind of the Church. Benedict XIV prohibited Latins to receive Holy Communion from Greek priests consecrated according to the Greek rite. In like manner Greeks were forbidden to receive in the Latin rite, although it was lawful to partake of the Sacrament consecrated with unleavened bread in localities where the Greeks had no churches of their own rite.[77] This was the general rule repeated many times by the Holy See. It was merely by way of exception or necessity that it was licit for the faithful to receive the Eucharist in another rite when there was a difference in the use of leavened or unleav-

---

75 Pius X, *Tradita ab Antiquis*, 14 Sept. 1912, *A. A. S.*, IV, 609-617.

76 Gasparri, *De SS. Eucharistia*, II, n. 1178; Wernz, *Jus Decretalium*, III, n. 741. The custom of some Orientals to communicate under both species is also sustained where it prevails. Cf. Benedict XIV, Const. *Etsi Pastoralis*, 26 Maii 1742, § VI, n. XV, *Coll.*, n. 338; Resp. S. Cong. Rituum, 31 Aug. 1839, n. 4875, apud Gasparri, *op. cit.*, II, n. 1177; Bona, *Rerum Liturg.* lib. II, cap. XVIII, n. 3; Antoine, *Theologia Moralis*, V, 184-185; Synodus Sciarfensis (1888), cap. V, art. IV, § 6, n. 1. Benedict XIV enforced certain precautions for the reservation and the renewal of the Sacred Species for Holy Viaticum among the Italo-Greeks. Cf. Benedict XIV *loc. cit.*, § VI, n. III, IV, V; Gasparri, *op. cit.*, II, n. 1177. The custom obtains among the Graeco-Ruthenians to communicate under both species. Cf. Synodus Ruthenorum (1891), tit. II, cap. III, nn. 4-6.

77 Benedict XIV, *Etsi Pastoralis*, 26 Maii 1742, § VI, n. XII, XIII, XIV, *Coll.*, n. 338. These norms with reference to the Holy Eucharist given for the Italo-Greeks could be applied elsewhere. This is evident from a resolution of the S. Cong. of the Inquisition, 19 Jul. 1752; cf. Zitelli-Solieri, *Apparatus Juris Eccles.*, n. 1188.

ened bread.[78] This discipline stands out in rigorous contrast to the lenient provisions of the Code.

Canon 866, § 1. "*Omnibus fidelibus cuiusvis ritus datur facultas ut, pietatis causa, Sacramentum Eucharisticum quolibet ritu confectum suscipiant.*"

The beginnings of this legislation appear under Leo XIII. He permitted all the faithful, whether Latins or Orientals, dwelling in places where they had neither church nor priest of their rite to partake of the Eucharist not only in cases of necessity, but for purposes of devotion they could communicate in the church and rite established in the place provided that it was Catholic.[79] Later the same Pontiff allowed the faithful even where there was a church and priest of their rite to approach the Holy Table in any church, although the matter of the Sacrament differed, when they were unable to attend their proper church because of the distance or some grave inconvenience.[80] The Ordinary was to be the judge of the circumstances of the case.[81] These norms are noticeable in Oriental Synods,[82] and are implied in the earlier decrees for the Orientals in this country.[83] The first paragraph of the present Canon is taken from the famous Constitution, *Tradita ab Antiquis* of Pius X. He granted to the faithful the privilege of receiving Holy Communion in any Catholic rite even for devotional motives.[84] This concession is now embodied in the Code and it grants to all faithful complete liberty in the reception of the Holy Eucharist in Catholic rites.[85] It is to be noted that this privilege cannot be restricted by authority

78 S. Cong. Officii, 4 Sept. 1721, *Coll.*, n. 296; S. Cong. de Prop. Fide, 11 Dec. 1838, ad 21am, 22am, 23am, *Coll.*, n. 879.

79 S. Cong. de Prop. Fide, 18 Aug. 1893, *Coll.*, n. 1846.

80 Leo XIII, *Orientalium Dignitas*, 30 Nov. 1894, n. 2. *Coll.*, n. 1883.

81 S. Cong. de Prop. Fide, 26 Feb. 1896, *Coll.*, n. 1919; Gasparri, *op cit.*, II, n. 1178.

82 Synodus Alex. Coptorum (1898), sect. II, cap. I, art. V, n VIII; Synodus Sciarfensis (1888), cap. III, art. IX, n. 14.

83 S. Cong. de Prop. Fide, 1 Maii 1897, n. 1, *Coll.*, n. 1966; Litt. Apost. *Ea Semper*, 14 Junii 1907, art. 21, *A. S. S.*, XLI, 8.

84 Const. 14 Sept. 1912, n. III, *A. A. S.*, IV (1912), 609-617.

85 Woywod, *A Practical Commentary*, I n. 765; Blat, *Commentarium*, Liber III, n. 185.

inferior to the Holy See because it is now a part of the common law.

2. *The Paschal Precept*

A very practical question may be raised with reference to the fulfillment of the Easter duty. The Code inaugurates a new principle on this point and makes a departure from past regulations.

Canon 866, § 2. *"Suadendum tamen ut suo quisque ritu fideles praecepto communionis paschalis satisfaciant."*

All former legislation, excepting cases of necessity which have been considered, insisted that the faithful must satisfy the Easter Communion in their own rite. Decrees of the Holy See [86] and Oriental Synods,[87] all mention this obligation. The wording of the Code must be noticed, *"suadendum est."* The phrase does not permit the same liberty as is given for the devotional Communion. The Church expects and desires that the faithful comply with their Easter duty in their proper rite. Should a person even deliberately act against the mind of the Church, he satisfies, nevertheless, the Paschal precept; hence, the exhortation cannot be enforced either under the threat of ecclesiastical penalty or guilt of sin. There was a tendency not to extend this milder discipline to the Orientals. The Apostolic Delegate to Egypt asked whether this Canon (866, § 2) abolished also for the Orientals the Constitution of Pius X, that all the faithful must fulfill the Paschal precept in their own rite. The answer was in the negative.[88] This implied that the Orientals were bound to receive the Easter Communion according to their rite and excluded them from the be-

---

86 Pius X, Const. *Tradita ab Antiquis,* 14 Sept. 1912, n. IV, *A. A. S.,* IV (1912), 616; S. Cong. S. Officii, 12 Dec. 1821, apud S. Cong. de Prop. Fide, 11 Dec. 1838, ad 23, *Coll.,* n. 879, footnote 1; 26 Feb. 1896, *Coll.,* n. 1919.

87 Synodus Alex. Coptorum (1898), sect. II, cap. I, art. V, n. VIII; Synodus Sciarfensis (1888), cap. III, art. IX, n. 14.

88 Resp. S. Cong. pro Eccl. Orient. (ad Delegatum Apost. Aegypti), 31 Oct. 1922.

nign law of the Code. A subsequent response stated that in the Orient the faithful of the Oriental rites were guilty of grave sin and did not comply with their obligation unless they communicated during the Paschal time in their proper rite.[89]

A later decree, however, changed this view entirely. The Congregation for the Oriental Church has declared that the Orientals are embraced by Canon 866, § 2.[90] Hence, any previous legislation, pontifical or synodal, opposed to this Canon is to be considered abrogated. The decree *Cum Episcopo* for the Greek-Ruthenians in the United States, demanded that the faithful receive the Paschal Communion in their own rite and from their own pastor.[91] In view of the above Canon and the recent response of the Holy See, this law can no longer be sustained.[92]

The conclusion follows that the Paschal precept may be fulfilled in any Catholic rite. Prudence demands that if a person necessarily or purposely complies with his obligation outside of his proper church, and especially in another rite, the fact should be brought to the notice of the pastor. The pastor has the duty to urge this obligation; therefore, he should know whether his parishioners have respected the law of the Church.

3. *The Holy Viaticum*

The Code introduces no change with regard to the reception of the Holy Viaticum. The Church has frequently insisted that the faithful must receive the Sacrament in their proper rite in danger of death, except in cases of necessity.

---

89 Resp. S. Cong. pro Eccl. Orient., 24 Aprilis 1924. These responses are to be found in Cicognani, *Commentarium* ad Lib. Ium Codicis, pp. 14-15; cf. also *El Monitore Ecclesiastico,* 1925, p. 101.

90 Decr. S. Cong. pro Eccl. Orient., 26 Jan. 1925, apud Cicognani, *op. cit.,* p. 338.

91 S. Cong. de Prop. Fide pro Negotiis, R. O., 18 Aug. 1914, art. 24, *A. A. S.,* VI (1914), 462.

92 Vermeersch-Creusen, *Epitome,* I (1927), n. 49; Cicognani, *op. cit.,* p. 338.

Canon 866, § 3. "*Sanctum Viaticum moribundus ritu proprio accipiendum est; sed, urgente necessitate, fas esto quolibet ritu illud accipere.*"

The wording of the Code is practically the same as is contained in the legislation of Pius X on this point.[93] Other decrees emanating from the Holy See do not differ in substance from the Code.[94] An instruction issued for the guidance of Greek-Ruthenian and Latin bishops in the province of Leopoli contains specific directions with reference to the reception of Holy Viaticum. The Sacrament must be administered by a priest of the rite of the sick person. In cases of necessity, when the proper priest cannot be present, the sick person may receive the Viaticum, consecrated with leavened or unleavened bread, from a Greek or a Latin priest.[95] The Oriental Catholics in the United States in places where they have not their own priests or churches, or in cases of necessity when the proper priest is not at hand, must avail themselves of this Canon.[96]

Since there is a divine precept which urges the reception of the Holy Viaticum at the hour of death, it is easily understood why the Church willingly permits the Sacrament to be received in any Catholic rite. Hence the Church must suspend what is merely ecclesiastical law, as is the reception of the Sacrament in one's own rite, in order that the faithful in danger of death may comply with the divine precept to receive the Holy Eucharist.[97]

---

93 Const. *Tradita ab Antiquis,* 14 Sept. 1912, *A. A. S.*, IV (1912), 616.

94 S. Cong. de Prop. Fide, 11 Dec. 1838, ad 23, *Coll.*, n. 879; S. Cong. de Prop. Fide, Instr. (ad Delegat. Apost. Egypti), 30 Aprilis 1862, ad 2am, 3am, *Coll.*, n. 1228.

95 S. Cong. de Prop. Fide, 6 Oct. 1863, C, d, *Coll.*, n. 1243.

96 S. Cong. de Prop. Fide, 1 Maii 1897, n. 1, *Coll.*, 1966; S. Cong. de Prop. Fide pro Negotiis R. O., 18 Aug. 1914, art. 25, *A. A. S.*, VI (1914), 462.

97 Cappello, *De Sacramentis,* I, n. 471; Gasparri, *De SS. Eucharistia,* II, 1142-1147; Synodus Sciarfensis (1888), cap. III, art. IX, n. 15; Synodus Alex. Syrorum (1898), sect. II, cap. I, art. V, n. IX.

CHAPTER X

THE SACRAMENT OF PENANCE

§ 1. The Reception of the Sacrament in Different Rites

1. *The Jurisdiction of the Confessor*

The Code provides that all priests who are approved to hear confessions in a certain place, whether they enjoy ordinary or delegated jurisdiction, may validly and licitly absolve all penitents who approach them; the Catholics of the various rites are explicitly included.

Canon 881, § 1. "*Omnes utriusque cleri sacerdotes ad audiendas confessiones approbati in aliquo loco, sive ordinaria sive delegata jurisdictione instructi, possunt etiam vagos ac peregrinos ex alia dioecesi vel paroecia ad sese accedentes, itemque catholicos cuiusque ritus Orientalis, valide et licite absolvere.*"

The text of this canon does not require a commentary; its meaning together with its purpose are obviously and clearly stated. Ordinarily the Oriental rites would not be affected by a mere ecclesiastical enactment for the Latin Church;[1] but in this instance, they are expressly mentioned by the legislator, wherefore, the Orientals are also governed by the common law in this matter. Cappello[2] observes, and rightly too, that since the prescriptions of the present Canon constitute the universal or pontifical law applicable to all, no authority inferior to the Holy See may derogate from the established norms. Consequently, if the local legislation of a Latin or Oriental Ordinary is opposed to the principles of the Code, it is without legal force. The Church has in view the good

1 Canon 1.

2 *De Sacramentis,* II, p. I, n. 406; Woywod, *A Practical Commentary,* I, n. 786.

of souls which is certainly fostered and protected when access to approved confessors in the sacred tribunal is unrestricted. Repeated declarations of the Holy See over a long period furnish the background of the present legislation. An instruction of the Holy See in 1626 to the Latin and Greek Ruthenian Ordinaries indicates that approved Latin or Greek Ruthenian confessors may absolve penitents of either rite.[3] When the Holy Office was asked whether Maronite priests approved by their Ordinaries may hear the confessions of all persons of whatever nation or Oriental rite dwelling in the locality, the Cardinals of the Congregation after a consideration of the consultors' vote responded: "*Maronitas non esse inquietandos.*"[4] More recent pronouncements of the Holy See plainly vindicate the freedom of penitents to confess their sins to approved confessors of another rite.[5]

It is a generally accepted principle that delegated jurisdiction may be conceded with certain limitations.[6] May the Ordinary, who gives delegated faculties to a priest to hear confessions in a given place, limit the faculties to such an extent that the confessor may absolve only penitents of a particular rite, for example, those of the Latin rite. In view of the explicit text of Canon 881, § 1 which permits the approved confessor to hear all penitents without distinction of rite, such a restriction of jurisdiction is not possible. In other words, a limitation of jurisdiction to hear confessions merely of persons of a particular rite is opposed to the Code and previous declarations of the Holy See.[7]

It is customary in European countries to grant limited faculties to some confessors because they have not attained the required qualifications; a confessor may have

---

3 S. Cong. de Prop. Fide, 2 Junii 1835, *Coll.*, n. 839; Zitelli-Solieri, *Apparatus Juris Eccl.*, n. 1187.

4 S. Cong. S. Officii, 5 Dec. 1715, *Coll. Lac.*, II, 506, n. XVII.

5 S. Cong. de Prop. Fide, 11 Dec. 1838, ad 12, 13, *Coll.*, n. 879; 16 Apr. 1862, ad 2, *Coll.*, n. 1228.

6 Canon 878, § 1. "Jurisdictio delegata aut licentia audiendarum confessionum concedi potest certis quibusdam circumscripta finibus."

7 Cf. footnotes 3, 4, 5, supra this chapter.

jurisdiction to hear only certain classes of penitents, for example, children or men. Such a restriction of jurisdiction is not opposed to the principles of the Code;[8] the limitation of faculties in this case is not a discrimination against any particular rite, but is founded upon the lack of the proper qualifications demanded for the confessor in the sacred tribunal. It might happen that a confessor is approved only to hear the confession of children, hence, he could not hear adults of any rite.

Beyond the restrictions of the common law, the Ordinaries in the United States, as a general rule, grant faculties to confessors with no limitations as to certain classes of penitents. The Oriental priests in this country who are subject to Latin Ordinaries receive the faculties to administer the Sacraments at the discretion of the respective local Ordinary.[9] The Greek-Ruthenian priests in America, since they are subject to the jurisdiction of the respective Ordinaries of their rite, obtain the necessary faculties to exercise the sacred ministry from their proper Ordinary.[10]

2. *Freedom of the Penitent*

An examination of the legislation promulgated by the Holy See reveals that the Church has constantly maintained the maxim, that in a matter so delicate as the reception of the Sacrament of Penance, the freedom of the faithful should not be restricted.[11] Under the most favorable circumstances sacramental confession is often burdensome and humiliating to human nature. In order to facilitate fruitful confessions, penitents are permitted to confess their sins to any priest, whomsoever they prefer, provided the minister is endowed with the requisite jurisdiction.

---

8 Cappello, *op. cit.*, II, p. I, n. 395.

9 S. Cong. de Prop. Fide, 10 Maii 1892, *A. E. R.*, VII (1892), 66; 12 Apr. 1894, *Coll.*, n. 1866.

10 S. Cong. de Prop. Fide pro Negotiis R. O., 17 Aug. 1914, art. 11-13, *A. A. S.*, VI (1914), 460-461.

11 S. Cong. de Prop. Fide, 2 Junii 1835, *Coll.*, n. 839; Augustine, *A Commentary on Canon Law*, IV, 282.

Canon 905. "*Cuivis fideli integrum est confessario legitime approbato etiam alius ritus, cui maluerit, peccata sua confiteri.*"

An opinion which tends to impede the freedom to confess to an approved priest does not appear plausible in view of the present law.[12] Neither may the ancient custom of confessing to one's proper pastor nor to his delegate during the Paschal season be sustained.[13] Since the Church permits all Catholics to approach any approved confessor, she desires also to remove any unnecessary odium which might be connected with the reception of the Sacrament of Penance.

The legislation of the Code reflects the mind of the Church for centuries. It is really not a new principle. A decree of the Congregation of the Propaganda in 1626 stated that Latin bishops must not prohibit their subjects to confess to uniate Greek-Ruthenian priests approved by the Ordinary of the place. Neither was it permitted for Greek-Ruthenian bishops to forbid their subjects to confess to approved Latin priests. The Holy See adds that the uniate Ruthenians are truly Catholics, and in such matters as confession a diversity of rite is not repugnant. The efforts to excite discord or disagreement on this score were severely condemned.[14] The same Congregation admonished the Patriarch of the Maronites that he cannot punish with excommunication Maronites who wish to receive the Sacraments from the missionaries of the Holy See.[15] More recent decrees of the Congregation of the Propaganda vindicate the liberty of all Catholics to choose any approved confessor of another Catholic rite for the reception of the Sacrament of Pen-

---

12 *AkKR*, 105 (1927), 201; Cappello, *op. cit.*, n. 406; Augustine, *A Commentary on Canon Law*, IV, 347.

13 S. Cong. de Prop, Fide, 17 Sept. 1792, *Coll.*, n. 610; S. Cong. de Prop. Fide, 30 Aprilis 1862, ad 2am, *Coll.*, n. 1228; *A Commentary on Canon Law*, IV, 347.

14 S. Cong. de Prop. Fide, 2 Junii 1835, *Coll.*, n. 839; Zitelli-Solieri, *Apparatus Juris Eccl.*, n. 1137.

15 S. Cong. de Prop. Fide, 5 Dec. 1544, *Coll. Lac.*, II, 503, n. VIII; Antoine, *Theologia Moralis*, V, 355.

ance.[16] Synodal legislation of the Oriental rites also stresses the lawfulness of confession to any approved priest without distinction of rite.[17] The legislation which provided for the status of the Greek-Ruthenian Catholics in the United States makes special mention of the liberty of Greek-Ruthenian Catholics to confess to approved Latin priests and of Latins to confess to approved Greek-Ruthenian priests.[18]

§ 2. The Orientals and the Reservations of the Code

The legislation of the Code pertains to the Latin Church and does not affect the Oriental Churches except when the Orientals are expressly mentioned, or when, *ex natura rei,* a declaration must be extended to them.[19] These norms, however, do not settle all difficulties with reference to the application of reservations of sin and censures found in the Code to the Orientals. Some years after the promulgation of the Constitution *Apostolicae Sedis,* the question was asked, to what extent does it affect the Orientals. The Holy Office, August 6, 1885, declared: *"Per Constitutionem Apostolicae Sedis, nihil esse innovatum circa censuras earumque reservationes pro fidelibus rituum Orientalium."* Moreover, in this declaration the Holy See followed the conclusion of the canonists and theologians mentioned in a previous chapter;[20] this is a noteworthy fact, since it has provided some very important principles:

---

16 S. Cong. de Prop. Fide, 2 Junii 1835, *Coll.,* n. 830; 11 Dec. 1838, ad 12, 13, *Coll.,* n. 879; 30 Aprilis 1862, ad 2, *Coll.,* n. 1228; 6 Oct. 1863, C, b, *Coll.,* n. 1243.

17 Synodus Ruthenorum (1891), tit. I, cap. IV, n. 2; Synodus Sciarfensis Syrorum (1888), cap. III, art. IX, n. 14; Synodus Alex. Coptorum (1898), sect. II, cap. I, art. V, n. XIV; Synodus Montis Libani (1736), pars II, cap IV, n. 8.

18 S. Cong. de Prop. Fide pro Negotiis R. O., 17 Aug. 1914, art. 22, *A. A. S.,* VI, 462; S. Cong. de Prop. Fide pro Negotiis R. O., 18 Aug. 1913, art. 28, *A. A. S.,* V, 397.

19 Canon 1.

20 Supra chap. V, § 1.

*"Eosdem (Orientales) fideles subjici omnibus censuris ab Apostolica Sede latis in materia dogmatum et in Constitutionibus in quibus implicite de iis desponitur, nempe ubi materia ipsa demonstrat eos comprehendi, quatenus non de lege mere ecclesiastica agitur, sed jus naturale et divinum declaratur * * * illos fideles subjici nominatim nedum censuris, sed etiam Apostolicis reservationibus latis in Const. Benedicti XIV Sacramentum Poenitentiae, in Constitutionibus contra sectae massonicae aliisque similibus addictos."* [21]

Cicognani [22] apparently inclines to the opinion that the Orientals are still bound by the reservations and censures of the Constitution *Apostolicae Sedis* [23] in so far as they may be affected in accordance with the principles quoted above. It is true that the declaration of the Holy Office was occasioned by the Constitution *Apostolicae Sedis.* It seems, however, more probable to conclude that the Holy Office established at this time a set of general principles which were to be used indefinitely for the application of pontifical legislation to the Orientals in the matter of reserved cases and censures. Mark the introductory words of the Congregation: *"Per Const. Apostolicae Sedis, nihil innovatum circa censuras earumque reservationes pro fidelibus rituum Orientalium."* In other words, the definite principles which were enunciated at that time have always been the same with reference to the Orientals.[24] Cappello,[25] quoting the above sentence, adds that the same is to be said of the reservations in the Code. According to his view the Code has not changed these principles and they remain today. Therefore, it seems the application of the reservations of sin and censures of the Code to the Orientals must be judged according to the same norms as those established by the Holy See, August 6, 1885.

---

21 S. Cong. de Prop. Fide, 6 Aug. 1885, *Coll.*, n. 1640; Synodus Alex. Coptorum (1898), sect. II, cap. III, art. V, *De peccatis reservatis.*

22 *Comment. ad Lib. Ium Cod.*, p. 11.

23 Pius IX, 12 Oct. 1869, *Coll.*, n. 1348.

24 Zitelli-Solieri, *Apparatus Juris Eccl.*, pars II, Supplementum, p. 315.

25 *De Censuris*, n. 22.

Hence, the Canons of the Code which inflict certain censures for crimes against faith or the unity of the Church, e. g., apostasy, heresy, schism or suspicion of heresy,[26] embrace all Catholics. Points of Catholic doctrine or teaching also implicitly apply to the Orientals; therefore, to reject the teaching of the Church based upon the natural or divine positive law, or to defend propositions condemned by the Holy See [27] which are contrary to sound morals or Christian ethics are crimes intimately connected with faith and Catholic doctrine; reservations of sin or censures to correct delinquents must *natura rei* apply to Orientals. The Holy See *nominatim* extends certain penalties of the Latin Church to the Orientals; these are more easily recognized.

The Church may abrogate or mitigate censures or reservations in these matters. In the light of the principles just quoted the Orientals are affected by any changes in the law. A practical case may be introduced. The Code mitigated the legislation with reference to forbidden societies in Canon 2335.[28] Do the Orientals profit by the new law or are they held by the more stringent law of the Constitution *Apostolicae Sedis?* Quigley strongly favors the opinion that they come within the scope of the Canon. He says: "The whole discussion hinges on the declaration of the Holy Office, August 6, 1885. The declaration does not mean that the constitutions against the Masons and other anti-social societies, promulgated prior to August 6, 1885, are alone to be the legislation for the Orientals hereafter, but it means that whenever there appears any new legislation about Freemasonry for the Latin church, *natura rei,* this is to apply also to the Oriental Church * * * as their proper legislation. * * * "[29]

26 Chelodi, *Jus Poenale*, nn. 57, 59.

27 E. g., Pius IX, Syllabus errorum (1864), *Fontes*, n. 543; Pius X, litt. encycl. *Pascendi*, 8 Sept. 1907, *Fontes*, n. 680.

28 Leech, *The Constitution, Apostolicae Sedis, and the Codex Juris Canonici*, pp. 57-59; Quigley, *Condemned Societies*, pp. 50, 51.

29 *Condemned Societies*, p. 73 seq.; Cicognani, *Comment. ad Lib. Ium Cod.*, p. 11.

The same argument might be advanced for all points included in the principles outlined by the Holy Office. Whatever, therefore, is the legislation and mind of the Church in these matters, it appears, should be extended to the Orientals. The Church has never shown a tendency to be stricter with the Oriental faithful, an added reason which forces uniformity. With these guiding principles in mind, it will be easier to establish the binding force of reservations and censures in the Code which affect the Orientals.

As a general rule canonists do not treat this matter in detail. This is, no doubt, a prudent procedure. It is to be imitated rather than condemned, because it is difficult to determine in some particular cases whether a certain reservation embraces the Orientals; a rather free application of reservations to the Orientals might easily exceed the mind of the supreme legislator. Since the odious is to be restricted, it is perhaps better not to extend too freely the penalties of the Code to the Orientals.[30]

Moreover, the Church has made certain distinctions, and officially maintains that the Orientals are not affected by all reservations of the Latin Church.[31] To ignore the principles of the Holy See in its decrees is to run counter to the attitude of the Church towards the Oriental Cath-

---

30 Maroto considers the Orientals affected by the penal laws of the Latin Church (*Institutiones Juris Can.*, n. 198, c). It does not seem probable to conclude from this statement that he extends all censures, reservations and penalties of the Code to the Orientals (Kelly, *Jurisdiction of Simple Confessor*, p. 66). Maroto surely had in mind the distinction made by the Holy See in the application of censures and reservations to the Oriental Catholics (S. Cong. de Prop. Fide, 6 Aug. 1885, *Coll.*, n. 1640). Hence, when he says, the Orientals are subject to the penal laws of the Latin Church, the statement must be interpreted strictly. The purpose of reserved sins, it seems, is disciplinary, rather than penal (Dargin, *Reserved Cases*, p. 10 seq.; S. Cong. S. Officii, 13 Julii 1916, *A. A. S.*, VIII, 313). Censures according to the Code are medicinal punishments (Canon 2216; Dargin, *op. cit.*, p. 41), whilst penal laws are remedies or measures established to remove scandal or a voluntary occasion of sin (Canons, 2306, 2307; Dargin, op cit., p. 41). In this final and strict sense, it appears, that the Orientals would be subject to the penal laws of the Church.

31 S. Cong. de Prop. Fide, 6 Aug. 1885, *Coll.*, n. 1640; Synodus Alex. Coptorum (1898), sect. II, cap. III, art. V, *De peccatis reservatis;* Zitelli-Solieri, *op. cit., loc. cit.*; Cappello, *op. cit.*, n. 22.

olics. The policy of the Church and the first Canon of the Code indicate that the Orientals are exempt from the reservations of sin and censures established by the Code unless the matter *natura rei* pertains to them, or the legislation refers to them nominally.

Cappello[32] is practically alone among canonists who deals with the subject at some length with an explanation of the principles of the Holy Office. He refers to the first Canon and states that the Orientals are bound by censures established by common law which inflict penalties for crimes against faith, e. g., apostasy, heresy, schism or whatever indicates a suspicion of heresy, in fact all pertinent crimes which come within the competency of the Holy Office.[33] After a consideration of the norms established by the Holy Office, Cappello concludes: *Hisce attentis, Orientales certe subsunt censuris, de quibus in canonibus* 2314, 2316, 2318, 2319, 2320, 2332, 2335, 2367, 2371. His deductions do not appear to be at variance with the mind of the legislator, and represent a logical interpretation of the Church's principles.[34]

The more important reservations enumerated below will serve to illustrate the principles of the Holy See and to determine whether a reserved sin or censure of the Code applies to the Orientals.

1. The only sin reserved *ratione sui* to the Holy See is given in Canon 894. The sin reserved by this Canon is the false accusation of an innocent confessor before an ecclesiastical tribunal of the crime of solicitation in

32 *De Censuris*, n. 22.

33 Canons 247 and 257, § 2.

34 Cappello also states (*op. cit.*, n. 22) that by reason of particular laws the Orientals may be subject to other censures. Cf. Synodus Sciarfensis Syrorum (1888), cap. V, art. VII; Synodus Alex. Coptorum (1898), sect. II, cap. III, art. 5, *De peccatis reservatis*; Synodus Montis Libani (1736), pars II, cap. V, VI; pars IV, cap. II, n. 12 seq.; Synodus Ruthenorum (1891), tit. II, cap. IV, n. 1. Would the Orientals be bound by the reservations of their particular law if they abandoned their domicile in the Orient and acquired new domiciles, e. g., in the United States? A distinction must be made: if the reservation is by Papal authority it would seem to bind the Orientals everywhere. Reservations made in the Orient by a local Patriarch or Ordinary apply in their respective territories and to their subjects. Hence, if an Oriental no longer comes under such jurisdiction, he would not be affected by the Oriental Ordinary's reservations.

connection with the Sacrament of Penance. There is no doubt of its extension to the Orientals, since they have been included *nominatim* in various decrees.[35]

2. The censure of excommunication *speciali modo* reserved to the Holy See (Canon 2363) is inflicted on all who falsely accuse an innocent confessor of the crime of solicitation in connection with Sacramental confession, even though the accusation is made to a mere superior. The Orientals have been explicitly included in this legislation.[36]

3. All confessors who absolve or pretend to absolve an accomplice in *peccato turpi* (Canon 2367) incur the censure of excommunication *specialissimo modo* reserved to the Apostolic See. The penalty of this Canon has been extended *nominatim* to the Orientals.[37]

4. The censure of excommunication *specialissimo modo* reserved to the Holy See is incurred by those who desecrate the Consecrated Hosts, or carry them away, or retain them for an evil purpose; persons guilty of this sacrilege are furthermore suspected of heresy (Canon 2320).[38] The Orientals are embraced by this censure since it pertains to matters of faith.[39]

5. Editors who publish books of heretics, apostates, and schismatics which defend heresy, apostasy and schism, incur excommunication *speciali modo* reserved to the Holy See (Canon 2318). This action is a formal cooperation in matters subversive of the true faith which is always strictly forbidden (Canon 1258), *natura rei* the

---

35 Canon 6, n. 2; Benedict XIV, Const. *Sacramentum Poenitentiae,* 1 Junii 1741, Documentum V in Codice; Const. *Etsi Pastoralis,* 26 Maii 1742, § IX, n. V, *Coll.,* n. 338; S. Cong. Officii, 1 Junii 1775, *Coll.,* n. 509; S. Cong. de Prop. Fide, 6 Aug. 1885, *Coll.,* n. 1640; S. Cong. Officii, 13 Junii 1710, *Coll.,* n. 279; Cappello, *De Sacramentis,* II, p. I, n. 707; *De Censuris,* n. 22; Cicognani, *Comment. ad Ium. Lib. Cod.,* p. 10; Antoine, *Theologia Moralis,* V, 329.

36 *Ibidem.*

37 *Ibidem;* Genicot-Salsmans, *Institut. Theol. Moralis,* II, n. 394 seq.; Cappello, *De Censuris,* n. 456; Chelodi, *Jus Poenale,* n. 91; Antoine, *op. cit.,* V, 323 seq.

38 Chelodi, *op. cit.,* n. 61.

39 Cappello, *De Censuris,* n. 22.

censure must extend to the Orientals. The same censure is incurred by persons who knowingly and without the proper permission retain or read such books or other books nominally condemned by the Holy See. They represent a common danger to Christian faith and principles; hence, the prohibition and the censure applies to all Catholics without distinction of rite.[40]

6. Those who appeal to a general council against the decrees, mandates, or laws of the Roman Pontiff incur the censure of excommunication reserved *speciali modo* to the Apostolic See (Canon 2332). The Code states that persons who make such an appeal to a general council are considered *suspecti de haeresi;* the penalty annexed to this sin must embrace the Orientals because it is intimately connected with Catholic faith and doctrine.[41]

7. Apostates, heretics, and schismatics incur the censure of excommunication *speciali modo* reserved to the Holy See (Canon 2314). There can be no doubt that this censure *ex natura rei* extends to the Orientals.[42]

8. Persons suspected of heresy who after six months have manifested no signs of amendment also incur excommunication *speciali modo* reserved to the Apostolic See (Canon 2315). After six months a suspect is considered as a heretic, and hence, he is liable to the same penalty.[43]

9. Those who join the Masons or similar societies which machinate against the Church or legitimate civil power incur the censure of excommunication *simpliciter* reserved to the Holy See (Canon 2335). This censure has been extended *nominatim* to the Orientals and com-

---

40 Pius IV, Const. *Dominici gregis,* 24 Mar. 1564, *Fontes,* n. 105; Leo XIII, Const. *Officiorum ac Munerum,* 25 Jan. 1897, cap. IV, V, *Fontes,* 632; S. Cong. pro Eccl. Orient., 26 Maii 1928, *A. A. S.,* XX (1928), 195; Cappello, *De Censuris,* n. 22; Wernz, *Jus Decretalium,* III, nn. 97, 109, 112.

41 Cappello, *De Censuris,* n. 22; Benedict XIV, Const. *Allatae Sunt,* 26 Julii 1755, n. 44, *Coll.,* n. 395.

42 S. Cong. de Prop. Fide, 6 Aug. 1885, *Coll.,* n. 1640; Cappello, *op. cit.,* n. 22.

43 Cf. Canons 2316, 2340, § 1; Chelodi, *Jus Poenale,* n. 59.

mentators do not hesitate to apply to them the penalty of this Canon.[44]

10. Catholics who contract marriage or renew matrimonial consent before a non-Catholic minister, acting as such, incur the censure of excommunication reserved to the Ordinary (Canon 2319, § 1, n. 1). Cappello extends this censure to the Orientals.[45] The fundamental principles enunciated by the Holy See support his conclusion. The prohibition is founded upon the natural and divine positive law [46] which always forbids an active communication *in sacris* with a non-Catholic sect.[47] Therefore, the penalty attached to the violation of this prohibition *natura rei* must apply to the Orientals. This is confirmed by responses of the Holy See which indicate that Orientals who have given matrimonial consent before heretical or schismatical minister in the sense of the Canon (*uti sacris addictus*) incur a censure, for it is stated that if they are sincerely repentant, they may be absolved from censure having first seriously promised to carry out the *cautiones*.[48] One of the conditions to obtain a dispensation for a mixed marriage demands that there shall be no non-Catholic ceremony (*qua talis*) before or after the Catholic ceremony.[49]

11. An excommunication reserved to the Ordinary is incurred by:

Catholics who contract marriage with the agreement, implicit or explicit, that any or all their children shall be educated outside of the Catholic faith (Canon 2319, § 1, n. 2).

---

44 Quigley, *Condemned Societies*, pp. 71-74; Blat, *Commentarium*, Liber V, n. 61; Augustine, *A Commentary on Canon Law*, VIII, 343; Cappello, *De Censuris*, n. 22.

45 *De Censuris*, n. 22.

46 Cerato, *De Matrimonio*, n. 57; Vlaming, *Praelectiones Juris Matr.*, I, n. 228; Cappello, *De Sacramentis*, III, n. 317; Wernz, *Jus Decretalium*, IV, n. 588, footnote 42; Pighi, *Censurae Latae Sententiae*, n. 102.

47 Canon 1258, § 1.

48 S. Cong. S. Officii, 10 Feb. 1892, ad 2am, *Coll.*, n. 1783; S. Cong. S. Officii, 5 Aug. 1846, ad 3am, *Coll.*, n. 1009; S. Cong. de Prop. Fide, 1858 (ad Episcopos Graeco-Rumenos), *Coll.*, n. 1154.

49 Instr. S. Cong. S. Officii, 12 Dec. 1888, nn. 5, 6, 7, *Coll.*, n. 1696.

Catholics who knowingly present their children to a non-Catholic minister for baptism (Canon 2319, § 1, n. 3).

Catholic parents or those taking their place who knowingly hand over their children to be educated in a non-Catholic religion (Canon 2319, § 1, n. 4).

Persons guilty of these crimes are suspected of heresy.[50] The prohibitions are all based upon the natural and divine positive law which require the Catholic education of the children.[51] When there is question of a mixed marriage, the Church by means of the *cautiones* or promises demands moral certainty that all the offspring shall be educated in the Catholic faith.[52] Since the Canon itself states that persons who fail in these obligations are suspected of heresy, the matter is certainly intimately connected with faith; hence, the censure attached to violation of the law *natura rei* embraces the Orientals.[53]

The application of the reservations of sin and censures established by the Code to the Orientals in the United States must be judged in the light of the principles outlined by the Holy See which have been discussed in this article.[54] Do other reservations *ex jure communi* which are merely ecclesiastical or disciplinary in foundation affect the Orientals in this country? The principles of the Holy See do not warrant the extension of such penalties to the Orientals, even if they are outside of their proper territory or if they are under the jurisdiction of Latin Ordinaries. It is true that the Congregation of the Propaganda has declared that Orientals in the United States who have not a proper Ordinary of their respec-

50 Chelodi, *Jus Poenale*, n. 59.

51 Sanchez, lib. VII, disp. 72, n. 6; Schmalzgrueber, tom. IV, pars II, tit. VI, n. 150; Reiffenstuel, lib. IV, tit. I, n. 371.

52 Vlaming, *op cit.*, I, nn. 218-220; Wernz-Vidal, *Jus Canonicum*, V, n. 177 seq.; Instr. S. Cong. S. Officii (ad omnes Episcopos ritus Orientalis), 12 Dec. 1888, nn. 4-6, *Coll.*, n. 1696.

53 Cappello, *De Censuris*, n. 22.

54 S. Cong. de Prop. Fide, 6 Aug. 1885, *Coll.*, n. 1640; Cappello, *De Censuris*, n. 22; supra this chapter, § 2.

tive rite are subject to the local Latin Ordinary.[55] But the Holy See did not say that they were subject to the common law of the Latin Church; therefore, one could not extend the reservations of the Code to the Orientals beyond the cases permitted by the supreme legislator.

§ 3. Episcopal Reservations and the Orientals in the United States

Examples of the reservations of sin and censures in the Code which affect the Orientals have already been considered. It is now in order to discuss briefly the cases which the local Ordinary is empowered to reserve to himself.[56] Reservations of sin or censure established by the local Ordinary for his particular territory are known as episcopal cases.[57]

The Holy See has placed all Orientals in the United States, The Greek-Ruthenians excepted,[58] under the jurisdiction of the local Latin Ordinaries in whose diocese they have their domicile.[59] Hence, they necessarily become subject to the particular law of the diocese in so far as it is not in prejudice to their proper rite or discipline. The episcopal reservations, therefore, which are in force in the diocese must extend to all Orientals who are subjects of the local Ordinary. The Greek-Ruthenian Ordinaries in this country have complete and ordinary jurisdiction over their respective subjects independent of the local Latin Ordinaries. They may, as a consequence, establish their particular reservations for their own subjects.[60]

---

55 S. Cong. de Prop. Fide, 1 Maii 1897, *Coll.*, n. 1966. The Congregation for the Oriental Church makes the same statement in a letter to the Apostolic Delegate, Washington, D. C., May 29, 1925. This letter is quoted in chapter IX, § 1.

56 Canons 893, § 1, 2247.

57 Cappello, *De Sacramentis*, II, p. I, nn. 511-515.

58 S. Cong. de Prop. Fide pro Negotiis R. O., 17 Aug. 1914, art. 2, *A. A. S.*, VI (1914), 458.

59 S. Cong. de Prop. Fide, 1 Oct. 1897, *Coll.*, n. 1966.

60 S. Cong. de Prop. Fide pro Negotiis R. O., 17 Aug. 1914, art. 2, 22, *A. A. S.*, VI, 458, 462.

§ 4. Faculties to absolve from Reservations

1. *Oriental Confessors subject to Latin Ordinaries*

The Oriental priests in this country who are under the jurisdiction of Latin Ordinaries are given their faculties to hear confessions at the discretion of the respective local Ordinary.[61] A difficulty is immediately in evidence. To what degree is the jurisdiction of the Oriental confessor in question restricted by the various classes of reservations? It must be noted at once that definite conclusions cannot be expected. Just as it seems quite impossible to determine the exact extent of the reservations in the Code to the Orientals, so also, it will be equally difficult to establish in every instance the exact limitation of the jurisdiction of the Oriental confessor relative to the different classes of reservations.

Certainly the reservations sin and censures in the Code which *natura rei* or *nominatim* affect the Orientals, whether reserved to the Holy See or to the Ordinary, in like manner limit the jurisdiction of the Oriental confessor to absolve from such cases.[62] It would follow as a logical consequence that all reservations of the Code which are merely disciplinary would not limit the jurisdiction of the Oriental confessor, since he is not affected by the purely disciplinary laws of the Latin Church unless there is an express mention to that effect.[63] Any approved Oriental confessor could absolve Latin penitents, it seems, from reservations of the Code which are merely disciplinary in foundation.[64]

It appears within the power of the Latin Ordinary who has Oriental priests under his jurisdiction to make a further restriction of their faculties to absolve from cases reserved to the Ordinary by the Code which would include even the disciplinary reservations of this class.

---

61 S. Cong. de Prop. Fide, 12 Aprilis 1894, *Coll.*, n. 1866.

62 Canon 1; S. Cong. de Prop. Fide, 6 Aug. 1885, *Coll.*, 1640; Dargin, *Reserved Cases*, p. 74; Kelly, *Jurisdiction of the Simple Confessor*, p. 64 seq.; Cappello, *De Censuris*, n. 22.

63 *Ibidem;* supra chapter V.

64 Kelly, *op. cit.*, p. 66.

The Oriental confessor in question obtains his faculties to hear confessions from the respective local Latin Ordinary. It should be, therefore, within the power of the local Ordinary to limit the jurisdiction of the Oriental confessor so that he could not absolve from any cases reserved to the Ordinary by the Code.[65]

The episcopal cases or reservations established by the local Ordinary for his particular territory offer no difficulty. The Orientals who are under the jurisdiction of Latin Ordinaries are bound by the particular reservations in force in the diocese of their domicile. Certainly the Latin Ordinary who grants faculties to Oriental priests may restrict their faculties to absolve from episcopal reservations effective in the diocese. Moreover, the limitation of the faculties of certain Oriental confessors relative to episcopal cases is already implied in the fact that they are under the jurisdiction of the Latin Ordinary, and consequently subject to the particular law of the diocese.

2. *The Greek-Ruthenian Confessors*

The Greek-Ruthenians in the United States have Ordinaries of their own rite[66] who exercise complete and ordinary jurisdiction over their respective subjects.[67] They are affected, therefore, by the following reservations: 1. The reservations of sin and censures in the Code which *ex natura rei* or *nominatim* apply to the Orientals, whether reserved to the Apostolic See or to the Ordinary by the Code. 2. The reservations of their respective Greek-Ruthenian Ordinary. They are neither bound by the mere ecclesiastical or disciplinary reservations of the Code nor are they subject to those of the local Latin Ordinaries.

Since the faithful may confess their sins to any approved confessor even of another rite, what restrictions,

---

65 S. Cong. de Prop. Fide 12 Aprilis 1894, Coll., n. 1866.

66 S. Cong. Consist., 20 Maii 1924, *A. A. S.*, XVI (1924), 243.

67 S. Cong. de Prop. Fide pro Negotiis R. O., 17 Aug. 1914, art. 2, *A. A. S.*, VI, 458.

for example, are placed upon the jurisdiction of the Greek-Ruthenian confessor to absolve from the reservations of sin and censures established by the Code. The single sin reserved *ratione sui* to the Holy See binds Latins and Orientals alike; consequently it limits the jurisdiction of all confessors.

The sins reserved *ratione censurae* by the Code which are mere disciplinary measures of the Latin Church offer some difficulty. A Greek-Ruthenian penitent may confess to an approved Latin priest a sin reserved *ratione censurae* by the Code to which the Orientals are not bound *natura rei* or *nominatim*. In this case the Oriental does not incur the censure, therefore, the sin is not reserved and the penitent may be absolved by the Latin confessor. There are other similar difficulties which may arise that seem to frustrate the purpose of certain censures reserved by the Code. If a Latin confesses to a Greek-Ruthenian priest a sin reserved *ratione censurae* impeding the reception of the sacraments, he may be absolved if the reservation in only a disciplinary one of the Latin Church, because the Greek-Ruthenian confessor's jurisdiction, it seems, is limited only by the reservations which *natura rei* or *nominatim* apply to the Orientals.[68]

Complications may occur in connection with episcopal cases of the Latin and Greek-Ruthenian Ordinaries. If a Latin penitent confesses a sin to a Greek-Ruthenian confessor which the local Latin Ordinary has reserved *ratione censurae*, in this instance, the confessor cannot be restricted by the Latin Ordinary in the exercise of his jurisdiction, and hence, *per se,* he may absolve the penitent from the censure. When a Greek-Ruthenian confesses to an approved Latin priest, the same principles might obtain in regard to reservations of the Greek-Ruthenian Ordinaries. This would certainly lead to difficulties and for practical purposes reservations would be ineffective. However, it must be remembered that an

68 Kelly, *op. cit.*, p. 66 seq.

Ordinary cannot restrict the faculties given by another Ordinary which may be seen from the present case. This must be done by a higher authority.[69] The Holy See has provided that priests must respect the reservations established by Ordinaries of another rite and they may not absolve from them without proper permission:

"*Presbyteri vero Latini absolvere non poterunt fideles Graeco-Rutheni ritus a censuris et casibus reservatis ab Ordinario Graeco-Rutheni statutis, absque venia ejusdem. Vicissim idem dicatur de presbyteris Graeco-Ruthenis quoad censuras et reservationes statutas ab Ordinariis Latini ritus.*"[70]

This restriction placed by the Sacred Congregation is not recent. A similar provision was made in 1838 at the request of the Apostolic delegates in the Orient[71] and the same legislation was enacted by Leo XIII.[72] The regulation does not solve all possible cases of jurisdiction. Kelly proposes a few which are not settled.[73] Does the above law, which restricts the jurisdiction of a Greek-Ruthenian confessor, extend to papal reservations of the Code, whether reserved to the Apostolic See or to the Ordinaries, to which the Orientals are not subject *natura rei* or *nominatim?* If it does not, the Ruthenian confessor may absolve a Latin penitent from any reserved censure of the Code which is merely disciplinary, because his jurisdiction is not limited except in those cases which restrict Orientals *nominatim* or *ex natura rei.*

According to the strict wording of the law, it can hardly be extended beyond reservations of the Ordinary which he establishes for his particular territory. If the legislator intended to settle all difficulties of jurisdiction, it seems to be his mind to include all reservations

---

69 Kelly, *op. cit.*, p. 68.

70 S. Cong. de Prop. Fide pro Negotiis R. O., 17 Aug. 1914, art. 22, *A. A. S.*, VI, 462; S. Cong. de Prop. Fide pro Negotiis R. O., 18 Aug. 1913, art. 28, *A. A. S.*, V, 397; Woywod, *A Practical Commentary*, I, n. 823.

71 S. Cong. de Prop. Fide, 11 Dec. 1838, ad Xam et XIam, *Coll.*, n. 879.

72 Const. *Orientalium*, 30 Nov. 1894, n. 6, *Coll.*, n. 1883; Zitelli-Solieri, *Apparatus Juris Eccl.*, n. 1186.

73 *Op. cit.*, p. 68.

whether constituted by the Code or by the local Ordinary. It is not evident that the reservations of the Code are included by the law. In practice, it appears, the confessor need only to respect the reservations of the local Ordinary. He could not be criticised for absolving in view of the milder interpretation. There exists a positive doubt as to the extension of the law, therefore, his absolution would be valid and licit.[74]

§ 5. Indulgences

The Church has at her disposal many spiritual favors to promote the welfare of souls, and it becomes her duty to dispense all means of grace to worthy subjects. Indulgences are among the favors which the Church offers upon the fulfillment of the requisite conditions. Since indulgences pertain directly to the spiritual good of souls, they must be intended for all Catholics. In this matter there is no distinction between the Oriental and the Latin Churches.[75]

Paul V, in 1616, assured the clergy and people of the Ruthenian nation in communion with the Apostolic See that they share with the rest of the faithful all indulgences upon the fulfillment of the prescribed conditions.[76] In recent years the same teaching has been reiterated by the Holy See. A certain Oriental bishop proposed the following question: May the faithful of the Oriental rites gain the indulgences granted by the Supreme Pontiff by universal decree? The Sacred Poenitentiary responded in the affirmative.[77] The indulgences and favors of the Jubilee Year may already be extended to the Orientals by the principle contained in the response of the Sacred Poenitentiary; however, the Church is usually

74 Kelly, *op. cit.*, p. 68; Canon 209: "In errore communi aut in dubio positivo et probabili sive juris sive facti, jurisdictionem supplet Ecclesia pro foro tum interno tum externo."

75 Cappello, *De Sacramentis*, II, p. I, n. 1030.

76 Cf. *Coll. Lac.*, II, 600, d.

77 S. Poenitent. Apost., 7 Julii 1917, *A. A. S.*, IX, 399; Maroto, *Institutiones Juris Can.*, I, n. 198; Vermeersch-Creusen, *Epitome* I (1927), n. 49; Cappello, *op. cit.*, n. 979.

very explicit in such points. They were expressly included in the recent Jubilee proclamation.[78]

Since these concessions refer only to indulgences granted to all the faithful by a universal decree, Vermeersch asks a very practical question:[79] May the Orientals by the use of scapulars and blessed beads gain the indulgences as the Latins? He is inclined to the affirmative opinion, even if the erection of a Confraternity is required. The opinion is based upon a response of the Sacred Congregation of Indulgences. The Congregation declared it was lawful for the Master General of the Order of Preachers without a special faculty of the Holy See to erect Confraternities proper to the Order also in Churches of a different rite with the previous consent of the Ordinary as among the Latins.[80]

---

78 Pius XI, Const., *Apostolico Muneri*, 30 Julii 1924, *A. A. S.*, XVI (1924), 314; Benedict XV, 15 Aprilis 1916, *A. A. S.*, VIII (1916), 137; Cappello, *op. cit.*, n. 1030.

79 *Periodica*, IX (1921), 67, 68.

80 S. Cong. Indulg., 21 Junii 1893, *Coll.*, n. 1837.

CHAPTER XI

THE SACRAMENT OF EXTREME UNCTION

A study of the discipline of the Oriental Churches and their rituals reveals that as a general rule the Eastern Churches admit a plurality of ministers for the Sacrament of Extreme Unction.[1] The various explanations of this custom hinge upon the interpretation of the Jacobean text, "*inducat presbyteros ecclesiae.*" Wernz remarks that the same practice existed in the West until the 13th century. It has not only disappeared in the Latin Church, but it is now unlawful according to the Latin rite for several priests to confer the Sacrament.[2] The Church does not condemn the Oriental custom where it exists, but she insists that a single minister, a priest, is sufficient to administer the Sacrament validly. Official pronouncements confirm this doctrine.[3] Pope Benedict XIV clearly defined the teaching of the Church on this point in his Constitution addressed to the Italo-Greeks: "*Nec refert, utrum eadem Extrema Unctio per unum vel plures presbyteros fiat, ubi hujusmodi viget consuetudo; dummodo credant et asserant, illud Sacramentum, servata debita materia et forma, ab uno presbytero valide et licite confici.*"[4] The Code stresses the same principle: "*Hoc Sacramentum valide administrat omnis et solus sacerdos.*"[5]

Where the custom obtains among the Orientals, it certainly is lawful for several priests to administer Extreme

---

1 Kilker, *Extreme Unction*, p. 86; Denzinger, *Ritus Orientalium*, I, 188.

2 Wernz, *Jus Decretalium*, III, n. 749, (note 11); Benedict XIV, *De Synodo Dioecesana*, lib. VIII, cap. IV, n. 4 seq.

3 C. 14, X, *de verb. signif.*, V, 40.

4 *Const. Etsi Pastoralis*, 26 Maii 1742, § V, n. III, *Coll.*, n. 338; Kilker, *op. cit.*, p. 87.

5 Canon 938, § 1.

Unction. This practice is especially noticeable in the Byzantine rite.[6] The number of priests may vary. Seven is the ideal number, although fewer may confer the Sacrament, five, three, and even one, according to the prescriptions of their rituals, which must always be followed.[7] Whatever the approved practice of the Oriental rites, they must all believe as defined by the Holy See, and restated by the Code, that a single priest may validly administer the Sacrament of Extreme Unction.[8] This teaching is usually incorporated in Oriental Synodal legislation which prescribes that a single priest must confer the Sacrament in cases of necessity.[9] It is to be noted, however, that some Oriental rites prescribe that only one priest may administer Extreme Unction. This holds for the Maronites[10] and Syrians.[11]

The blessed oil used for the anointing of the sick furnishes another mooted question. Must the oil for the sick be blessed by the bishop, or does the blessing of the simple priest suffice? As far as the Latin Church is concerned, positive law demands that the *Oleum Infirmorum* must have the episcopal blessing, or the blessing of a priest who has obtained his faculty from the Holy See.[12] Pope Eugene IV in the Council of Florence declared to the Armenians that "*oleum olivae per Episcopum consecratum,*" is the matter for Extreme Unction.[13] The

---

6 Benedict XIV, Const. *Etsi Pastoralis*, 26 Maii 1742, § V, n. III, IV, *Coll.*, n. 338; Synodus Montis Libani (1736), pars II, cap. VIII, n. 8, *Coll. Lac.*, II, 152; Synodus Ruthenorum (1720), tit. III, § VI; Synodus Ruthenorum (1891), tit. II, cap. V; Synodus Alex. Coptorum (1898), sect. II, cap. III, art. VI, n. 7, I.

7 Antoine, *Theologia Moralis*, V, 376.

8 Eugene IV, Const. *Exultate Deo* (in Conc. Florent.), 22 Nov. 1439, § 14, *Fontes*, n. 52; Benedict XIV, ep. encycl. *Ex quo*, 1 Mar. 1756, § § 45, 46, *Fontes*, n. 438.

9 *Ibidem;* Antoine, *Theologia Moralis*, V, 376; *AkKR*, VIII (1862), n. 4, p. 172; Kilker, *op. cit.*, p. 88 seq.

10 Synodus Mont. Libani (1736), pars II, cap. VIII, n. 8, *Coll. Lac.*, II, 152.

11 Synodus Sciarfensis (1888), cap. V, art. VIII, n. 3.

12 Canon 945.

13 Eugene IV, Const. *Exultate Deo*, 22 Nov. 1439, § 14, *Fontes*, n. 52.

Council of Trent[14] and certain popes[15] made similar declarations. The custom of the Byzantine rite evidences the fact, nevertheless, that the Greek priests have blessed the oil for the sick since the earliest times. This is emphasized by historical records,[16] and the Holy See, at various times, has approved the ancient custom which obtains amongst them.[17] Ordinarily, the Maronite priests are forbidden to bless the oil of the sick. However, if the supply consecrated by the bishop fails, simple priests in this case enjoy the faculty to bless the *oleum infirmorum*.[17a]

Who is in duty bound to administer Extreme Unction to those in danger of death? Generally speaking the pastor of the place is under grave obligation to administer to the sick within the limits of his parish. In cases of necessity, with at least presumed permission of the pastor or Ordinary of the place, any priest may do so.[18] Such is the law for the Latin Church which does not differ substantially from the legislation of the Oriental rites.[19] It is the mind of the Church that Catholics receive the Sacraments according to their proper rite. Hence, even in the United States, if the Orientals have a church and priest of their rite, the pastor is bound to administer the Sacrament to his people. It may happen that Orientals are situated in localities where they have neither church nor priest of their rite; in such cases they depend entirely upon the ministration of the

---

14 Sess. XIV, *de sacramento extr. unct.* cap. I, Denzinger-Bannwart, *Enchiridion Symbolorum*, n. 908.

15 Decr. S. C. Officii, sub Paulo V, 13 Jan. 1611, et Gregorio XVI, 14 Sept. 1842, Denzinger-Bannwart, *op. cit.*, nn. 1628, 1629.

16 Migne, P. L., 99, 929; Allatius, *Eccl. Occid. et Orient. Consens.* lib. III, cap. 16; Kilker, *op. cit.*, p. 301 seq.

17 Benedict XIV, *De Synodo Dioecesana*, lib. VIII, cap. I, n. 4; Clement VIII, Instr. *Sanctissimus*, 31 Aug. 1595, § 3, *Fontes*, n. 179; Benedict XIV, Const. *Etsi Pastoralis*, 26 Maii 1742, § IV, n. I, *Coll.*, n. 338; Benedict XIV, ep. encycl. *Ex quo*, 1 Mar. 1756, § § 45-47, *Fontes*, n. 438.

17a Synodus Montis Libani (1736), pars II, cap. VIII, n. 2.

18 Canon 938, § 2.

19 Synodus Montis Libani (1736), pars II, cap. VIII, n. 12, *Coll. Lac.*, II, 153; Synodus Ruthenorum (1720), tit. III, § VI; Synodus Sciarfensis Syrorum (1888), cap. V, art. VIII, n. 5; Synodus Alex. Coptorum (1898), sect. II, cap. III, art. VI, n. 7, IX, X.

local Latin pastor who has the same obligations towards his Oriental subjects.[20] An instance of unusual urgency may occur even when the various rites have their proper church and priest. In an extraordinary case the Latin or Oriental priest may not be present to administer to his dying parishioners. The Code seems to be plain that in such circumstances, any priest with at least the presumed permission of the pastor, must in charity, administer the Sacrament.[21] The Holy See has provided a norm for such emergencies. In certain places of Europe where the Ruthenians and Latin Catholics intermingle, this very case is mentioned. Whenever a sick person cannot have a minister of his own rite, a priest of another may confer Extreme Unction. He must follow, however, the prescriptions of his particular ritual.[22]

---

20 Leo XIII, Const. *Orientalium Dignitas,* 30 Nov. 1894, n. 9, *Coll.,* n. 1883; S. Cong. de Prop. Fide, 1 Maii 1897, n. 1, *Coll.,* n. 1966; S. Cong. de Prop. Fide pro Negotiis R. O., 17 Aug. 1914, art. 19, *A. A. S.,* VI, 461.

21 Canon 938, §§ 2, 3.

22 S. Cong. de Prop. Fide, 6 Oct. 1863, C, d, *Coll.,* n. 1243; Canon 733, §§ 1, 2.

CHAPTER XII

THE FORM OF MARRIAGE

Christ our Lord elevated the marriage contract of Christians to the dignity of a Sacrament, wherefore between baptized persons a valid matrimonial contract is simultaneously a Sacrament.[1] The two necessary elements of the Sacrament, matter and form, may be distinguished in the sacramental matrimonial contract. Benedict XIV defines them thus: "*Mutua nempe ac legitima corporum traditio, verbis ac nutibus, interiorem animi assensum exprimentibus, materia; et mutua pariter a legitima corporum acceptatio, forma.*"[2]

Matrimony, whether considered as a Sacrament or as a contract, essentially consists in the mutual consent of the contracting parties sufficiently manifested. Practically among all peoples of every age the manifestation of the nuptial consent has been characterized by certain solemn ceremonies.[3] The Church cannot change the matter and form of the Sacrament, but she may determine under what conditions the matrimonial contract may be considered valid.[4] These consist of certain established solemnities which must be observed as a *sine qua non* for the validity of the nuptial contract, otherwise known as the substantial or juridical form.[5]

The Church has always abhorred and prohibited secret or clandestine matrimonial unions.[6] Since ancient times the marriage of Christians has been considered a pub-

1 Canon 1012.

2 In epist. ad Archiep. Goanum, 19 Mart. 1758, apud Gasparri, *De Matrimonio*, I, n. 33.

3 Prümmer, *Manuale Theol. Moralis*, III, n. 742.

4 Prümmer, *loc. cit.*

5 Vlaming, *Praelectiones Juris Matr.*, II, n. 553; Gasparri, *De Matrimonio*, II, n. 1027.

6 Conc. Trident., *sessio* XXIV, *de reform. matr.*, cap. I; Tertullian, *De pudicitia*, cap. IV, Migne, P. L., II, 987; I, 1302; St. Ambrose, epist. XIX, *ad Virgilium*, cap. VII, Migne, P. L., II, 984.

lic religious act subject to ecclesiastical regulation.[7] Historical facts testify, nevertheless, that prior to the Council of Trent, no substantial form was exacted for the matrimonial contract under pain of nullity. Even if a capable Christian man and woman by mutual agreement clandestinely entered upon a common life for the purpose of procreating children and mutual assistance, this fact constituted a one and indissoluable Christian marriage.[8] Although valid the Church constantly proclaimed secret marriages illicit and contrary to her desire and ideal. A lawful union demanded the public services and intervention of the Church.[9]

The Fathers of the Council of Trent in order to prevent the many evils consequent upon clandestine marriages enacted the legislation of the decree *Tametsi* which provided a substantial form for the matrimonial contract. It declared not only illicit, but invalid a marriage which was not celebrated before the proper pastor of the parties, or another priest delegated by the pastor or the Ordinary, and at least two witnesses.[10] This legislation was to be extended universally at least to the Latin Church. Before the decree could be enforced a promulgation was necessary in every parish, and only after thirty days was the law to become effective. The fact remains that the Tridentine law was never published in many places. Certain territories were governed by the decree, others were not subject to its legislation. As a consequence, clandestine marriages were valid in many places where the law was never promulgated.[11] Later

---

7 Ayrinhac, *Marriage Legislation*, n. 232; Ojetti, *Jus Pianum*, n. 5 seq.

8 De Smet, *De Spons. et Matr.*, I, nn. 103, 20; Wernz-Vidal, *Jus Canonicum*, V, n. 526.

9 Conc. Trident., *loc. cit.*; Conc. Later., IV (1215), cap. 51, apud cap. 3, *de clandest. desp.*, X, IV, 3; Cappello, *De Sacramentis*, III, n. 658; Chelodi, *Jus Matr.*, n. 128.

10 "Qui aliter quam praesente parocho, vel alio sacerdote de ipsius parochi seu ordinarii licentia, et duobus, vel tribus testibus matrimonium contrahere attentabunt, eos sancta synodus ad sic contrahendum omnino inhabiles reddit; et hujusmodo contractus irritos et nullos esse decernit, prout eos praesenti decreto irritos facit et annulat." (*Sess.* XXIV, cap. I, *de reform. matr.*).

11 Telch, *Epitome Theol. Moralis*, 455 seq.

the declaration *Benedictina* provided further exceptions,[12] and exempted mixed marriages and those of heretics among themselves from the law in certain localities where the decree *Tametsi* already obtained. A considerable lack of uniformity prevailed which engendered many difficulties.[13]

Necessity forced a new uniform and general legislation. This reformation was effected by the promulgation of the decree *Ne Temere* for the Latin Church. It declared valid only those marriages contracted before the pastor of the place, or the Ordinary or a priest delegated by either, and at least two witnesses according to the rules given in the decree.[14] This new law distinguished between valid and licit assistance, and provided for valid marriages in extraordinary cases. These norms were embodied in the Code almost without change.[15] An attempted marriage in the Latin Church celebrated without the substantial form provided in the Code, save the exceptions admitted by law, is considered null and void.[16]

The form of the matrimonial contract among the Oriental Catholics is not governed by such definite Canons as are found in the Code for the Latin Church. Only a few of the uniate rites demand a juridical form for the nuptial contract, for example, the Maronites observe the decree *Tametsi,* the Greek-Ruthenians in the United States the form of the decree *Ne Temere.* The question is somewhat complex, and even after considerable discussion the norms in many instances do not prove satisfactory. General principles applicable to all Oriental rites are quite impossible. What do the different Oriental rites consider the required form necessary for a valid

---

12 Benedict XIV, 4 Nov. 1741, *Coll.*, n. 333.

13 Cappello, *op. cit.*, III, n. 659; Ojetti, *op. cit.*, nn. 10-24.

14 S. Cong. Conc., 2 Aug. 1907, nn. III, IV.

15 Canons 1094-1099.

16 The prevalent legislation for the Latin Church does not enumerate a clandestine marriage or the failure to observe the prescribed juridical form as an impediment to the matrimonial contract. The Code prescribes a juridical form as a *condition sine qua non,* for the recognition of a valid marriage contract (Canon 1094).

matrimonial union? The subsequent norms may be useful to determine the more common and possible cases which may occur among the Orientals found in the United States.

Clearness suggests a three-fold division and a separate treatment of each class: 1. Orientals who are not bound to observe a juridical form for a valid matrimonial contract. 2. Orientals who are bound by the decree *Tametsi.* 3. Orientals who are bound by the decree *Ne Temere.*

§ 1. Orientals not bound to observe a juridical form

Even if the legislation of the decree *Tametsi* was intended to regulate the matrimonial contract of all Christians, the fact remains that the Tridentine law never became universal among the Orientals. They were permitted to retain their ancient laws and customs; common opinion also considered the Orientals exempt from the disciplinary decrees of the Latin Church unless they were explicitly mentioned.[17] The decree *Ne Temere* did not change their approved legislation,[18] and the present form of the Code does not affect them except when they contract with Latins.[19]

The laws and customs of the Orientals in many instances do not correspond to the Latin practice. It is not strange, therefore, to find that their notion of clandestine marriages is not the same as recognized in the Latin Church. The Oriental concept of clandestinity seems to imply a marriage entered into against the will of the parents and without witnesses, although blessed by a priest.[20] Such a marriage would be valid, but illicit. Generally speaking, Orientals never marry without the blessing of the priest. Their insistence of the sacerdotal

---

17 Benedict XIV, Const. *Allatae Sunt,* 26 Julii 1755, nn. 3, 44. *Coll.,* n. 395; supra chap. V, § 1.

18 S. Cong. Conc., 1 Feb. 1908, *A. S. S.,* XLI, 108.

19 Canons 1, 1099, § 1, n. 3.

20 Benedetti, *Votum,* n. 9, footnote, *A. S. S.,* XLI, 260. The *Votum* of Benedetti is also found in the *Thesaurus Resolutionem, S. Cong. Concilii,* CLXVII, 180-202.

benediction as a *sine qua non* for a valid marriage is based upon the once probable opinion that the priest was the minister of the Sacrament.[21] The uniate Orientals have rejected this opinion, and in conformity to the teachings of the Church hold that the contracting parties to the marriage are themselves the ministers of the Sacrament.[22] Even to this day apparently many of the uniate Orientals regard the blessing and presence of a priest necessary for a valid matrimonial contract.[23]

The Instruction of the Congregation of the Propaganda, addressed to the Greek-Roumanian bishops, discusses the question of clandestine marriages in the Oriental Church.[24] Since the advent of Christianity, the celebration of marriage as a Sacrament of the New Law demanded the sacred rites of the Church and the blessing of the priest. Secret unions were strictly forbidden. However, if the sacramental union is entered into contrary to the accepted custom, it is impossible to prove from the ecclesiastical documents of the Oriental Church, whether such marriages are not only illicit, but also invalid. The necessity of the priestly blessing seems to be founded in a decree of the civil law. Emperor Leo, the Philosopher, in 893, enacted a law that a matrimonial contract required the sacredotal blessing under pain of nullity. Authorities indicate that the Emperor at this time merely prescribed the conditions of a marriage which would be recognized by the civil law, and protected as to the subsequent legal effects. The imperial sanction could in no wise change the ecclesiastical law or introduce a diriment matrimonial impediment. It is not surprising that this civil sanction was accepted as ecclesi-

21 *De Synodo Dioecesana*, lib. VIII, cap. 13, n. 4; lib. XIII, cap. 22, n. 67; Gasparri, *De Matrimonio*, I, n. 32; Papp-Szilagyi, *Enchiridion Juris Eccl. Orient.*, § 88.

22 Benedetti, *Votum*, n. 21, *A. S. S.*, XLI, 267; S. Cong. de Prop. Fide,—Junii 1858, cf. par. *Ceterum posterioribus*, *Coll.*, n. 1154; Papp-Szilagyi, *op. cit.*, § 88.

23 Benedetti cites testimony of Oriental prelates (*Votum*, n. 2. *A. S. S.*, XLI, 254); Mansella, *De Impedimentis Dirim. ac Processu Judiciali*, pp. 152-155.

24 Instr. S. Cong. de Prop. Fide, 28 Junii 1858, *Coll.*, n. 1154.

astical law among many Orientals; with the outbreak of the schism the civil canons enjoyed a higher esteem than the canons of the Church.[25]

Benedetti, who treats this point extensively, introduces historical evidence to show that even prior to civil enactment of Leo the Philosopher, and after his time, the Orientals considered nuptials celebrated without the blessing of the priest invalid.[26] Milasch mentions three conditions which must be verified for a valid marriage among the Greek-Orthodox: (a) The mutual consent of the parties to institute a common life. (b) The manifestation of this consent by a solemn promise made before a priest. (c) The confirmation of this promise by the blessing of the priest.[27]

The common opinion prevails among the Orientals whether uniates or schismatics that the blessing of the proper pastor is only necessary for the lawfulness, and the blessing of any priest suffices for the valid celebration of marriage. This is the prevalent discipline according to the Archbishop of Smyrna in a letter addressed to the Propaganda. The information submitted by the Prelate gives added force to the practice that Orientals, whether schismatics or heretics, as well as Catholics,[28] insist upon the sacerdotal blessing for the confirmation of a valid matrimonial union.

There are also Oriental authorities who hold that the blessing of a priest is only required for the lawfulness, and is not necessary for the validity of the marriage. This is the opinion of Papp-Szilagyi; he rightly draws a distinction between impediment of clandestinity of the Council of Trent, and the notion of clandestinity accepted in the Oriental Church: "*Quod jam Ecclesiam Orientalem adtinet, probe distinguenda est clandestinitas antiqui juris, a clandestinitate per Concilium Tridentinum ex-*

---

25 *Ibidem;* Ojetti, *Jus Pianum,* p. 9 (note); *A. S. S.,* XLI, 255; Woywod, *A Practical Commentary,* I, n. 1099.

26 *Votum,* n. 4 seq. *A. S. S.,* XLI, 256.

27 Milasch, *Das Kirchenrecht der Morgenländischen Kirche,* § 179.

28 Lettera alla S. C. di Prop. Fide, del 18 maggio 1847, *A. S. S.,* XLI, 259; del 19 maggio 1859, *A. S. S.,* XLI, 259.

pressa, certumque est, jus Orientale non agnoscere nisi clandestinitatem antiqui juris, videlicet prohibitionem contrahendi matrimonium absque publicis ceremoniis ab Ecclesia pro ejusdem celebratione praescriptis, quae quidem necessariae sunt ut matrimonii celebratio licita evadat et non prohibita. Utrum vero benedictio aut coronatio necessaria sit ad matrimonii validitatem, decisum ac definitum non fuit ab Ecclesia.'' [29] It is true that the Church has never declared whether the sacerdotal blessing is necessary for a valid marriage of certain Orientals.[30] Theoretically the latter conclusion is sound, but in practice it seems the question must be solved by an appeal to the immemorial observance of the Oriental law or custom which considers the sacerdotal blessing an absolute formality for valid nuptials.

The Instruction of the Congregation of the Propaganda to the Greek-Roumanian bishops [31] also considers the point of Oriental discipline which seems to demand the blessing of the priest for a valid matrimonial contract. It is not the intention of the Congregation, as it states, to disapprove in any way or pass judgment upon the religious rites which are to be desired at all nuptials. The difficulty of the question is admitted and some explanation is required. Silence is not advisable, lest the Congregation would seem to admit, that the Orientals consider the priest as the minister of the Sacrament of Matrimony,[32] and that the priestly blessing is necessary for the validity of the matrimonial contract. In matters of doctrine there must be agreement between the Eastern and Western Churches. In the Latin Church the blessing of the priest and sacred rites connected with the celebration of marriage are not demanded for validity. (The Congregation is not speaking here of the priest as the

29 *Enchiridion Juris Eccl. Orient. Cath.*, § 118, p. 274.
30 Mansella, *op. cit.*, pp. 152-155.
31 Junii 1858, *Coll.*, n. 1154.
32 The Congregation in the same Instruction shows that the Orientals consider the contracting parties to the marriage as the ministers of the Sacrament. Cf. par. *Ceterum posterioribus, Coll.*, n. 1154; Papp-Szilagyi, *op. cit.*, § 88.

authorized witness to assist at the marriage.) The blessing of the marriage which is prescribed by the Oriental Church is not a matter of doctrine, but of discipline; hence, if nuptials are contracted by the Oriental faithful without the blessing of a priest, they should not immediately be declared null and invalid.

This is not a definite answer, and does not solve the question entirely. Although the Holy See does indicate that some marriages of the Orientals contracted without the blessing of the priest are valid, it must be noted that the distinction was given to the Greek-Roumanians who consider clandestinity merely an impedient impediment.[33] No doubt among the Roumanians a nuptial contract is valid without the blessing of the priest, since there is positive evidence to that effect.

What is to be said about the Catholic Orientals whose laws or customs require the sacerdotal benediction for the confirmation of a valid matrimonial contract? In most instances, there is no question of the Tridentine law or subsequent legislation of the Latin Church which demands a juridical form for a valid union. This legislation does not apply to them as a rule, according to the Latin concept of clandestinity, therefore, secret marriages among certain Orientals should be valid. That is true *objectively,* but *subjectively* most Orientals who are not bound to observe a juridical form have the conviction and persuasion that a marriage is not valid when contracted without the blessing of the priest,[34] it becomes necessary to consider what the different rites require for a valid marriage. This information must furnish the practical norm of action for the individual case.

1. *Greek-Roumanians.* There is no authentic document which proves the existence of the Tridentine law among the Greek-Roumanian Church. This information was given to the Congregation of the Propaganda by an Ordi-

---

33 Benedetti, Votum., n. 12, *A. S. S.*, XLI, 261.

34 Benedetti, *Votum,* nn. 2-9, *A. S. S.*, XLI, 254; Smolikowski, *Votum, A. S. S.*, XLI, 252 seq; Mansella, *op. cit.*, pp. 152-155; Zhisman, *Das Eherecht der Orientalischen Kirche,* p. 686.

nary of that rite. Secret marriages were always considered illicit, and clandestinity is merely an impedient impediment. The public celebration of marriage according to the sacred rites of the Church is urged. A provincial council introduced clandestinity as a diriment impediment according to the decree *Tametsi,* but this did not obtain the approval of the Holy See.[35]

2. *Greeks (puri).* The Greek uniates in the vicinity of Constantinople are few in number. As Orientals they are not subject to the decree *Tametsi.* They, as the Greek schismatics, demand the blessing of the priest for the confirmation of a valid matrimonial contract. The same applies to the Greek-Bulgarian Catholics who are also influenced by the schismatic customs.[36]

3. *The Greek Melkites.* They maintain that the matrimonial contract is invalid unless blessed by the pastor, or the Ordinary or a priest delegated by either.[37]

4. *The Uniates of the Syrian rite (puri).* In a synodal decree (1888) they established the diriment impediment of clandestinity according to the Tridentine legislation. This action was not approved by the Congregation of the Propaganda; hence, it was deleted from the synodal legislation. A remnant of clandestinity, however, exists among them. The impediment of clandestinity is enumerated by the synod, but its nature is not explained.[38] This seems to exclude the Tridentine impediment. The synod also states that a marriage is invalid through the omission of the proper form prescribed by the Council of Trent in places where the decree was published; still there is no mention whether the Tridentine law was promulgated among the Syrians.[39] The matter appears

35 Benedetti, *Votum,* n. 12, *A. S. S.,* XLI, 261.

36 Benedetti, *op. cit.,* nn. 14, 15, *A. S. S.,* XLI, 263.

37 Synodus nation. Melchitarum (1806), cap. IX, can. 9, Mansi, XLVI, 764; Conc. Patr. Hierosolm (1849), cap. VII, can. 6, n. 9, Mansi, XLVI, 1056; Cappello, *op. cit.,* III, n. 924; Benedetti, *op. cit.,* n. 16, *A. S. S.,* XLI, 263.

38 Benedetti, *Votum,* n. 19, *A. S. S.,* XLI, 266; Synodus Sciarfensis Syrorum (1888), cap. V, art. XV, § 8, n. 1.

39 Synodus Sciarfensis Syrorum, cap. V, art. XV, § 10, n. 3.

doubtful,[40] and it seems reasonable to conclude the Syrians refer to the Oriental concept of clandestinity, and that they require merely the priestly blessing for the confirmation of a valid matrimonial contract.[41]

5. *The Catholics of the Chaldean rite.* They do not differ in practice from the other Orientals, and also maintain that a nuptial contract must be blessed by the priest.[42]

6. *The Catholics of the Coptic rite.* The Coptic Church in their Synod (1898) renewed the old custom of their rite which declares that the matrimonial contract is null and void unless blessed by the priest (not necessarily the pastor) and in the presence of at least two witnesses.[43]

7. *The Armenians.* Apparently the uniate Armenians require that a marriage be celebrated before the proper pastor, and two witnesses.[44]

§ 2. The Orientals bound by the decree Tametsi

1. *The Maronites*

It may be taken for granted that the Maronites in their native land are governed by the legislation of the decree *Tametsi* relative to the form of marriage.[45] The synod of Mount Lebanon (1736) declared that clandestinity is a diriment impediment which hinders a valid matrimonial contract: "*Nullum est matrimonium clandestinum, id est, quod aliter contrahitur, quam praesente parocho vel sacerdote de ipsius parochi vel ordinarii licentia et duobus vel tribus testibus.*"[46]

It is to be noted that the acts and decrees of the synod were approved by Benedict XIV *in forma specifica,*[47] and

---

40 Telch. *op. cit.*, p. 464.

41 Benedetti, *loc. cit.*; Cappello, *De Sacramentis*, III, n. 924.

42 Benedetti, *Votum*, n. 19, *A. S. S.*, XLI, 266.

43 Benedetti, *Votum*, n. 20, *A. S. S.*, XLI, 267; Synodus Alex. Coptorum, (1898), sect. II, cap. III, art. VIII, § 5, n. XVI.

44 *Acta et Decreta Conc. Arem.* (1911), n. 575.

45 Cappello, *De Sacramentis*, III, n. 925; Wernz-Vidal, *Jus Canonicum*, V, n. 552.

46 *Acta et Decreta*, pars II, cap. XI, n. XII, *Coll. Lac.*, II, 166; pars II, cap. XI, n. 28, *Coll. Lac.*, II, 178.

47 Const. *Singularis*, 1 Sept. 1741, § 10, *Coll. Lac.*, II, 488 seq.

by virtue of this approbation the synodal enactments assume the character of pontifical law.[48] In order to understand the nature and the extent of the Tridentine legislation in its application to the Maronites, some of the legal principles which the decree involves must be recalled.

The decree *Tametsi* has primarily a *territorial* or *local force;* that is, all within the territory subject to the decree must contract marriage under pain of nullity before their proper pastor, or before a priest authorized by the pastor or Ordinary of the parties, and two or more witnesses. Secondly, the law may also have a *personal force.* Suppose a man and a woman have their domiciles where the Tridentine law prevails. If the parties in question *in fraudem legis* contract a clandestine marriage in a locality where the decree *Tametsi* was not promulgated, such an attempted marriage is invalid, since the contracting parties are subject to the law and must observe the Tridentine form. However, if the parties have acquired a domicile or quasi-domicile where the law of Trent was not promulgated, they might contract a valid clandestine marriage provided no other impediments hinder the union.[49]

Another principle is also of paramount importance. If one party to a marriage has a domicile or quasi-domicile where the decree *Tametsi* obtains, and the other party has a domicile in a locality not subject to the Tridentine law, and if the marriage is contracted in the latter place which is not governed by the decree *Tametsi,* neither party is bound under pain of nullity to observe the juridical form prescribed by the Council of Trent. In this case the law admits the principle that the party who is not subject to the decree communicates to the other the

[48] *De Synodo Diocesana*, lib. XII, cap. 5, n. IX seq; Benedetti, *Votum*, n. 18, *A. S. S.*, XLI (1908), 265; Mansella, *De Impedimentis Matr. Dirim. et Processu Judiciali*, p. 151, n. 26.

[49] S. C. S. Officii, 14 Dec. 1859, apud Gasparri, *op. cit.*, II, n. 1066; S. Cong. de Prop. Fide, 7 Junii 1867, *Coll.*, n. 1305; Benedict XIV, litt. apost. 19 Martii 1758, *Coll.*, n. 410. Gasparri, *op. cit.*, II, nn. 1066 seq. 1166 seq.; Wernz, *Jus Decretalium*, IV, n. 159, footnote 98; Mansella, *op. cit.*, pp. 127 seq., 140 seq.

privilege of exemption *ratione individuitatis* of the matrimonial contract.[50] The same exemption would also apply in the following case. Suppose a Maronite in this country has a domicile where the decree *Tametsi* was promulgated. If he contracts marriage even in the place of his domicile, for example, with Oriental woman who is not subject to the Tridentine law, the juridical form of the decree *Tametsi* is not required *sub poena nullitatis.* The second party to the contract who is not embraced by the law communicates to the Maronite the privilege of exemption *ratione individuitatis* of the nuptial contract.[51]

The competent pastor according to the decree who may validly assist at the marriage is the proper pastor of either of the contracting parties by reason of domicile or quasi-domicile.[52] He may validly assist at the marriages of his subjects anywhere.[53] It matters not whether he is irregular, under ecclesiastical censure, merely a tonsured cleric, or only a putative pastor.[54] Again, passive assistance does not hinder the validity of the nuptial contract, even though the pastor is compelled to witness the marriage.[55]

In order to determine whether the Maronites in this country in a particular case are bound to observe the Tridentine form or are exempted from it, apparently the principles mentioned above must be applied. However, if the Maronites who have a domicile or quasi-domicile where the Tridentine decree was not promulgated, they are not obliged under pain of nullity to contract marriage before the proper pastor and the required wit-

---

50 S. Cong. de Prop. Fide, 11 Jan. 1817, *Coll.*, n. 716; Benedict XIV, *De Synodo Dioecesana*, lib. VI, cap. 6, n. 12 seq.; Mansella, *op. cit.*, p. 144.

51 S. Cong. de Prop. Fide, 21 Mar. 1759, *Coll.*, n. 415; 11 Jan. 1817, *Coll.*, n. 716; Mansella, *op. cit.*, p. 144, Gasparri, *op. cit.*, II, n. 1167; Zitelli-Solieri, *op. cit.*, n. 930.

52 Vlaming, *Praelectiones Juris Matr.*, II, n. 556; Cronin, *op. cit.*, p. 43; Ojetti, *Jus Pianum*, n. 25; Gasparri, *op. cit.*, II, n. 1075.

53 Vlaming, *loc. cit.*, Cronin, *op. cit.*, p. 93 seq.

54 Cronin, *op. cit.*, p. 85; Ojetti, *op. cit.*, n. 25; Gasparri, *op. cit.*, II, n. 1123.

55 Ojetti, *op. cit.*, n. 26; Cronin, *op. cit.*, p. 171 seq.; S. Cong. Conc. (1581), ad 3, 4, 5, apud *De Synodo Dioecesana*, lib. XIII, cap. XXIII, n. 1.

nesses. Chelodi does not hesitate to say that the impedi ment of clandestinity binds or does not bind the Maronites according to the accepted principles relative to the decree *Tametsi*.[56] "*Maronitae ligantur decr. Tametsi, quod suam vim localem retinet in eorum territoriis, personalem etiam extra erga eos qui exeunt in fraudem legis. Secus ipsi quoque possunt valide contrahere sine forma.*"

It must be noted that in the United States the decree *Tametsi* was published in some dioceses, and in others it was never promulgated. Later in certain dioceses where the decree was in force, the declaration *Benedictina* was extended which provided for the validity of clandestine marriages of heretics among themselves, and also of mixed unions with Catholics.[57]

The promulgation of the decree *Ne Temere*, Easter, 1908, abrogated the Tridentine legislation; after that date it no longer obtained for the Latin Church. Did this fact in any way affect a matrimonial contract of the Maronites in certain localities of the United States? Since the decree *Tametsi* was no longer effective beginning with Easter 1908, it would seem to follow that even a marriage of Maronites, after that date, who have their domiciles and who contract in localities previously governed by the Tridentine law, would not require the juridical of the decree *Tametsi* under pain of nullity.

This solution offers further complications. If the Maronites in the case given above must still observe the Tridentine form *sub poena nullitatis*, then, the juridical form for the matrimonial contract for the Maronites apparently resolves itself into a particular law. There is reason to believe, it seems, that the form of marriage required for the Maronites is a particular law intended for them as a personal society or group, therefore, it should oblige them everywhere. The diriment impediment relative to the form of marriage established by the

56 Chelodi, *Jus Matrimonale*, n. 139.

57 *Acta et Decreta C. Plen. Balt. III*, p. CVII seq.; Cronin, *op. cit.*, p. 256; Zitelli-Solieri, *Apparatus Juris Eccl.*, n. 933; Augustine, *A Commentary on Can. Law*, V, 267-270.

Synod of Mount Lebanon (1736) substantially agrees with the Tridentine enactment.[58] There is a noticeable difference in regard to the manner of publication. The decree *Tametsi* required definite promulgation in every parish.[59] The synod of Mount Lebanon does not mention this method of promulgation,[60] but when the acts of the synod, however, received papal approval *in forma specifica,* the Tridentine form had the force of a pontifical law.[61]

Although the form of marriage prescribed for the Maronites appears to be similar to a particular law, and as such, should bind them everywhere, in view of authority mentioned in the first part of this article, it could hardly be enforced in all parts of the United States. The juridical form of marriage for the Maronites in this country probably must be determined in harmony with the accepted principles relative to the decree *Tametsi* according to the authority already given.[62]

2. *Italo-Greeks*

The diriment impediment of clandestinity established by the Council of Trent was introduced among the Italo-Greeks by Clement VIII [63] and Benedict XIV maintained the same legislation.[64] Hence, the Italo-Greeks were obliged to observe the same form for valid matrimonial contracts as the Latins. When the decree *Ne Temere* was promulgated, the new law affected all dioceses of the Latin Church. It would seem that the Italo-Greeks were also bound by the decree *Ne Temere,* since they were subjects in Latin dioceses and under the jurisdiction of Latin Ordinaries. It must be noted that the Italo-Greeks have not been subject to Latin bishops temporarily or accidently, but permanently for centuries. It appears rea-

58 Synodus Montis Libani, pars II, cap. XI, n. 28, *Coll. Lac.*, II, 178; pars II, cap. XI, n. XII, *Coll. Lac.*, II, 166.

59 Con. Trident., *sess.* 24, cap. 1, *de reform. matr.*

60 *Ibidem*, cf. footnote 58.

61 Benedict XIV, Cont. *Singularis*, 1 Sept. 1741, § 10, *Coll. Lac.*, II, 488; Mansella, *op. cit.*, p. 152.

62 Cf. this chap., § 2.

63 Instr. *Sanctissimus*, 31 Aug. 1595, § 5, *Fontes*, n. 179.

64 Const. *Etsi Pastoralis*, 26 Maii 1742, § VIII, n. I, *Coll.*, n. 338.

sonable to say that they are in their place of origin.[65] If the Italio-Greeks were subject to the *Ne Temere* it follows that they should be governed by the present law of the Code for the juridical form of the matrimonial contract. This may be the case *de facto,* but no decree of the Holy See indicates that the Italo-Greeks are governed by the juridical form of marriage established by the decree *Ne Temere* or the Code.

Before the advent of the *Ne Temere* it is certain that the Italo-Greeks were bound to observe the Tridentine law. Th Sacred Congregation of the Council expressly declared, without an exception, that the decree *Ne Temere* did not bind the Orientals,[66] and by virtue of Canon 1 they are not subject to disciplinary laws of the Code.

Since the Italo-Greeks remain Orientals, it seems to follow that they are still bound by the *Tametsi.*[67] Hence, in the United States they would be governed by the principles of the Tridentine law which have already explained with reference to the Maronites.[68]

---

65 A diocese has recently been established for the Italo-Greeks, but for those only in Calabria; they now have an Ordinary of their own rite. (Benedict XV, Const. *Catholici fideles,* 13 Feb. 1919, *A. A. S.*, XI, 222). There seems to be no published source of their present status. The Italo-Greeks, at least many of them, do not constitute an Oriental Church properly so called. (There is no mention of the Italo-Greek Church in the sense as one speaks of the Greek-Ruthenian, Coptic or other Eastern Churches, with their proper hierarchy, organization, etc.). They are a group somewhat unique; they have lived in Lower Italy for centuries under the dependence of the Latin Ordinaries. Around 1468, many Greeks fled from Albania to Italy, and settled chiefly in Calabria and Sicily. Popes Leo X, Paul III, and Julius III provided certain ecclesiastical privileges for them. These, however, were all withdrawn by Pius IV in 1564, and this Pontiff placed the Greek colonists under the jurisdiction of the local Latin Ordinaries. Cf. Silbernagl-Schnitzer, *Verfassung . . . Kirchen des Orients,* p. 325. They ceased to be an independent Oriental Church with their own hierarchy, etc. The Constitution *Etsi Pastoralis* of Benedict XIV (26 Maii, 1742, *Coll.*, n. 338) provides for their situation. This document established certain norms given to the Latin Ordinaries which enable them to administer properly for their Greek subjects.

66 Resp. S. Cong. Conc., 1 Feb. 1908, ad Iam, *A. S. S.* (1908), XLI, 108, 109.

67 Cappello, *De Sacramentis,* III, n. 925.

68 Cf. this chap., § 2, n. 1.

§ 3. The Decree Ne Temere, the form of Marriage for the Greek-Ruthenians in the United States

The scope of the present article does not require a comprehensive treatise with reference to the valid form of the matrimonial contract among the Greek-Ruthenians in Europe. It is to be noted that the Tridentine law was not promulgated, nor did custom bring about its acceptance among all uniate Greek-Ruthenians. A provincial synod of the Ruthenians in 1626 enacted a law which prohibited clandestine marriages under pain of nullity. It decreed that marriages must be contracted before the proper pastor and at least two witnesses. The synodal decree, however, was without force, since it did not receive the specific approval of the Holy See. In 1629, Urban VIII addressed a communication to the Archbishop of Kief and declared that the synod mentioned above was incompetent to establish a diriment impediment or prescribe a new form for the nuptial contract. Hence the enactment was ineffective.[69] The Pontiff did not condemn the endeavor to prevent clandestine unions, but he did not deem it expedient to publish the Tridentine decree universally among the Greek-Ruthenians on account of certain differences between the uniates and the schismatics at that time.[70]

The provincial synod of the Ruthenians which convened in Zamos [71] expressly mentions the Tridentine decree promulgated amongst them.[72] A decree of the Congregation of the Propaganda in 1863 [73] and the recent provincial synod of the Greek-Ruthenians held at Leopoli [74] leave no doubt that the Tridentine legislation was accepted as the juridical form of marriage. It must be

69 Mansella, *op. cit.*, pp. 150-151.

70 Benedetti, *Votum, A. S. S.*, XLI (1908), 260; *De Synodo Dioecesana*, lib. XII, cap. 5, nn. 7-11.

71 This synod received the approval of Benedict XIII, 19 July, 1724, *in forma specifica* (Synodus Ruthenorum [1720], p. VII), therefore, its decrees have the force of pontifical law.

72 Synodus Ruthenorum (1720), tit. III, § VIII.

73 S. Cong. de Prop. Fide, 6 Oct. 1863, D, *Coll. Lac.*, II, 564; *Coll.*, n. 1243.

74 Synodus Ruthenorum, Galiciae (1891), tit. II, cap. VII.

noted, however, that the decree *Tametsi* was only followed in the dioceses of Galicia.[75] There is no evidence of the Tridentine law among the Greek-Ruthenians in Hungary.[76] Although the decree *Ne Temere per se* did not extend to the Orientals, since it was a disciplinary law for the Latin Church,[77] in the course of time the Greek-Ruthenians in certain dioceses with the approval of the Holy See, adopted this legislation; e. g., the Greek-Ruthenians in Galicia.[78]

These historical antecedents conjure up the situation which faced the Greek-Ruthenian pastors with regard to the valid form of marriage for their countrymen who emigrated to the United States from the different countries and dioceses of Europe. The Rt. Rev. Soter S. Ortynski, bishop of the Greek-Ruthenian rite in the United States, directed a letter to the Congregation of the Propaganda and described the existing difficulties and the doubtful validity of many marriages of his people. The influence of the schismatics complicated the situation. They readily assisted at the marriages of uniates and openly declared the validity of such unions. In some instances this was probably true, but the communication of Catholics with schismatics could not be tolerated. His Lordship requested the extension of the decree *Ne Temere* to all the uniate Greek-Ruthenians in the United States; this would effect a uniform discipline with reference to the form of marriage, and also counteract the influence of the schismatics.[79]

The Holy See in 1914 reorganized the status of the Greek-Ruthenians in the United States. At this time the decree *Ne Temere*[80] was embodied in the new legislation. This action provided a uniform discipline for the juri-

---

75 Telch, *Epitome Theol. Moralis*, p. 456.

76 Benedetti, *Votum*, n. 11, *A. S. S.*, XLI, 261.

77 Ferreres, *Los Esponsales y el Matrimonio*, nn. 500-511, nn. 550-559.

78 S. Cong. de Prop. Fide pro Negotiis R. O., 5 Maii 1911, apud *AkKR.*, XCII, 484; S. Cong. Conc., 1 Feb. 1908, ad Iam, *A. S. S.*, XLI, 108, 109.

79 Letter of Rt. Rev. S. S. Ortynski, May 21, 1912. Cf. Acta S. Cong. de Prop. Fide pro Negotiis R. O., Augusti 1912.

80 S. Cong. de Prop. Fide pro Negotiis, R. O., 17 Aug. 1914, art. 30, *A. A. S.*, VI, 463.

dical form of marriage which is still in force.[81] The Greek-Ruthenians in Canada [82] and South America [83] are also governed by the same legislation.[84] The norms of this decree are quite familiar, and they represent substantially the same principles found in the Code.[85]

Hence, the Greek-Ruthenians in the United States can only contract a valid marriage before the pastor or the Ordinary, or by a priest delegated by either, and at least two witnesses according to rules expressed in the decree; exceptions are admitted also in certain cases.[86]

If a Greek-Ruthenian wishes to marry another Oriental who is not bound to the form *Ne Temere,* it must, nevertheless, be observed. The legislator has expressly stated that even if one party is not bound, the validity of the matrimonial contract demands the observance of the decree *Ne Temere,* since the communication of exemption is no longer admitted.[87]

When the parties to the marriage are members of different rites, as a rule, the ceremony should take place before the pastor of the groom, and according to the rite of the groom, unless a particular law provides otherwise.[88] This exception applies to some Greek-Ruthenians; it is prescribed that the marriage be celebrated according to the rite and before the pastor of the bride.[89] This,

---

81 The decree *Cum Episcopo* has been indefinitely extended by the Oriental Congregation, 21 June, 1924. Cf. Letter of the Apostolic Delegate to the Ordinaries in the United States, August, 1924, No. 2633-G.

82 S. Cong. de Prop. Fide pro Negotiis R. O., 19 Aug. 1913, art. 36, *A. A. S.*, V, 398.

83 Decr. S. Cong. de Prop. Fide pro Negotiis R. O., 27 Mar. 1916, art. 17, *A. A. S.*, VIII, 107.

84 Chelodi, *Jus Matrimoniale,* n. 139.

85 Canon 1094 seq; cf. Wouters, *Commentarius in Decr. Ne Temere,* p. 6 seq.

86 S. Cong. Conc., 2 Aug. 1907, n. III seq; cf. Wouters, *op. cit.*, p. 6 seq; Cronin, *The New Matrimonial Legislation,* p. 1 seq.

87 S. Cong. Conc., 30 Martii 1908, ad Iam, *A. S. S.*, XLI, 287, 288; Wouters, *op. cit.*, p. 78 seq; Ferreres, *Los Esponsales y el Matrimonio,* nn. 550-559, 567, 569; Vidal, *Votum, A. S. S.*, XLI, 272 seq.

88 Canon 1097, § 2.

89 S. Cong. de Prop. Fide pro Negotiis R. O., 17 Aug. 1914, art. 30, *A. A. S.*, VI, 463. Augustine's (*A Commentary on Canon Law,* V, 292) conclusions are based upon the earlier decree of 1907 for the Greek-Ruthenians in the United States. A later decree, quoted above, necessitates a slight change with reference to the lawfulness of the celebration.

however, is a point which deals with licit assistance and the validity of the contract does not depend upon it, but upon the substantial juridical form which the parties must observe. A practical case may be considered. A Greek-Ruthenian man wishes to marry a Greek-Bulgarian woman. The Greek-Bulgarians are not bound by the impediment of clandestinity and they consider a marriage blessed by the priest even without witnesses sufficient for validity.[90] In accordance with the legislation for the Greek-Ruthenians the marriage should be celebrated before the pastor of the bride.[91] Hence, the Greek-Bulgarian pastor should assist at the marriage. What juridical form must be used? Since the man, a Greek-Ruthenian, is subject to the form of the *Ne Temere* which admits no communication of exemption, although the other party to the contract is not bound to observe it, the marriage must take place before the pastor of the place, or his delegate, and two witnesses under pain of nullity. This is a consequence of the principles contained in the decree, and the interpretation of the legislator who insists that the stricter form must be followed.[92]

§ 4. Certain Principles with Reference to the Marriage of Orientals

1. *Marriage Form when Orientals contract among themselves*

It is evident that most Orientals when they contract marriage *inter se* are exempted from the observance of a substantial form which is required in the Latin Church.[93] This is true with few exceptions; however, if a particular Oriental group has adopted, with the approval of the Holy See, a juridical form for the matrimonial

90 Benedetti, *Votum*, n. 15, *A. S. S.*, XLI, 261, 267; Cappello, *De Sacramentis*, III, n. 925.

91 S. Cong. de Prop. Fide pro Negotiis R. O., 17 Aug. 1914, art. 30, *A. A. S.*, VI, 463.

92 S. Cong. Conc., 30 Martii 1908, ad Iam, *A. S. S.*, XLI, 287, 288; Ferreres, *op. cit.*, nn. 556, 557, 567-569.

93 Canon 1; S. Cong. Conc., 1 Feb. 1908, *A. S. S.*, XLI, 108, 109; supra this chap. § 1.

contract, it must be followed under pain of nullity. The Greek-Ruthenians in the United States, for example, must conform to the prescriptions of the decree *Ne Temere.*[94] As a consequence the Oriental uniate rites in the United States who constitute a parish or mission in charge of a priest of their proper rite, must observe their particular laws or customs required for the validity of the matrimonial contract. The Orientals who are not bound to observe a juridical form, as a rule, demand the sacerdotal blessing as a confirmation that a valid matrimonial consent has been given by the contracting parties.[95] This is the required form (if it may be called that; certainly not in the sense of the Code) necessary among them to recognize the validity of the nuptial contract.

With reference to the liturgical celebration of marriage among the Orientals it is necessary to distinguish two ceremonies: 1. *Desponsatio.* This consists in the blessing of the rings and the manifestation of the matrimonial consent. 2. *Coronatio.* The solemn benediction of the marriage which includes the blessing of certain wreaths or crowns, and the coronation of the couple, and also the blessings of the nuptial garments, etc.[96]

Some Orientals in the United States have their domiciles in localities where they have neither church nor priest of their proper rite to provide for their spiritual welfare. In such instances they must depend upon the ministrations of the local Latin pastor. Suppose two Orientals of a certain rite are parties to a matrimonial contract, and who are not bound to observe a juridical form under pain of nullity. What form must be followed by the Latin pastor if he is asked to assist at the marriage?

Since the Orientals in question are not obliged to ob-

---

94 S. Cong. de Prop. Fide pro Negotiis R. O., 17 Aug. 1914, art. 30, *A. A. S.* VI, 463.

95 Smolikowski, *Votum, A. S. S.*, XLI, 253; Benedetti, *Votum*, n. 21, *A. S. S.*, XLI, 267.

96 Cappello, *De Sacramentis*, III, n. 926; Denzinger, *Ritus Orientalium*, I, p. 176.

serve a juridical form *sub poena nullitatis* it seems sufficient if they manifest their mutual consent before the Latin pastor, and if he blesses the union in accordance with the prescriptions of the Roman ritual. It is not evident that the Orientals in the above case must observe the Latin form; however, in practice to assure the validity of the matrimonial contract, the Latin pastor should assist at the marriage of Oriental subjects according to the norms of Canon 1094 seq. If this is done, the validity of the marriage could not be attacked for the lack of essential form; since the strictest juridical form which the Church requires has been observed.

2. *The Form of Marriage when Orientals contract with Latins*

All Orientals must observe the juridical form prescribed by the Code if the contract marriage with any person bound by the present form of the Latin Church.[97] Hence, whenever Latin and Oriental parties intermarry, the validity of the matrimonial contract requires that the marriage be celebrated before the pastor of the place, or his delegate, and the necessary witnesses according to the norms of Canon 1094 and subsequent canons.[98] The Code,[99] as the decree *Ne Temere,*[100] excludes the privilege of exemption which is admitted by the Tridentine law if one party to the marriage is not bound to observe the form under pain of nullity.[101]

3. *Requisites for the Licit Celebration of Marriages for Catholics of Different Rites*

A lawful celebration of marriage in the Latin Church ordinarily requires that the ceremony take place before the pastor of the bride.[102] There is a departure from

97 Canon 1099.

98 Woywod, *A Practical Commentary,* I, nn. 1126, 1114; Petrovits, *New Church Law on Matrimony,* n. 502; Wernz-Vidal, *op. cit.,* V, n. 551, III.

99 Wernz-Vidal, *Jus Canonicum,* V, n. 551, II.

100 Resp. S. Cong. Conc., 28 Martii 1908, ad Iam, *A. S. S.,* XLI, 287, 288.

101 Mansella, *op. cit.,* p. 144.

102 Canon 1097, § 2.

this rule when Catholics of different rites are parties to a marriage: "* * * *Matrimonia autem Catholicorum mixti ritus, nisi aliud particulari jure cautum sit, in ritu viri et coram ejusdem parocho sunt celebranda.*"[103]

It is important to notice that the prescriptions of this Canon refer only to matters which concern the lawfulness of the matrimonial contract.[104] It must be noted that for all who are embraced by the Code,[105] or the Orientals who are also bound to follow a prescribed juridical form, for example, the Greek-Ruthenians in the United States, the validity of the matrimonial contract depends upon the observance of their respective juridical form, and it matters not according to what rite the ceremony is celebrated.[106]

It seems to be an Oriental custom which gives preference to the rite and pastor of the groom to assist at the marriage of Catholics of different rites.[107] If a Syro-Maronite woman, for example, is to marry a Latin spouse, the licit celebration requires that the pastor of the groom assist at the marriage. The marriage, then, should be contracted before the Latin pastor, and the prescriptions of the Roman Ritual followed for the ceremony.[108] Suppose, for instance, the groom is a Greek-Melkite and the bride a Latin. The pastor of the groom has the right to assist at the nuptials and the ceremony is in accordance with his particular Oriental rite. The exception which the Canon provides for the particular law of certain Orientals, for example, the Greek-Ruthenians in the United States[109] and in Galicia.[110] When they contract marriage with persons of another Catholic rite,

---

103 *Ibidem.*

104 Canon 1097, § 1.

105 Canon 1099.

106 Woywod, *A Practical Commentary,* I, n. 1114.

107 Synodus Sciarfensis Syrorum (1888), cap. III, art. IX, n. XI; Synodus Alex. Coptorum (1898), sect. II, cap. I, art V, n. XXIV; Woywod, *A Practical Commentary,* I, n. 1110.

108 Canon 1100.

109 S. Cong. de Prop. Fide pro Negotiis R. O., 17 Aug. 1914, art. 30, *A. A. S.,* VI (1914), 463; Petrovits, *op. cit.,* n. 492.

110 S. Cong. de Prop. Fide, 6 Oct. 1863, D, b, *Coll.,* n. 1243.

the ceremony takes place according to the rite and before the pastor of the bride.[111]

The new law of the Code permits the wife whose rite is different from that of her husband, to adopt the rite of her husband, at the time of the marriage, or at any time whilst the union perdures. After the marriage is dissolved, she is free to return to her native rite, unless particular law ordains otherwise.[112] The exception applies for the Italo-Greeks.[113]

4. *Mixed Marriages*

The Church solicitously guards the faith of her children and as a consequence any contract with heretics or infidels which might jeopardize the virtue of faith is viewed with alarm. The marriage of Catholics with those baptized in heretical and schismatical sects or with infidels is considered a common danger to the faith, and where this exists, divine positive law prohibits a union with those not of the household of the faith. Mixed marriages are strictly forbidden to all Catholics because the law is founded upon a divine sanction.[114] This doctrine of the Church is fully explained in the Instruction of the Holy Office [115] to all the bishops of the Oriental rites. This document summarizes the legislation touching mixed marriages for the Oriental Catholics. The Congregation distinguishes the impedient impediment which arises between a Catholic and a heretic or a schismatic (mixta religio), and the diriment impediment which arises between any baptized person and a non-baptized person (disparitas cultus) according to the legislation of the Oriental Church.

---

111 *Ibidem.*

112 Canon 98 § 4; Cf. supra chap. VI; Leo XIII, Const. *Orientalium*, 30 Nov. 1894, n. 8. *Coll.*, n. 1883.

113 Benedict XIV, Const. *Etsi Pastoralis*, 26 Maii 1742, § VIII, n. IX Petrovits, *loc. cit.*

114 Deut. VII, 1-4; Papp-Szilagyi, *op. cit.*, § 102; Bellarmine, lib. I, *de Sacr. Matr.*, cap. XXIII, *Op. Omnia*, Tom. V; II Cor. VI, 14; I Cor. VII, 39; I Cor. V, 11; Rom. XVI, 17; Tit. III, 10; II John X, 11.

115 12 Dec. 1888, *Coll.*, n. 1696.

Mixed Religion. The impediment of mixed religion existing between parties to a matrimonial contract renders the marriage illicit; nevertheless, it is valid, since it is a nuptial contract between Christians. As in the Latin Church, mixed religion is an impedient impediment among the Oriental Catholics.[116] Despite the strict prohibition of the Church, she sometimes grants a dispensation so that Catholics may licitly marry a person baptized in a non-Catholic sect. There must be a grave canonical reason, however, for the marriage, and the usual promises must be given: 1. The non-Catholic party must remove all danger of perversion to the Catholic spouse. 2. Both parties must promise to have all the children baptized and educated in the Catholic faith. 3. Moral certainty must give assurance that the promises will be fulfilled.[117]

Disparity of Cult. There exists among all the faithful of the Oriental rites, the diriment impediment which renders null and void a marriage between a baptized and a non-baptized person.[118] This distinction no longer prevails in the Latin Church.[119] According to the Oriental Church, the diriment impediment of disparity of cult obtains between any baptized person whether Catholic or non-Catholic and any non-baptized person. Hence, if any Oriental wishes to marry a non-baptized person, the

---

116 Synodus Alex. Coptorum (1898), sect. II, cap. III, art. VIII, § 5, p. 165; Synodus Sciarfensis Syrorum (1888), cap. V, art. XV, § 7; Cappello, *op. cit.*, III, nn. 898-900.

117 Cf. Instr., S. Cong. de Prop. Fide, 12 Dec. 1888, n. 5, *Coll.*, n. 1696. The Congregation explains the conditions thus: "*Exigendae enim praeterea sunt opportunae a contrahentibus cautiones de amovendo a conjuge catholico perversionis periculo, de conversione conjugis a-catholici ab illo pro viribus curanda, ac de universa prole utriusque sexus in catholicae religionis sanctitatae omnino educanda. Has autem cautiones jus naturale ac divinum cumpostulet, nulla unquam humana auctoritate mixtae nuptiae sine ipsis permitti possunt.*" With reference to the impediment of mixed religion there is substantial agreement with the law of the Code contained in Canons 1060-1064. Synodus Sciarfensis *loc. cit.*; Synodus Alex. Coptorum, *loc. cit.*

118 Synodus Ruthenorum (1720), tit. III, § 8; Synodus Montis Libani (1736), pars II, cap. XI, n. VII; Synodus Sciarfensis Syrorum (1888), cap. V, art. XV, § 8, n. 14; Synodus Alex. Coptorum (1898), sect. II, cap. III, art. VIII, § 5, n. 4, XIII. Cappello, *op. cit.*, n. 906; Papp-Szilagyi, *op. cit.*, § 102.

119 Canon 1070; Cappello, *op. cit.*, n. 414.

validity and lawfulness of such a contract demands a dispensation from the diriment impediment of disparity of cult. The conditions, promises, and canonical reasons are the same as for mixed religion.[120]

Assistance at mixed marriages. Since mixed marriages are not favorably viewed by the Church even after the proper dispensations have been granted, ordinarily no religious rites or ceremonies are permitted at the marriage.[121] If there is a danger of, or an active participation in a non-Catholic sect, sacred rites are never allowed.[122] The Congregation of the Propaganda warns that parties to a mixed union are not allowed to go before a heretical or schismatical minister (*sacris addictus*); this would be a communication in sacris forbidden to the Catholic party.[123]

The priest who assists at the mixed marriages of Oriental subjects is forbidden to impart the sacredotal blessing, or to perform the sacred rites of the Church.[124] However, sometimes certain ceremonies might be permitted in order to prevent a greater evil, and where custom allows them.[125] A practical case might be to prevent assistance of a heretical minister. But this is always done with the greatest reluctance on the part of the Church.[126] The Code does not absolutely prohibit certain ceremonies, always exclusive of Holy Mass, when custom demands them to avoid a more serious evil. It is left to the judgment of the Ordinary to determine the merits of a particular case.[127]

---

120 Cf. supra this article; Cappello, *op. cit.*, III, n. 906; Canons 1060-1063, and Canons 1070-1071.

121 Canon 1102, § 2; Papp-Szilagyi, *op cit.*, § 102.

122 Canon 1258, § 1; Woywod, *op. cit.*, I, n. 1131. S. Cong. S. Officii, 15 Nov. 1858, *Coll.*, n. 1169. S. Cong. S. Officii, 29 Sept. 1899; 10 Sept. 1820; S. Cong. de Prop. Fide, 11 Mar. 1868.

123 Instr., 12 Dec. 1888, nn. 5, 6, 7, *Coll.*, n. 1696.

124 Papp-Szilagyi, § 102; Synodus Sciarfensis Syrorum cap. V, art. XV, § 7, n. 5, p. 174; Synodus Alex. Coptorum, sect. II, cap. III, art. VIII, § 5, IV, d.

125 Synodus Sciarfensis Syrorum, *loc. cit.*, Synodus Alex. Coptorum, *loc. cit.*

126 Instr. S. Cong. de Prop. Fide, Junii 1858, *Coll.*, n. 1154.

127 Canon 1102, § 2; Petrovits, *op. cit.*, nn. 512, 530.

5. *The Assistance of a Schismatic Minister*

Sometimes it happens in the Orient that when uniate Catholics have been refused the matrimonial blessing of a Catholic priest, they proceed to have their union blessed by a schismatical priest. Orientals who are not bound by a juridical form and who seem to demand only the blessing of the priest to confirm their matrimonial consent, may contract a valid marriage before the schismatical priest, although it is gravely forbidden. It is required, however, that he be not suspended by proper ecclesiastical authority.[128] The Holy See has maintained the validity of such marriages of certain Oriental Catholics.[129] There is on record a practical case touching this point which was submitted by the Bishop of Helena to the Holy See.[130]

In the year 1897 an Oriental girl was baptized in the rite of her parents as a uniate Greek-Melkite. Together with the family she emigrated to America in 1899. The parents took the girl to a Latin church when she was five years of age and she was instructed, received the Sacraments of Penance, Holy Eucharist, and Confirmation according to the Roman rite. Since 1902 she had not ceased to frequent the Latin Church and, moreover, expressed her intention to continue a Latin. In 1912, the girl married a Greek-Schismatic before the Greek-Schismatic bishop and two assisting priests in the city of Brooklyn. Three questions were proposed: 1. Whether the woman is to be considered a Latin or an Oriental. 2. If she belongs to the Latin rite, is not the marriage to be considered invalid on account of the impediment of clan-

---

128 Smolikowski, *Votum, A. S. S.*, XLI, 253; the Chaldeans, however, consider such a marriage invalid. (*Ibidem.*)

129 S. Cong. de Prop. Fide, 21 Martii 1759, *Coll.*, n. 415; S. Cong. de Prop. Fide, 18 Feb. 1783, *Coll.*, n. 562; S. Cong. Officii, 5 Aug. 1846, ad Iam et 2am, *Coll.*, n. 1009; S. Cong. de Prop. Fide, Junii 1858, in fine, *Coll.*, n. 1154; Cf. letters of the Archbishop of Smyrna to S. Cong. de Prop. Fide, 18 maggio 1847; 19 maggio 1859, apud Benedetti, *Votum, A. S. S.*, XLI, 259.

130 Letters to S. Cong. of Holy Office, 11 Sept. 1924; 20 Dec. 1924, apud Vermeersch, *Periodica*, XIV (1926), 99-101, and *A. E. R.* LXXIII (1925), 305 seq.

destinity. 3. If she remains an Oriental, is she not bound *sub poena nullitatis* to contract marriage before a Catholic Oriental priest.

The Congregation of the Holy Office responded: *Non constare de matrimonii nullitate.*[131] From this answer all the questions proposed may be solved. The Code states that a person belongs to the rite in which he was baptized, and there can be no transfer to the Latin rite without the permission of the Holy See; the custom of receiving Holy Communion in another rite does not bring about a change of rite.[132] This has been permitted under stress of necessity, and likewise the reception of the other Sacraments.[133]

When certain Orientals contract marriage among themselves, they are not bound to follow the juridical form under pain of nullity.[134] Since the woman is a Greek-Melkite, and her spouse a Greek-Schismatic, the validity of the marriage depends upon the observance of their Oriental laws and customs. In this particular case, the matrimonial contract confirmed by the blessing of the priest, suffices for the validity. This is indicated by the decision given by the Holy Office. The communication with schismatics is not approved, and even an Oriental Catholic who contracts marriage before a schismatic priest incurs a censure.[135]

§ 5. Faculties to Dispense Orientals from Matrimonial Impediments

The Code states that the Roman Pontiff alone is competent to abolish or change the established ecclesiastical impediments, both diriment and impedient; neither can anyone dispense from these impediments, except to the

---

131 1 Maii 1925, apud Vermeersch, *Periodica, loc. cit.*; *A. E. R., loc. cit.*

132 Canon 98, § 1, § 3, § 5.

133 Leo XIII, Const. *Orientalium*, 30 Nov. 1894, nn. 2, 9, *Coll.*, n. 1883; S. Cong. de Prop. Fide, 1 Maii 1897, nn. 1, 2, *Coll.*, n. 1966.

134 Resp. S. Cong. Conc., 1 Feb. 1908, *A. S. S.*, XLI, 108; Canon 1; Vermeersch, *Periodica*, XIV (1926), 102.

135 S. Cong. Officii, 10 Feb. 1892, *Coll.*, 1783; S. Cong. Officii, 5 Aug. 1846, ad 3am, *Coll.*, n. 1009.

extent of the faculty granted by common law or indult of the Holy See.[136] The various ecclesiastical impediments enumerated in the Code by virtue of Canon 1 obtain only for the Latin Church. It is a juridical axiom "*nihil inovandum esse*" with reference to Oriental discipline.[137] This applies also to their ecclesiastical matrimonial impediments which differ in many instances from prevalent discipline in the Latin Church; there is an added difficulty since the ecclesiastical impediments may differ again in the various Oriental rites.[138] Each rite, however, is bound to observe its particular discipline and is not at liberty to change it.[139] Ordinarily, without the express permission of the Holy See, for a legitimate transfer to another rite, an Oriental remains a member of his proper rite and is subject to its discipline.[140]

It may not be amiss to recall that Oriental Patriarchs enjoy and exercise extensive jurisdiction over all their subjects, whether laymen, clergy or bishops; consequently, they may dispense their subjects within or outside of their territory.[141] Oriental Ordinaries also possess liberal faculties, by concession of the Holy See, to dispense from matrimonial impediments. The synodal legislation of the Syrians [142] enumerates certain principles which in practice apply to other Orientals. Through the concession of the Holy See, in danger of death or insufficient time to have recourse to the Apostolic See, the Ordi-

---

136 Canon 1040.

137 Benedict XIV, Const. *Allatae Sunt*, 26 Julii 1755, n. 3, *Coll.*, n. 395.

138 Cf. the following commentators for ecclesiastical impediments existing in the different Oriental rites: Mansella, *De Impedimentis Matr. Derimentibus eo de Processu Judiciali;* Antoine, *Theologia Moralis*, VI, 119, seq; Cappello, *De Sacramentis*, III (1927), Appendix; *Conference Bulletin of the Archdiocese of New York*, Vol. VI (1928), p. 18 seq. Zhisman, *Das Eherecht der Orientalischen Kirche.*

139 Benedict XIV, *Etsi Pastoralis*, 26 Maii 1742, § VIII, n. V, VI, *Coll.*, n. 338, Cicognani, *Comment. ad Lib. Ium Cod.*, 11; Vermeersch-Creusen, *Epitome*, II, n. 298.

140 Canon 98, § 3; Leo XIII, Const. *Orientalium Dignitas*, 30 Nov. 1894, nn. 7-9, *Coll.*, n. 1883; S. Cong. de Prop. Fide, 1 Maii 1897, n. 2, *Coll.*, n. 1966.

141 Benedict XIV, ep. encycl. *Satis Vobis*, 17 Nov. 1741, *Fontes*, n. 319; Cappello, *De Sacramentis*, III, n. 922; *Conference Bulletin of the Arohd. of N. Y.*, Vol. VI (1928), p. 36.

142 Synodus Sciarfensis Syrorum (1888), cap. V, art. 15, § 9, n. 1.

nary may either personally or by delegate, e. g., a pastor, dispense from all diriment ecclesiastical impediments, whether occult or public, except priesthood and affinity in the direct line arising from consummated marriage. The faculty may also be used in favor of persons living in concubinage, who, for peace of conscience, wish to contract marriage according to the laws of the Church. The bishop may dispense, too, in the sacramental and extra sacramental forum from occult impediments when just and lawful reasons urge, and the following conditions are verified: 1. When the marriage was celebrated according to the laws of the Church and has been consummated. 2. When contracted in good faith and in ignorance of the existing impediment. 3. If a just cause renders it difficult to obtain the dispensation from the Holy See or the Patriarch, or their delegate. 4. If scandal would arise should the parties separate.[143] The same faculties are exercised by the Ordinaries of the Coptic Rite.[144] Although nothing expressly is mentioned by other Oriental rites in this regard, it is evident from the statement of the Holy Office [145] that all Oriental Ordinaries possess the faculties just enumerated.[146]

The legislation of the Maronites varies to some extent. The Patriarch by concession of the Holy See dispenses from all diriment matrimonial impediments, also from the simple perpetual vow of chastity and the vow to enter religion. Ordinaries, however, may dispense in the forum of conscience when conditons similar to the Syrian legislation are verified.[147]

Cappello [148] observes that the extent of the faculties enjoyed by Oriental Ordinaries to dispense from matrimonial impediments, at the present time, should be judged according to the norms of Canons 1043 and 1045.

143 Cappello, *loc. cit.*

144 Synodus Alex. Coptorum (1898), sect. II, pars II, art. 8, § 6, n. 5 seq.

145 S. Cong. S. Officii, 20 Feb. 1888, *Coll.*, n. 1685.

146 Cappello, *op. cit.*, III, n. 922.

147 Synodus Montis Libani (1736), pars II, cap. 11, n. 15; cf. supra this article.

148 *Op. cit.*, III, n. 923.

The Oriental pastor, confessor, etc., in like manner may determine their faculties in cases of urgency in accordance with the prescriptions of Canons 1044 and 1045, § 3. Likewise, Cappello concedes to the Orientals the use of the principles contained in Canon 15[149] and 209.[150] He observes that these are general principles of law and the Church has always in mind the *bonum animarum,* hence, the generous faculties granted by the Code to dispense in urgent and extreme cases should be available for all Catholics even of the Oriental rites. The opinion does not appear to be in opposition to the mind of the supreme legislator. In harmony with these conclusions it seems the Latin Ordinary may use the faculties granted by the common law to dispense his Oriental subjects in the cases mentioned in Canons 1043 and 1045, and the Latin pastors and confessors would be guided by the norms of Canons 1044 and 1045, § 3.

Is the Latin Ordinary in the United States competent to dispense his Oriental subjects from matrimonial impediments which obtain among the different Eastern rites outside the cases of urgency? It has already been noted that if the Latin Ordinary wishes to dispense his subjects of the Latin rite from the established matrimonial impediments, he must request faculties from the Holy See.[151] The several Roman Congregations, the Holy Office, the Congregation of the Sacraments, the Congregation of the Propaganda, and the Sacred Poenitentiary usually issue quinquennial faculties to the Ordinaries to dispense from certain matrimonial impediments.[152]

The Latin Ordinary possesses no jurisdiction to dispense Oriental subjects from matrimonial impediments in the faculties granted by the above mentioned Roman

---

149 Canon 15. "Leges, etiam irritantes et inhabilitantes, in dubio juris non urgent; in dubio autem facti potest ordinarius in eis dispensare, dummodo agatur de legibus in quibus Romanus Pontifex dispensare solet."

150 Canon 209. "In errore communi aut in dubio positivo et probabili sive juris sive facti, jurisdictionem supplet ecclesia pro foro tum externo tum interno."

151 Canon 1040.

152 Vermeersch-Creusen, *Epitome,* II, n. 871, Appendix.

Congregations. The Code states clearly that the Congregation for the Oriental Church has the cumulative faculties of all other Congregations combined. To this Congregation are reserved all affairs which pertain to persons, discipline, and rites of the Oriental Churches; cases of a mixed nature which affect Oriental and Latin Catholics also come within its competency. The only exception is made in favor of the Holy Office whose jurisdiction remains intact.[153] All faculties, therefore, which would enable Latin bishops to dispense Oriental subjects must be sought through the Oriental Congregation.

With reference to matrimonial impediments, the Holy Office maintains exclusive competency in matters of the Pauline privilege, mixed religion, and disparity of cult. This jurisdiction also extends to Orientals.[154] There was a time when the section of the Congregation of the Propaganda which had charge of Oriental affairs was also competent to grant faculties to dispense from the impediments of disparity of cult and mixed religion.[155] Although there is now a distinct Congregation for the Oriental Church,[156] *de jure* the Code has limited its jurisdiction in these matters. In practice if Latin Ordinaries require faculties to issue dispensations in favor of their Oriental subjects they must apply to the Oriental Congregation. When requested, no doubt, limited faculties are granted by the Congregation to Latin Ordinaries in order to dispense Oriental subjects from certain matrimonial impediments. Even for dispensations reserved to the Holy Office, proper procedure seems to demand the intervention of the Oriental Congregation which will obtain the required faculty from the Holy Office or the concession of the requested dispensation.[157] The Apostolic delegate

153 Canons 257, § 2, 247.

154 Canon 257, § 2.

155 Resp. S. Cong. Consist., 12 Nov. 1909, ad VI, *A. A. S.*, I, 149, 151; Pius IX, Const. *Romani Pontifices*, 6 Jan. 1862, *Coll.*, n. 1223.

156 Jus Pontificium, VII (1927), 128.

157 Benedetti, *Schema Facultatum S. Cong. pro Eccl. Orientali* (sub praelo).

most probably possesses certain faculties to whom application may also be made.[158]

A practical case may now be considered. There are in the United States two Greek-Ruthenian Ordinaries who have complete jurisdiction over their subjects. Suppose a Greek-Ruthenian man and a Latin woman wish to contract marriage, but are related within forbidden degrees of consanguinity. Who is competent to issue the necessary dispensation, the Latin or Greek-Ruthenian Ordinary? If both Ordinaries have the proper faculties from the Oriental Congregation, it would seem, either Ordinary is competent to grant the required dispensation. A particular law, however, prevails for the Greek-Ruthenians in the United States. In case Catholics of mixed rites marry and dispensations are required they are to be given and requested from the Ordinary of the bride.[159]

When Catholics of mixed rites must obtain dispensations from matrimonial impediments the general rule indicates that the favor is to be granted by the Ordinary of the bridegroom.[160] If the impediment is such that only one party to the marriage is directly affected, for example, a simple vow of chastity, the correct procedure seems to be that the person should seek the required dispensation from his proper Ordinary.

---

158 Leo XIII, Const. *Orientalium Dignitas*, 30 Nov. 1894, n. 12, *Coll.*, n. 1883.

159 S. Cong. de Prop. Fide pro Negotiis R. O., 17 Aug. 1914, art. 31, *A. A. S.*, VI (1914), 463.

160 Synodus Sciarfensis (1888), cap. III, art. IX, n. 11; Synodus Alex. Coptorum (1898), sect. II, cap. I, art. 5, n. XXIV.

BIBLIOGRAPHY

Juridical Sources

A. A. S.=*Acta Apostolicae Sedis,* 19 vols., Romae, 1909——.

A. S. S.=*Acta Sanctae Sedis,* 41 vols., Romae, 1865-1908.

Acta Pii IX, Pontificis Maximi, vol. V, Romae, 1907.

Acta Pii X, Pontificis Maximi, vol. I, Romae, 1854.

Acta et Decreta Concilii Plenarii Americae Latinae (1899), 2 vols., Romae, 1900.

Acta et Decreta Concilii Armenorum (1911), Romae——.

Acta et Decreta Synodi provincialis Ruthenorum Galiciae (1891), Romae, 1895.

Coll. Lac.=*Acta et Decreta Sacrorum Conciliorum Recentiorum, Collectio Lacensis,* 7 vols., Friburgi Brisgovae, 1870-1890.

Bullarium Romanum, 24 vols., Augustae Taurinorum, 1857-1872.

Canones et Decreta Concilii Tridentini, 19 ed., Taurini (Italia), 1913.

Codex Juris Canonici, Romae, 1919.

Fontes=*Codicis Juris Canonici Fontes,* 4 vols., Romae, 1923-1926.

Coll.=*Collectanea S. C. de Prop. Fide,* 2 vols., Romae, 1907.

Concilii Plenarii Baltimorensis II, Baltimorae, 1857.

Concilii Plenarii Baltimorensis III, Baltimorae, 1886.

Corpus Juris Civilis, ed. P. Drueger, Berolini, 1922.

Corpus Juris Canonici, ed. Richter Friedberg, 2 vols., Lipsiae, 1922.

Decreta Authentica Congregationis Sacrorum Rituum, 6 vols., Romae, 1898-1912.

Denzinger-Bannwart, *Enchiridion Symbolorum,* Friburgi Brisgoviae, 1922.

Mansi, Joannes Dominicus, *Sacrorum Conciliorum Nova et Amplissima Collectio,* 59 vols., Paris, 1901-1927.

Missale Romanum, ed. III juxta typicam Vaticanam, Ratisbonae, 1920.

Rituale Romanum, ed. typica, Romae, 1925.

Synodus Alexandrina Coptorum (1898), Romae, 1899.

Synodus Provincialis Ruthenorum Zamosciae (1720), 3 ed., Romae, 1883.

Synodus Sciarfensis Syrorum (1888), Romae, 1897.

Thesaurus Resolutionum Sacrae Congregationis Concilii, 167 vols., Romae, 1718-1908.

Works of Reference

Allatius, Leo, *De Ecclesiae occidentalis et orientalis perpetua Consensione,* libri tres, Cologne, 1648.

Allies, Thomas W., *The See of Peter, The Rock of the Church, The Source of Jurisdiction and the Center of Unity,* London, 1850.

Alphonsus de Liguori, *Theologia Moralis,* 11 ed., 3 vols., Bassani, 1816.

Antoine, Paul Gabriel, *Theologia Moralis Universa,* ed. novissima et nitida, 6 vols., Avenione, 1818.

Assemani, Joseph, *Codex Liturgicus Ecclesiae Universae,* 17 vols., Romae, 1749.

Assemani, Joseph, *Bibliotheca Juris Orientalis, Canonici et Civilis,* 3 vols., Romae, 1725-28.

Augustine, Charles, *A Commentary on the New Code of Canon Law,* 8 vols., St. Louis, 1918-1922.

Ayrinhac, H. A., *Marriage Legislation in the New Code of Canon Law,* New York, 1919.

————————, *Penal Legislation in the New Code of Canon Law,* New York, 1920.

————————, *General Legislation in the New Code of Canon Law,* New York, 1923.

Azor, *Institutionum Moralium Partes Tres,* Romae, 1610-11.

Bardenhewer, Otto, *Patrology, The Lives and Works of the Fathers of the Church,* Translated from the German by Shahan, Thomas J., St. Louis, 1908.

Benedict XIV (Prosper Lambertini), *De Synodo Dioecesana,* 2 vols., Romae, 1806.

Benedetti, H., *Schema Facultatum S. Cong. pro Ecclesia Orientali ad Normam Codicis Juris Canonici,* Romae, (sub praelo).

Binders, Matthaeus Joseph, *Praktisches Handbuch des Katholischen Eherechts,* 4 ed., Freiburg im Breisgau, 1891.

Blat, Albertus, *Commentarium Textus Codicis Juris Canonici,* 6 vols., Romae, 1921-1927.

Bliley, Nicholas Martin, *Altars According to the Code of Canon Law,* Washington, 1927.

Bona, Joannes Cardinal, *Rerum Liturgicarum,* Romae, 1671.

Braun, Joseph, *Liturgisches Handlexikon,* 2 ed., Regensburg, 1924.

——————, *Der Christliche Altar, in seiner geschichtlichen Entwicklung,* 2 vols., Munich, 1924.

Brightman, F. E., *Liturgies, Eastern and Western,* vol. I, London, 1896.

Burke, Thomas Joseph, *Competence in Ecclesiastical Tribunals,* Washington, D. C., 1922.

Cappello, Felix M., *De Curia Romana,* 2 vols., Romae, 1911.

——————, *De Sacramentis, Tractatus Canonico-Moralis, juxta C. I. C.,* vol. I, 2 ed., 1928, vol. II, p. 1, 1926, vol. III, 2 ed., 1927, Taurinorum Augustae.

Cappello, Felix, M., *De Censuris juxta Codicem Juris Canonici,* editio altera, Taurinorum Augustae, 1925.

Catholic Encyclopedia, 16 vols., and *Supplement,* New York, 1907-1914.

Catholic Directory, The Official, New York, 1928.

Catholic Dictionary, A, Addis-Arnold-Scannell, revised ed., New York, 1893.

Cerato, P., *Censurae Vigentes,* Patavii, 1921.

————, *Matrimonium,* 4 ed., Patavii, 1927.

Chelodi, Joannes, *Jus Matrimoniale,* 3 ed., Tridenti, 1921.

————, *Jus de Personis,* Tridenti, 1925.

————, *Jus Poenale,* Tridenti, 1920.

Cicognani, H., *Commentarium ad Librum I Codicis,* Romae, 1925.

Cronin, Charles J., *The New Matrimonial Legislation,* 2 ed., New York, London, 1909.

Dargin, Edward Vincent, *Reserved Cases according to the Code of Canon Law,* Washington, D. C., 1924.

Denzinger, Henricus, *Ritis Orientalium, Coptorum, Syrorum et Armenorum in Administrandis Sacramentis,* 2 vols., Wirceburgi, 1863.

De Smet, Aloysius, *De Sponsalibus et Matrimonio,* 4 ed., Burgis, 1923.

Dictionary of Christian Antiquities, 2 vols., London, 1880.

Dictionary of Greek and Roman Antiquities, 3 ed., 2 vols., London, 1901.

Doheny, William J., *Church Property: Modes of Acquisition,* Washington, 1927.

Duchesne, Louis, *Christian Worship,* 3d French ed., translated by McClure, M. L., London, 1903.

————, *Early History of the Christian Church,* translated from 4 French ed., 2 vols., New York, 1909-1912.

————, *The Churches Separated from Rome,* translated from the French by Mathew, Arnold Harris, New York, 1907.

Dugan, Henry Francis, *The Judiciary Department of the Diocesan Curia,* Washington, D. C., 1925.

Ferraris, F. Lucii, *Prompta Bibliotheca Canonica,* 9 vols., Romae, 1885-1892.

Ferreres, Joannes B., *Casus Conscientiae,* 5 ed., 2 vols. Barcinone, 1926.

——————, *Los Esponsales y el Matrimonio, Commentario Canonico-Moral sobre el Decreto Ne Temere,* 6 ed., Madrid, 1916.

Farrugia, Nicolaus, *De Matrimonio et Causis Matrimonialibus Tractatus Canonico-Moralis Juxta C. J. C.,* Taurini-Romae, 1924.

Fortescue, Adrian, *The Lesser Eastern Churches,* London, 1913.

——————, *The Mass, a Study of the Roman Liturgy,* London, 1922.

——————, *The Orthodox Eastern Church,* London, 1907.

——————, *The Uniate Eastern Churches,* edited by Smith, George B., London, 1923.

——————, *The Early Papacy,* London, 1920.

Funk, F. X., *A Manual of Church History,* Translated from the 5 German edition by Luigi Cappadelta, 3 ed., 2 vols., St. Louis, 1912.

Gasparri, Petrus, *Tractatus Canonicus de Sanctissima Eucharistia,* 3 ed., 2 vols., Parisiis et Lugduni, 1897.

——————, *Tractatus Canonicus de Matrimonio,* 3 ed., 2 vols., Parisiis et Lugduni, 1904.

Hedley, John Cuthbert, *The Holy Eucharist,* London, 1923.

Hefele, Carl Joseph, *Conciliengeschichte,* 2 ed., Freiburg im Breisgau, 1873-1890.

Heiner, Franciscus, *Benedicti XIV Papae Opera Inedita,* Friburgi Brisgoviae, 1904.

Hitti, Philip K., *The Syrians in America,* New York, 1924.

Keller, Charles Frederick, *Mass Stipends,* Washington, D. C., 1925.

Kelly, James Patrick, *The Jurisdiction of the Simple Confessor,* Washington, 1927.

Kilker, Adrian Jerome, *Extreme Unction,* Washington, 1926.

Lectures on The History of Religious, 5 vols., London, 1910-11.

Laemmer, Hugo, *In Decreta Concilii Ruthenorum Zamosciensis Animadversiones, Theologico - Canonicae,* 1865, Friburgi Brisgoviae.

Lexicon Totius Latinitatis, Faciolati-Torcellini, revised by Corradini, Palavii, 1887.

Leech, George Leo, *A Comparative Study of The Constitution Apostolicae Sedis and the Codex Juris Canonici,* Washington, 1922.

MacKenzie, Eric F., *The Canonical Status of the Ruthenian Rite in the United States,* Washington, 1919.

Mansella, Joseph, *De Impedimentis Matrimonium Dirimentibus de Prosessu Judiciali,* Romae, 1881.

Maroto, Philippus, *Institutiones Juris Canonici,* 3 ed., 2 vols., Romae, 1921.

Maximilianus, Princips Saxoniae, *Praelectiones de Liturgiis Orientalibus,* vol. I, Friburgi Brisgoviae, 1908.

Migne, P. G.=*Patrologia Graeca,* 161 vols., Paris, 1857-1866.

Migne, P. L.=*Patrologia Latina,* 221 vols., Paris, 1844-1855.

Milasch, Nikodemus, *Das Kirchenrecht der Morganlaendischen Kirche,* translated by Alexander R. Pessic, 2 ed., Mostar, 1905.

Missiones Catholicae, S. Cong. de Prop. Fide, Romae, 1907.

Motry, Hubert Louis, *Diocesan Faculties According to the Code of Canon Law, Washington,* D. C., 1922.

Neuberger, Nicholas, J., *Canon 6, or The Relation of the Codex Juris Canonici to Preceding Legislation,* Washington, 1927.

Nilles, Nicolaus, *Symbolae ad Illustrandam Historiae Ecclesiae Orientalis,* 2 vols., Oeniponte, 1885.

Noldin, H., *Summa Theologiae Moralis,* 7 ed., 3 vols., Oeniponte, 1924.

Ojetti, Benedictus, *Jus Antepianum et De Forma Matrimonii,* Romae, 1908.

Papp-Szilagyi, Josephus, *Enchiridion Juris Ecclesiae Orientalis Catholicae,* 2 ed., Magno Varadini, 1880.

Petrovits, Joseph J. C., *The New Church Law on Matrimony,* 2 ed., Philadelphia, 1926.

Pighi, J. B., *Censurae Sententiae Latae et Irregularitates quas habet Codex Juris Canonici,* 7 ed., Veronae, 1922.

Pouget, Franciscus A., *Institutiones Catholicae in Modum Catecheseos,* 9 ed., 12 vols. in 4; Avenione, 1837.

Prümmer, Dominicus M., *Manuale Theologiae Moralis,* 2 et 3 ed., 3 vols., Friburgi Brisgoviae, 1923.

Quigley, Joseph A. M., *Condemned Societies,* Washington, 1927.

Renaudot, Eusebius, *Liturgiarum Orientalium Collectio,* 2 ed., 2 vols., London, 1847.

Reiffenstuel, Anacletus, *Jus Canonicum Universum,* 4 vols., Romae, 1833.

Rossi, Joseph, *De Matrimonio Celebratione juxta Codicem Juris Canonici,* Romae, 1924.

Sanchez, Th., *De Sancto Matrimonii Sacramento Disputationum,* tomi tres, Lugduni, 1669.

Scott, W. L., *The Reunion of the East,* Cincinnati, 1926.

Shahan, Thomas J., *Outline of Church History,* New York (n. d.).

Shipman, Andrew J., *The Ruthenian Greek Catholics,* New York, 1913.

Schmalzgrueber, Francisco, *Jus Ecclesiasticum Universum,* 12 vols., Romae, 1844.

Silbernagl-Schnitzer, *Verfassung und gegenwärtiger Bestand sämtlicher Kirchen des Orients,* Regensburg, 1904.

Streit, C. P., *Atlas Hierarchicus,* Friburgi Brisgoviae, 1913.

Tanquerey, A., *Synopsis Theologiae Dogmaticae,* 11 ed., 3 vols., Romae, 1922.

Telch, C., *Epitome Theologiae Moralis,* 6 ed., Oeniponte, 1924.

Van Espen, A. Zegeri Bernardi, *Jus Ecclesiasticum Compendium,* Oberhauser, Benedictus, compiler, 2 vols., Bassoni, 1784.

Van der Stappen, J. F., *Sacra Liturgia,* 2 ed., 5 vols., Mechliniae, 1902-1905.

Vering, F. H., *Theologische Bibliothek, Lehrbuch des katholischen, Orientalischen und Protestantischen Kirchenrechts,* 2 ed., Freiburg im Breisgau, 1881.

Vermeersch-Creusen, *Epitome Juris Canonici,* 3 vol., Mechliniae-Romae, 1924.

Vermeersch, Arthurus, *Compendium Theologiae Moralis,* 1 and 2 ed., 3 vols., Romae, 1924-1928.

Wapelhorst, Innocent, *Compendium Sacrae Liturgiae,* 6 ed., New York, 1904.

Wernz, Franciscus, X., *Jus Decretalium,* 6 vols., Prati, 1913.

Wernz-Vidal, *Jus Canonicum,* vols., II, V, VI, Romae, 1923-1927.

Will, Cornelius, *Acta et Scripta De Controversiis Ecclesiae Graecae et Latinae,* Lipsiae et Marpurgi, 1861.

Wouters, Ludovicus, *Commentarius in Decretum Ne Temere,* 4 ed., Amsterdam, 1912.

Woywod, Stanislaus, *A Practical Commentary on the Code of Canon Law,* 2 vols., New York (n. d.).

Zhisman, Joseph, *Das Eherecht der Orientalischen Kirche,* Wien, 1864.

Zitelli-Solieri, *Apparatus seu Compendium Juris Ecclesiastici,* Romae, 1907.

Periodicals

A. E. R.=American Ecclesiastical Review, Philadelphia, 1889——.

AkKR=Archiv für katholischen Kirchenrecht, Mainz, 1857——.

Conference Bulletin of the Archdiocese of New York, New York, 1923——.

Dublin Review, Dublin, 1836——.

Gregorianum Commentarii de Re Theologica et Phisolophica, Romae, 1920——.

Homiletic and Pastoral Review, New York, 1900——.

Il Monitore Ecclesiastico, Romae, 1888——.

Jus Pontificum Juridica Ephemeris, Romae, 1921——.

Periodica, de re Canonica et Morali, Romae, et Burgis, 1911——.

Stoudion-Bullettino delle Chiese di Rito Bizantino, Romae, 1923——.

Universitas Catholica Americae

Washingtonii, D. C.

Facultas Iuris Canonici

1927-1928

No. 48

TITULI

DEUS LUX MEA

TITULI

QUOS

AD DOCTORATUS GRADUM

IN

JURE CANONICO

Apud Universitatem Catholicam Americae

CONSEQUENDUM

PUBLICE PROPUGNABIT

IOANNES ALOISIUS DUSKIE

SACERDOS DIOECESIS CONCORDIENSIS

LICENTIATUS IN IURE CANONICO

HORA IX A. M. DIE I IUNII A. D. MCMXXVIII

DE IURE CANONICO

I. De Dissertatione.
II. De Historia Iuris Canonici.
III. De Relatione inter Ecclesiam et Statum.
IV. Canones 8-30 De Legibus Ecclesiasticis et Consuetudine.
V. Canones 31-35 De Temporis Supputatione.
VI. Canones 36-62 De Rescriptis.
VII. Canones 63-79 De Privilegiis.
VIII. Canones 80-86 De Dispensationibus.
IX. Canones 356-362 De Synodo Dioecesana.
X. Canones 363-390 De Curia Dioecesana.
XI. Canones 423-428 De Consultoribus Dioecesanis.
XII. Canones 445-450 De Vicariis Foraneis.
XIII. Canones 451-470 De Parochis.
XIV. Canones 471-478 De Vicariis Paroecialibus.
XV. Canones 479-486 De Ecclesiarum Rectoribus.
XVI. Canones 951-967 De Ministro Sacrae Ordinationis.
XVII. Canones 968-991 De Subjecto Sacrae Ordinationis.
XVIII. Canones 1019-1034 De iis quae Matrimonii Celebrationi Praemitti Debent.
XIX. Canones 1035-1057 De Impedimentis in Genere.
XX. Canones 1058-1066 De Impedimentis Impedientibus.
XXI. Canones 1067-1080 De Impedimentis Dirimentibus.
XXII. Canones 1081-1093 De Consensu Matrimoniali.
XXIII. Canones 1094-1103 De Forma Celebrationis Matrimonii.

XXIV. Canones 1110-1117 De Matrimonii Effectibus.

XXV. Canones 1118-1132 De Separatione Conjugum.

XXVI. Canones 1133-1141 De Matrimonii Convalidatione.

XXVII. Canones 1556-1568 De Foro Competenti.

XXVIII. Canones 1572-1596 De Tribunali Ordinario Primae et Secundae Instantiae.

XXIX. Canones 1597-1605 De Ordinariis Apostolicae Sedis Tribunalibus.

XXX. Canones 1608-1645 De Disciplina in Tribunalibus Servanda.

XXXI. Canones 1646-1666 De Partibus in Causa.

XXXII. Canones 1667-1705 De Actionibus et Exceptionibus.

XXXIII. Canones 1706-1725 De Causae Introductione.

XXXIV. Canones 1726-1741 De Litis Contestatione et Instantia.

XXXV. Canones 1747-1769 De Probationibus.

XXXVI. Canones 1960-1969 De Foro Competenti et Tribunali Constituendo in Causis Matrimonialibus.

XXXVII. Canones 1970-1973 De Iure Accusandi Matrimonium et Postulandi Dispensationem super Rato.

XXXVIII. Canones 1974-1989 De Probationibus et Publicatione Processus.

XXXIX. Canones 1993-1998 De Causis contra Sacram Ordinationem.

XL. Canones 2147-2161 De Modo Procedendi in Remotione Parochorum Inamovibilium et Amovibilium.

XLI. Canones 2162-2175 De Modo Procedendi in Translatione Parochorum et contra Clericos non Residentes.

XLII. Canones 2176-2181 De Modo Procedendi contra Clericos Concubinarios.

XLIII. Canones 2186-2194 De Modo Procedendi in Suspensione ex Informata Conscientia Infligenda.

XLIV. Canones 2214-2240 De Poenis in Genere.

XLV. Canones 2241-2254 De Censuris in Genere.

ROMAN LAW

XLVI. Sources of Roman Law.

XLVII. The Roman Concept of Personality.

XLVIII. Slavery.

XLIX. Citizenship.

L. The Roman Family.

LI. Marriage.

LII. Adoption and Adrogation.

LIII. Guardianship.

LIV. Dominium.

LV. Acquisition of Property.

LVI. The Roman Obligation.

LVII. Contracts in General.

LVIII. Real Contracts.

LIX. Verbal Contracts.

LX. Written Contracts.

VIDIT FACULTAS:

PHILIPPUS BERNARDINI, S.T.D., J.U.D., Decanus.

LUDOVICUS H. MOTRY, S.T.D., J.C.D., a Secretis.

VALENTINUS T. SCHAAF, O.F.M., J.C.D.

FRANCISCUS J. LARDONE, S.T.D., J.U.D.

VIDIT RECTOR UNIVERSITATIS:

+THOMAS J. SHAHAN, S.T.D., J.U.L., LL.D.